EDUCATION FOR TRAGEDY

KENNETH D. BENNE

EDUCATION FOR TRAGEDY

*Essays in Disenchanted
Hope for Modern Man*

UNIVERSITY OF KENTUCKY PRESS

Lexington
1967

CONTENTS

Introduction
vii

Education for Tragedy
1

Education in the Quest for Identity
37

Education in the Quest for Community
68

The Uses of Fraternity
89

Man and Moloch
107

The Re-education of Persons in
Their Human Relationships
137

From Polarization to Paradox
151

The Arts of Democratic Citizenship
187

Notes
197

Acknowledgments
203

Introduction

FOR MORE than a half century, I have lived as a participant in American life and as an observer and critic of that life. During much of that time, I have viewed the conduct and institutions of American people from the vantage point of a worker in education. Since my early student days, I have taught in elementary and secondary schools, in colleges and universities, and in a large variety of undertakings in adult education, formal and informal, traditional and experimental. As I have sought to invest myself deeply and reconstructively in American education, I have become inescapably involved in the contemporary crisis of American and world civilization. In its educational policies and programs, the ideals and realities of a culture, in consensus and in conflict, are brought to light perhaps more clearly than in policies governing any other aspect of a people's common life. For education, in a far from perfunctory sense, represents a society's considered departure from its past and its rendezvous with an uncertain and clouded future. The perpetuity and growth, the stagnation and decline, the dramatic eclipse or rebirth of a society and its people depend basically upon decisions about how and toward what ends members of that society will be educated.

Choices about the future of American and world society —the two sets of choices cannot today be separated sanely —are now multiplying more rapidly than confident, competent, and common resolutions are being achieved. This dwindling of common bases of action and valuation, this accumulation of unsettled alternatives, constitute a condition of social and cultural crisis. The crisis is revealed in every cranny of contemporary experience for those who have the sensibility and will to feel, to see and reflect. It is revealed in each individual's aggravated difficulty in achieving an adequate and viable personal identity. It is reflected in deepening fragmentation of community life, in accentuated intergroup struggles and conflicts. It manifests itself in overinvestment of resources and energies, personally and nationally, in defensive operations. The more energy a person, group, or nation invests in defensive operations, the less energy is available to devote to the clarification and pursuit of its own purposes and to the creation and pursuit of common purposes across current lines of cleavage and conflict.

Thus, the crisis of cultures presents itself as threat to contemporary man, individually and collectively—as threat to his integrity, his growth, and his perpetuity. But the crisis also presents itself as opportunity for people not too anxious and defensive to see avenues of growth and progress within a context of conflict, demolition, and fundamental revaluation. Opportunity is in the crisis for creation by individuals of personal identities that are unique and novel and not mere reflections of one dominant historic tradition or another. The deliberate development of community, open to the world of events and to the influx and assimilation of new knowledges, and at the same time supportive of unique personal and subgroup adaptations to these events and resources is now possible, as the hold of provincial and custom-controlled communities upon the minds and loyalties of men is relaxed. Science and technology, largely physical, have been used by men to destroy the bases of traditional community and to precipitate the uneasy confrontation of culture with culture, race with race, class with class—the confrontation which now appalls us. Science and technology, physical, biological, psychological and social, can be used—by men with the necessary vision and commitment—to build and undergird a sane world society, with poverty and war abolished—a society dedicated to the growth and nurture of various and creative persons, groups, and communities.

Men with the requisite vision and commitment will not develop automatically out of uncriticized and unevaluated experiences in our crisis culture. I have become disenchanted, as most men have, with the notion of inevitable progress. But I have not lost hope that the idea of social progress is meaningful or attainable. The clarification of its meaning and the ordeal of its attainment will lay heavy toll upon the ingenuity, the research, the education, the choices and the actions of all men and women now alive.

The sane management of cultural crisis, as I see it, requires the building of methods and mechanisms for the creative resolution of interpersonal and intergroup conflicts into the future of society at various levels of social organization—local, regional, national, and international. No longer can we rely upon nondeliberate processes of historical selection and equilibration to restore community among men where it is eroded or eclipsed, as did the tradition-directed societies of our past. We must, as men, deliberately organize and plan for building and maintaining community of choice and action where community has been threatened or lost, if cultural crisis is not to become cultural disintegration.

It is in finding and building mechanisms and methods for effectively and humanely resolving conflicts with respect to the major alternatives of contemporary culture that the general directions of social progress are now to be found. And it is in developing persons adequate to build and use such mechanisms and methods, creatively and adaptively, in the patterns of their daily lives, that directions for progress in the general or liberal education of people are now indicated.

Programs of general education should be focused at all levels upon the serious and thoughtful study of contemporary cultural issues, as these manifest themselves personally, interpersonally, socially, and politically. All members of our society should be helped to feel, to express, and to understand the crisis in contemporary culture. Such efforts should extend to members of other national societies as well. But we would do well to *begin* with ourselves in our own society. People should be helped to probe the complexities, the threats, and the hopes, in the major issues of our time—the place of national and supranational effort and authority in an interdependent world, problems centering around the place of government in our economic life, questions connected with the control of population and with the conservation and development of human and natural resources, problems in guaranteeing an optimum level of health, mental and physical, and of nutrition to all peoples, opportunities and barriers in the creative use of leisure time, problems of authenticity within and among the roles which channel human activity in a specialized mass society. People should be helped to become responsible participants in the resolution of these issues and in the solution of the problems that grow out of them.

An educative orientation to cultural and social crisis

should be fostered in institutions devoted primarily to
education. But the orientation should come to permeate
other institutions of our society and other societies, if
men and women of adequate vision and resolution are to
become the expected product of social life. We should
not forget John Dewey's wisdom in our time of troubles.

> Getting from the present the degree and kind of
> growth there is in it is education. This is a con-
> stant function, independent of age. . . . The heart
> of the sociality of man is in education. The idea
> of education as preparation and of adulthood as
> a fixed limit of growth are two sides of the same
> obnoxious untruth. If the moral business of the
> adult as well as the child is a growing and devel-
> oping experience, then the instruction that comes
> from social dependencies and interdependencies
> is as important for the adult as for the child.
> Moral independence for the adult means arrest of
> growth, isolation means induration. . . . Govern-
> ment, business, art, religion, all social institutions
> have a meaning, a purpose. That purpose is to
> set free and to develop the capacities of human
> individuals without respect to race, sex, class or
> economic status. And this is all one with saying
> that the test of their value is the extent to which
> they educate every individual to the full stature of
> his possibility. Democracy has many meanings,
> but if it has a moral meaning, it is found in re-
> solving that the supreme test of all political insti-
> tutions and industrial arrangements shall be the
> contribution they make to the all-around growth
> of every member of society.

Some such orientation toward the crisis in contemporary
life lends an underlying unity to the apparently diverse

essays in this volume, written over a period of nearly twenty years. I have probed various aspects of contemporary life and education, seeking to reveal barriers to human growth which they embody and to envision ways in which thoughtful grappling with these barriers might become part of the educational discipline of all men and women, young and old. I welcome the efforts of others to reveal and correct whatever inadequacies may exist in my suggestions. For such responses will focus the thought and deliberation of students of man and of his education upon issues where sustained dialogue now is desperately needed. Only out of such dialogue can come a disenchanted hope adequate to guide men in and through the cultural crisis in which they are now living.

Education for Tragedy

CONTEMPORARY EXPERIENCE is filled with the stuff of tragedy. We decide and act, and as a consequence fellow men are torn from the human relationships and affiliations which gave their life meaning, made them men. We decide and act, and as a consequence many men are shattered in body and in person. And we are not exempt from comparable suffering as a consequence of the decisions and actions of ourselves or of other men. Nor is it only that agony comes to meritorious and nonmeritorious agents alike. Even more fundamentally we realize that there is now no confident common standard for the determination of merit or demerit. Our valuations of the choices and actions of ourselves and others, often when those are most vehemently and desperately assured, are cankered with hollowness and doubt.

Yet, if contemporary experience is filled with the *matter* of tragedy, our actions seldom embody the *form* of tragedy. On any view of man which asserts or assumes his dignity and responsibility, which sees man as master or even as partner in the determination of his destiny, the function of human action is to give form to the matter of human experience. Only as our actions seek seriously to give form to our experience does either action or suffering acquire meaning. Only as the form of human action is designed to incorporate adequately the matter of contemporary experience can integrity be restored to human life. The thesis which I am broaching in this essay is that the tragic matter of contemporary experience requires an appropriate form of human action, if it is to become humanly intelligible, compatible with human dignity, and contributory to the learning by men of wisdom through suffering. The form of human action required is tragedy. If I am right, contemporary efforts to avoid or avert tragedy—and they are many and vocally vigorous— had better become efforts to achieve tragedy. In coaching contemporary efforts of men to achieve the form of tragedy in choice and action, education will today find its central purpose and responsibility.

In suggesting that our time is peculiarly a "time of troubles," replete with the largely unformed matter of tragedy, I did not mean that potential tragedy is ever absent from the lives of individuals. Even in settled periods of history each man must come to terms with a world not seldom indifferent to, or inimical to, his most cherished purposes and projects; men must make their bargain with a life the ending, if not the consummation, of which is death; men may come to face the easily forgotten fact that every choice is a denial as well as a fulfillment of possibilities and to mourn the potential selves slain through the denial attendant upon all choice; men may learn, through the suffering following action which denies them, the limitations of man, individual and generic. I am not denying the omnipresence of tragic matter in human experience in the senses just suggested when I assert that our period is emphatically one of potentially pervasive tragedy. Nor do I claim that the tragic form of action is the only fully appropriate form for the wise comprehension of human experience at any time and place. I am proposing rather a strategy in the humane management of contemporary experience, not attempting to prescribe norms for humanity for all time.

The diagnosis of the contemporary predicament of men which underlies my proposal of a tragic strategy reflects the growing witness, offered by students of human arrangements and derangements, that human society is today in a state of crisis, in transition from one structural system of fundamental order to some other. An order of relationships between life conditions, institutions, and a system of ideas and ideals, an order linking these factors in some semblance of meaningful and livable integration, has been challenged deeply. No viable new order has succeeded in establishing itself. The disorder of contemporary culture is not confined to the human *middle ground* of political economy, but penetrates also to the human *microcosmos*. Men everywhere confront the basic questions, "Who am I?" and "What model of 'right' interpersonal relations should guide my interactions with other men?" Only the unsane and insensitive among men today find easy, confident answers to these questions. Disorder extends to the outer limits of the human *cosmos*. Consensus concerning the implicit basic assumptions, at once ontological and normative, which operate at the core of stable human cultures to make sense of man's relations to the totality of things, to justify his commitments to this life policy or that, has been challenged in all major contemporary civilizations. In restoring order to human life, men in a period of crisis must reshape their relations to the cosmos, as well as to self and society. The wisdom which men must learn or relearn must be at once a "religious," an "ethical" and a "political" wisdom.[1]

To CLARIFY some of the generic characteristics of "tragedy," as I see them, a schema of human motivation and action is required. I can think of no better name for this schema than a *dramatistic* view of human motivation and action, a name given it by Kenneth Burke.[2] Burke developed his formulation in attempting to answer this question: What terms are necessary in order to talk adequately about what people are doing and why they are doing it? He claimed that a minimum of five terms is necessary to discuss intelligibly human action and motivation, whether that action is played out in literature, in laboratories, or in what educational theorists like to call real life situations. We need some name for the *act*, designating what took place in the deed and in antecedent, accompanying, and subsequent thought. There must be indicators for the *scene*, the background of the act, the set of conditions in which it occurred. Nor can we fail to name the *agent*, characterizing the kind of person or group who performed the act. In our technological age, we could hardly fail to recognize and name the *agency*, the means and instruments and methods which the agent used in working out his act, though pre-technological thinkers may have sought to assimilate agency to "natural" purpose or final cause. And, finally, for Burke, we need terms to name what is aimed at in the act, its *purpose*. It is Burke's claim that this pentad of terms—act, scene, agent, agency and purpose, or synonyms for them—is necessary in any rounded or "dramatistic" discussion of human doings and the motivations for them.

To Burke's pentad of terms, however, I would add another, the *chorus*, since I find it impossible to think about tragedy or, indeed, any other form of human action, without involving people other than the agent or agents in the act. I realize, as Burke does, that an act may include

4

many agents, coagents and counteragents. I realize, and would insist, that with appropriate extensions and qualifications, the term "agent" may be applied to groups of various sizes as well as to individuals. Even so, there is always, I believe, a chorus, actual or ideal, involved in developing the drama of the human act. It would be difficult to envisage any act today, save perhaps war, which might involve as agent all the people now living in the world. Yet, if such an act were to be perpetrated, the people not yet born would be involved and, as ideally present, would constitute a chorus to the act. Nor should we forget the chorus of people now dead who, as representatively present, would inevitably coach the choice and action of the agents. At the other extreme, the solitary individual decider, and actor, if much of modern social psychology is to be believed, would proceed in his decision and action with the advice, bad or good, of an internalized chorus, whether we prefer in naming it to use the language of "alterego," "generalized other," "ideal companion," or "reference group."

Whatever else tragedy involves, it involves a dialectic between the act of an agent and the counterassertions of conditions as they "judge" the act in terms of the suffering imposed as a consequence. Every action involves a co-responding passion. From the suffering of the passion arises an understanding of the act and its motivation. The tragic character, if conditions are right, acquires a clearer vision of the complex elements involved in human motivation and action. As his tragic destiny becomes clear, and it can only through choice and action, intrinsic and previously extrinsic factors in motivation merge into a new vision. Circumstances no longer are felt as merely elements of the *scene*. Circumstances now are seen to conspire with the character of the actor, the agencies available to him, the chorus available for coaching and interpreting his motives and his acts, to shape a just vision of the actions appropriate and possible to him and to others in his time and place.

Suffering coming to the passive victim of circumstance may be deplorable and pathetic. It is not tragic suffering unless seen in relation to human choice and act, as part of a destiny which the agent is a partner in shaping. There is no assertion of a motive, of a venturesome interpretation of the means, conditions and aims of human action by the passive victim of circumstances. The suffering imposed on the victim, by what may be called an act of God, is meaningless in human terms, "silly" and whimsical, however deplorable. Only as the assertion of chosen action calls forth the counterassertion of consequences can a tragic vision arise which includes an understanding of the act, a deepened sense of the interinvolvements of the scene and of incompletely tested agencies in the workings out of contemporary destiny, a summary view of the character of the agent in his strengths and weaknesses.

It would be wrong to assume that the tragic vision becomes fully clear in one or even in a series of tragic actions. Clarity comes but it may be spurious. Rationalizations come with all of the attractiveness of self-evident "truths." This the fully tragic agent knows, and he knows that the only antidote for the speciously self-evident lies in evidence gained through the test of further committed choice and action.

A favorite metaphor among critics in discussing drama is the judicial trial or testing. In the trial the elements of an action under scrutiny are summed up dramatically, evaluated and judged in terms of some existing body of legal or moral norms. From the tragic point of view, every major choice and its consequent action is both a trial of the agent and the attendant chorus. All elements in the action collaborate in passing judgment on the act and carrying out the sentence. Where the sentence is death, as it is in many cases of tragic action, the learning of wisdom, the rewriting of the norms of judgment which the sentence embodies, is the responsibility of the chorus. But the tragic agent need not literally die. Oedipus, blinded and exiled, lived to show at Colonus the regenerated character, the new wisdom, which his tragic ordeal had taught him. Lear lived long enough to sum up the new character he had achieved through his tragic experience. Dr. Stockman in Ibsen's *An Enemy of the People* survived his ordeal to voice his new wisdom concerning the strategy of cooperative loneliness in the reeducation of bourgeois society. Dialectically, a dying occurs each time tragic judgment is passed upon the character and chorus in an action and each time a rebirth of character and chorus occurs. Fundamental relearning from experience always involves, in this sense, death and rebirth.

This formulation of the dialectic of tragedy invites comparison with the experimental method of laboratory science. For here, too, the test of warranted assertion lies in the arena of asserted action and its consequences. I would suggest that laboratory method is a species of the broader method of tragedy. It is an ascetic mode of tragedy in which the agent denies himself the making of assertions other than those which, under appropriately constructed conditions, can be tested by the answers given by the things being studied. The scientist-agent does not seek a judgment of his whole character in the laboratory test. His play is a humanly attenuated play. Nor does the chorus that coaches his scientific action, the community of scientists, make judgments of his total character as they interpret his laboratory reports. As a matter of fact, the coaching of the chorus works to exclude those preferences that make up most of his character, other than his preference for "objectively true" statements, from the agony of laboratory testing.

While the findings from experimental science of impersonal and impartial knowledge and of methodical discipline appropriate to the production of such knowledge are indispensable ingredients of the wisdom which guide tragic action today, the tragic agent on the world or theater stage cannot depend for wisdom upon scientific knowledge alone. For, in the essentially moral agony of his choice and action, he submits his inclusive character to the judgment of circumstances and of other men. His dearest preferences and his faiths are part of what has been questioned and is now being tested. He must suffer the full consequences of his action, guided by whatever preparatory assertions and counterassertions have given it shape. He must continue to learn a more inclusive wisdom than the scientist as scientist seeks, and he must learn it under conditions of action appropriate to the learning sought.

What of the dialectic of comedy by way of contrast and, possibly, clarification? Eric Bentley leads toward at least one answer in discussing Shaw's comic dramaturgy. Shaw believed that only in the drama of fixed morality was there need for outward action. In that drama the agents must be tested by fire and water, by what Shaw named "the tomfooleries called action." Once the emphasis shifts from a drama of fixed morality to a drama concerned with the discovery of what is right, "outward eventfulness becomes superfluous and therefore vulgar."[3] The "right" presumably is to be discovered by the play of ideas upon ideas. It is to be found through the ironic exposure of the falseness and hollowness of moral pretensions and prides, by the ironic pointing up of the insincerities and stupidities in inadequate moral positions. Shaw himself characterized his method for the dramatic discovery and illumination of what is right as "a forensic technique of recrimination, disillusion, and penetration through ideals to the truth, with a free use of all the rhetorical and lyrical arts of the orator, the preacher, the pleader and the rhapsodist."

I would argue that Shaw is suggesting here not the *only* form of drama which can follow the decline or disappearance of a fixed morality. He is rather pointing to a *comic* form of drama appropriate to those conditions. What is it that constitutes it *comic?* The view that our insight into the pretensions, sentimentalities, the ludicrousness of the insincere, the untutored and the stupid in life comes best though the interplay of mind upon mind, of idea upon idea, through inspired verbal commentary and dialectic. Learning through comedy does not come by suffering as in tragedy. It comes through the verbal unmasking of the inadequacies and ludicrousness of human agents, agents typical of a class of men or of humanity as a whole. It may be that Shaw showed a personal idiosyncrasy in underrating the place of simulated action even in comic drama. There is unavoidably some action in Shavian drama, though action is underplayed there. In other comedy, action may be abundant and riotous, bordering on farce, as in Aristophanes. But its function is not that of action in tragedy. And here Shaw was true to the spirit of the comic in modern drama. *Comic action* teaches nothing to the agent. And the observer of comedy, and its author, learn not through identification with the action and suffering of the agent. Through the folly of the action, the relatively detached chorus is reminded of or develops a standard or insight, grounded in (or at least supplied through) some play of verbal dialectic, apart from the heat and suffering of committed action.

So FAR the attempt to characterize the tragic has been somewhat abstract, in terms of a dialectic in which the six aspects of human action appear as terms in a general pattern of development. To give more concreteness to the characteristic features of tragic action, it will be useful to comment in some detail on each of the aspects as they appear from a tragic point of view.

1. THE NOBLE AGENT IN SEARCH OF LIMITS

Tragic action always centers on a great crisis in a great human life. Whitney Oates found,[4] in his attempt to characterize all tragedy that one of its basic assumptions is the dignity and importance of man. I would add two others. One is that man's dignity lies in the irreducible fact of human choice, choice which joins freedom and responsibility. The second is that the human agent in his decision and action is not alone. In his choosing he must come to terms with other men and with forces greater than his own, greater indeed than the power of man, collectively or generically. The tragic agent, whatever the specific content of his character (and this must vary with culture, time and place), has intrinsic importance. Only through the collaboration of his choice does human action acquire form and meaning. Yet, facing as he must a crisis, the limits of his power to influence his destiny always are indeterminate. This problem of limits seems to focus, in the greatest tragedies, at three levels—the level of the individual, of man in society, and of Man in Nature. The perplexities of the tragic hero center in the setting of

proper limits to his choice and action. In these perplexities, questions, ethical, political, and religious, are
involved. The tragic action finds its resolution in the
simultaneous clarification, if not the settling, of the
problem of human limitation at these three levels. As
Theodore Spencer remarks concerning the *Oresteia* of
Aeschylus—"When Athena solves the problem of Orestes'
individual guilt she at the same time solves the problem
of man's relation to the supernatural by appeasing the
Furies, and she solves the problem of justice in the state
by establishing the court of the Areopagus. The three
realms of ethics, religion and government are all brought
together in one solution, in one reconciliation."[5] Spencer
shows, I think conclusively, that tragedy has always dealt
with problems of human adjustment at these three levels.
Significantly, his example from the nineteenth century—
a tragic novel, *War and Peace*—results in a clarification,
not a reconciliation, of the problem of human limitation,
freedom, and responsibility as it focused for that time.

From misplaced answers to the problem of human limits
flows the painful suffering of the tragic action. From the
achievement of tragic clarity as to the limits of "the
human" appropriate to a time and place follow order and
hope.

2. THE DEMONIC SCENE

The tragic agent recognizes superhuman forces moving
in his scene, forces that sweep him into action, that ask
for his unthinking allegiance and devotion, that tempt
him away from his aspiration to humanity, freedom and
responsibility. Reinhold Niebuhr, Peter Drucker[6] and
others have given to such modern forces as nationalism
and racism the name demonic forces. (In more "scientific"
language, such forces may be described as "trends.") Re-

peatedly in tragedy, painful suffering flows from the hero's listening to the demons who promise much as a price for the surrender of his essential humanity—Doctor Faustus and Mephisto, Macbeth and the witches, Othello and Iago (whom I would interpret as a demonic force masquerading as an agent), Hummel and capitalism as vampire in Strindberg's *Ghost Sonata*. How to win in the struggles with demonic forces in the scene—and as demonic (as quasi-personalized passion) the scene also within the agent—for possession of the agent's soul, how to maintain in the agent, against the power of the demonic, the essential attribute of the human—free and responsible choice—remains a major theme in the tragic drama.

3. THE CLOUDED AND CONFLICTING DESTINY

The tragic situation does not permit man easily to perceive the outlines of his destiny. Euripides thought so much of the following insight that he put it into the mouths of the chorus at the ending of five of his extant plays.[7] "For the way men saw opened not / And a way was there which no man thought— / Thus hath it fallen here." The tragic view of man discounts the virtue of individual clarity of purpose in the midst of human confusion. Clarity of purpose in genuine crisis is bought through suffering, and the clarity of purpose must become eventually a collective clarity as the suffering that evokes it is a collective suffering.

This counsel of wisdom is underlined by Hegel's insight that the tragic struggle is not a struggle between good and evil, right and wrong. It is rather a struggle between rival principles of right. Nowhere is this clearer than in the *Oresteia*. Clytemnestra had murdered her husband, Agamemnon. Orestes, the son, killed his mother to avenge his father's death. Orestes had obeyed the rule that a son should avenge his father. The Furies condemned him on the basis of the rule that the most heinous murder is to kill one's own kin. In Aeschylus' view, the gods were themselves divided on the issue. The Athenian jury divided six to six in trying to settle it. We have seen that the tragic solution demanded reconstruction and reconciliation of norms at the ethical, political and religious levels. Orestes could not have worked the solution out by and for himself.

4. THE CHORUS AND THE COMMON WISDOM

There seems to be no clear critical consensus on all of the dramatic functions of the chorus in Greek tragedy, not to mention the functions or even the existence of equivalents to the chorus in later tragedy. But the following generalities about the chorus are probably true, though I am more interested in the conclusion built upon them. At many points the chorus expressed the common wisdom, seeking either to influence the tragic agent in his choice or to influence the audience in their interpretation of the tragic action. We may also admit that the *chorus* at times was "the symbol of the mass of people moved by Dionysian excitement,"[8] the worthy opponent to Apollonian reason and restraint, as Nietzsche saw it. We need not admit with Nietzsche that the chorus as symbol of Dionysian frenzy provided a way to deeper wisdom than could rational human choice. In terms of our previous discussion, the chorus sometimes represents a "demonic force in the scene" in the development of the tragic action. And demons are not to be followed by men, but rather to be treated by some methods of rational exorcism.

The truth is probably that the "chorus" has been used to offer various counsel to tragic agents as it does in actual tragic action off the stage. My point here is that I do not believe the lesson of tragedy assigns any "final" wisdom to the chorus in the working out of the drama. Whatever of "final" wisdom the chorus possesses, it speaks in summation at the end, having learned it through the experience and suffering of agents. It can probably be safely said further that the learning possible through tragedy is not complete until the chorus, along with the agents, has achieved regeneration.

5. THE OVERPOTENT OR UNDERPOTENT AGENCY

The literature of tragedy seems not to have achieved the confident humanization of the agencies which man has contrived through his ingenuity any better than our culture has managed the task of humanization. "Technology" in the literature of Western tragedy was never fully disengaged from "black magic" in men's deeper thinking about the human lot and about human adjustment to crisis, as indeed the two were not effectively disengaged, historically speaking, until the modern period. Deep anxiety concerning the evil effects of man's exceeding his proper limitations, committing the sin of *hubris,* pervaded Greek tragedy, and, if indeed I have been right in my argument, is a persistent and valid tragic concern. This anxiety typically has supported the identification of any unusual mastery by a man of techniques (or of the knowledge which supports them) with the "demonic." Thus Medea's possession of arts not possessed by other Corinthians was combined with a character unrestrained and controlled by humanly uncontrollable passions. The tragic wisdom (achieved through the action of the *Medea*) condemned at once the technology and the character which possessed it (or was possessed by it). The same identification persists in the Faustian theme in modern drama.

Man must surrender (sell) his essential humanity to gain the mastery of technology and its supporting knowledge. (This same identification may underlie at some depth my earlier comparison of scientific method with the method of tragedy.) With all of Marlowe's sympathy with Faustus, a sympathy echoed philosophically without tragic misgivings by Francis Bacon with his deification of knowledge as power and his identification of human progress with progress in science and its application, Marlowe's conclusion was traditional. In Goethe's treatment of the Faustian legend there seems to be some ambiguity in the tragic conclusion, with the hint that at least partial expiation for Faust might lie in using his overdeveloped mastery of technology in transforming the scene in a way which served meritorious human purposes (draining the swamps). There may be a comparable ambiguity in Aeschylus' treatment of Prometheus. It may not be too farfetched in this perspective to say that Ibsen in *The Master Builder* had achieved some transformation of the perceived place of agency in human tragedy. Was not what made Solness admirable in some large measure his mastery of architecture and of its methods of intelligent adaptation in building? His inadequacy lay in lack of comparable adaptability in facing his moral problems.

It I am right, most of tragic literature has identified unusual development and use of out-of-the-ordinary agencies with the service of dark and inhumane unnatural purposes. Clear-eyed thinking and just feeling about the problems of managing technology in ways compatible with human dignity and responsibility under these conditions is impossible. In modern tragedy, the suggestion appears that technology, partly detached from demons, becomes an ingredient of human tragedy through recognition of the overpotency of agencies. Agencies serve more purposes than those for which they are consciously designed. The unintended consequences of overpotent agencies make them matters of tragic concern. Perhaps the suggestion of the underpotency of available means, in serving purposes for which agencies are needed, is, as in Ibsen, entering our underlying conceptions of the modern tragic situation. Meanwhile, the problem of humanizing technology and of technologizing the humanities remains a central element in contemporary tragedy outside the theater.

6. THE PAINFUL WISDOM

In saying "Man shall learn wisdom, by affliction schooled," Aeschylus suggests that one approach to the fundamental meaning of tragic action is to see it as the way in which men learn wisdom, if at all. This is the approach which I have tried to use but from the opposite direction. How can men learn wisdom at a time when they need very much to learn it, or to relearn it? This is a question which must be clarified or answered before meaning can be given to the question "How can we educate for wisdom in a time of crisis?"

These questions have led me to study the tragic form of human action. The fruits of my study, garnered ironically enough largely through "comic" methods, may be summarized all too briefly. The occasion for relearning wisdom is a time when fundamental disorder threatens human agents at three levels—at the level of his relations to himself and others, at the political level, and at the level of the relations of man and nature. In any adequate learning of wisdom, order must be sought at all three levels and the levels of learning, of reconciliation and reconstruction seen in interrelationship. The problem of the agent confronted by disorder may be defined, at least in part, as the discovery of his limitations, which again must be widened from the limitations of the person to the limitations of Man, collectively and generically. Only in relation to limitations adequately seen and felt can an agent define his freedom and responsibility as to time and place, or chart confidently his relationships with the other elements inescapably involved in his action and suffering.

The "method" of tragedy is the dialectic of chosen action and suffering, leading to vision in which all the interrelated elements of the action acquire meaning, in which clarity concerning the unsettled questions motivating the action is generated, and in which both acceptance of the finite human lot and celebration of man's greatness are blended.

The tragic agent is capable of human dignity and dignity demands active participation in the determination of human destiny. Yet for the tragic agent destiny is clouded. The clarification of the clouded human destiny is not the task of the agent alone. The chorus, though perhaps in command of traditional wisdom, is frequently divided and confused and, though necessary to the development of the action and to learning from it, is undependable. The chorus must learn along with the agents. The clarification of destiny must be a collective as well as an individual achievement. The tragic agent is harried by demons which in troubled times find their way into agent and chorus as well as the scene of action. No agent is free from the threat of demonic possession, though the tragic agent, consistently with his insistence on choice as indispensable to human dignity, must cultivate strategies of rational exorcism. The tragic agent is beset with qualms about the agencies which he must use in developing his action—questions concerning the adequacy of agencies to be employed built upon the recognition of both the overpotency and underpotency of means. Such, formally stated, are the conditions of tragic action as I see them. And these also are the formal conditions for learning wisdom in our time.

ALTHOUGH "tragedy," we may say, is the dramatic posture toward man and events to be accepted and cultivated in our age of crisis, can and will its values become the motivating factors in human action? This question calls for prediction rather than prophecy. So far I have been concerned mainly with prophecy. If we were to predict, and I do not know enough to do so, we would have to assess the barriers in our human situation, its actors and its chorus, its agencies and its purposes, barriers to the realization of tragedy in human action. And, though I cannot undertake any detailed assessment here, a pointing toward three such barriers may help to put my thesis in perspective for the criticism which perhaps it deserves. Since each barrier named will spawn its own dramatic forms, alternative to the tragic, for the over-all adjustment of man in his choices and actions, we are concerned here with the contemporary lure of dramatic alternatives.

1. THE LURE OF EXISTENTIAL DRAMA

One ground theme in Western literary art of the twentieth and the late nineteenth centuries has been alienation. Individual man wanders lonely, alien, among his fellow men. He may seek the communion of sustaining common feeling and action. He may have surrendered the quest. But the lack of shared values by which to sustain and ground his choices and actions, whether in conformity or in revolt, tends to rob his choices of significance, to keep him a prisoner within a private world. How does a man choose and live within a moral vacuum? What does he do and how does he do it? Such have been the questions working in and behind the constructions of much serious modern literature. To document this claim, one might cite the works of such writers as Kafka, Proust, Gide, Joyce, Melville, Dostoyevsky, Eliot, Sherwood Anderson, Dos Passos, Nathaniel West, Pirandello, Strindberg, and Chaplin, among others, in evidence.

Perhaps no playwright has put the dilemma of the lonely agent more clearly, and consequently more absurdly, than Jean Paul Sartre. The clarity, if not the absurdity, may be due to the fact that he is a philosopher as well as a playwright and novelist. I do not wish here to examine the basis of existentialist philosophy. I wish to examine only the existentialist doctrine of human choice, the lonely choice of the lonely agent. With Sartre's insistence that the most distinctively human act is choosing, I would agree. Nor would I question that the basic moral notions of freedom and responsibility are meaningless apart from the ability of man to choose the direction of his action. And, with appropriate qualifications, I would agree that man creates the meaning and significance of the world through his choosing—apart from choice, the world loses significance, at least to human values.

It is when the total subjectivity of human choice is emphasized, when the utter and complete lack of intersubjectivity in any human resolve that merits the name of "free" is asserted, that the terror and basic anxiety of the existentialist view of man in the world is brought home to us. Marjorie Grene's description of the philosophic "program" of existentialism prepares us for the denial of religious and scientific supports to our choices, our value judgments.

Existential philosophy, then—or that branch of it which Sartre calls "atheistic existentialism"—is an attempt to reinterpret human nature in terms of human subjectivity itself, not through superhuman religious or subhuman material categories. It is this attempt to show how human values are derived from a totally human—in fact, a desperately human—situation that makes some of the analyses of Sartre or Heidegger, if not valid, at least terribly relevant to the dilemma of those who can find comfort in no creed of God or science.[9]

But Grene here hardly has prepared us for the existentialists' further rejection of any place for the chorus, other men, in shaping a man's dreadfully free resolve. Sartre himself can speak most eloquently on this subject.

. . . Ordinarily, my attitude with respect to values is eminently reassuring. The fact is, I am engaged in a world of values. The anguished apperception of values as sustained in being by my liberty is a posterior and mediated phenomenon. . . . We discover ourselves, then, in a world peopled with exigencies, at the heart of projects "in the course of realization": I am writing, I am going to smoke, I have an appointment tonight with Pierre, I must not forget to answer Simon, I have no right to hide the truth any longer from Claude. . . . For the rest there are, concretely, alarm clocks, signboards, tax returns, policemen—so many barriers against dread. But as soon as the undertaking fails me, as soon as I am sent back to myself because I must await myself in the future, I suddenly find myself to be the one who gives its meaning to the alarm clock, who forbids himself, at the instance of a signboard to walk on a flower-bed or a lawn, who lends its urgency to the chief's order, who decides on the interest of the book he is writing, who brings it about, finally, that values exist to determine his action by their exigencies. I emerge alone and in dread in the face of the unique and first project which constitutes my being; all the barriers, all the railings, collapse, annihilated by the consciousness of my liberty; I have not, nor can I have, recourse to any value against the fact that it is I who maintain values in being; nothing can assure me against myself; cut off from the world and my essence by the nothing that I am, I have to realize the meaning of the world and my essence: *I decide it, alone, unjustifiable, and without excuse.*[10]

What of other people in relation to this leap out of dread into free decision which I must take *"alone, unjustifiable, and without excuse?"* Onlookers, to Sartre (other men are onlookers, potential spies, never genuine collaborators in Sartre's examples), by making *me* an object and thus threatening the world which I have built out of my subjective liberty, can only be greeted with fear, shame or pride. Collaboration is impossible, since other people threaten the basis of my liberty. I can accept it only if I am willing to cease to be a man. As Garcin summed it up in Sartre's play, *No Exit,* "Hell is other people." (I know Sartre has more recently sought to justify his philosophy as admitting different relationships between self and others in response to criticisms from Marxists and Roman Catholics, among others. But these seem to be unconvincing and external defenses as long as he holds to the assumption of his philosophy as he seems to do.)

It is easy to ridicule existential philosophy as frequently has been done.[11] But we hardly will learn from it by ridiculing it. It is human and, therefore, deserves an effort to understand it and to learn from it. I can see how such a construction upon human choice and action might make sense under the conditions of underground life in an occupied country—especially a country with a tradition of personal liberty. These were the conditions under which Sartre's philosophy took shape. There the scene is set against me and my conscience. Collaboration with the occupiers and with those of my countrymen who have softly accepted the legitimacy of the occupation can be purchased only by surrendering my most priceless, my only, *human* possession, my right to choose. The old superficial certainties, which once blinded me to the dreadful venture involved in the prior choice upon which my conventional world of values rests, are now denied me. They give me no guidance in the extraordinary scene of my present action. Collaboration with my friends is proscribed, hunted down and punished mercilessly by the occupying Furies. Besides—who are my friends—which are stool-pigeons or proto-stool-pigeons for the hatred occupier? Yet I must choose or cease to be a man. How can I coach my action to wisdom from the scene, from agencies, from collective purposes—traditional and passé or current and deeply distrusted, or from the chorus, speaking through loud-speakers controlled by the occupiers. I must depend upon myself and make the leap of choice, *"alone, unjustifiable, and without excuse."* I must do so or cease to be a man, that is, to choose my destiny.

The form of action prescribed for man out of the underground of modern society is understandable, but it is far from tragic. Fortunately, its dramatic meaning has been explored by Sartre most aptly in *The Flies.* Here he has treated the tragic matter of the Orestes legend. We noted earlier Aeschylus' dramatic wisdom gleaned from the development of the same material. The tragic wisdom, "by affliction schooled," was that the situation could be resolved only by reconciliation and reconstruction at personal, collective-political, and cosmic levels. Only in the vision of a world restored to order at all levels could the suffering of Orestes and the others in the action be justified and given meaning. Sartre's Orestes kills his mother and the usurping king as an assertion of his individual liberty, an act born out of despair toward his previously "conventional" view of life. When Jupiter questions Orestes concerning the meaning of his act, he confesses his personal motive. When questioned about the meaning of his act for the other men of Argos, he replies that they can be led by the act to despair and perhaps to the self-assertion of their own subjective and arbitrary freedoms. More meaning he cannot or will not find in his act.

No, the existential drama is not tragedy. It surrenders the hope of learning from human action and its attendant suffering by shutting off all the other terms of the developing action, save the isolated agent, as possible resources of wisdom in our choices. Yet it may seem a sensible form of action within the underground of industrial society.

Before we take the metaphor of the "underground" too literally and come to believe wrongly that the exclusion of literal totalitarian occupiers will banish it or its stifled and distorted view of human choice and action from our midst, we should remember that there is an "underground" in all urbanized societies. Alienation and the lure of existential drama are not easily eliminated from our midst.

Grene, in criticizing existentialism as a universal philosophy, reminds us of at least one of the sociological bases of our modern underground.

The particular given situation out of which I make my world is not itself entirely private; and, though it becomes a world primarily for me, there are still, even in our society, some occasions on which it becomes a world genuinely for us. One can see this still, for instance, in some agricultural operations, such as a threshing, where the demands of the facts themselves produce for a few hours a genuine unity in the men who deal with them. Obviously, those occasions were most frequent in the old days of barn-raisings, hand-haying, and so on; and obviously, too, there are in modern urban society no such events at all. Here, indeed, there is the "one" and the despairing freedom of the Mathieus who would not be lost in it—and perhaps no more. But if we have lost those activities—part work, part ritual—in which men genuinely stand together to wrest the goods they need from a cooperative, yet unwilling, nature, we have no right, in consequence, to call our sophisticated loneliness a universal condition of mankind.[12]

Those of us who would depotentiate the lure of existential drama as a form of human action for our time cannot neglect to work toward abolishing the "underground" that helps give it its appeal.

2. THE LURE OF THE MORALITY PLAY

The disarticulation between the human agent, the scene of his action, and the human chorus that always characterizes periods of cultural crisis need not necessarily lead to elevation of the isolated agent as creator, enactor, and enjoyer of all values, and to the derogation of scene and chorus, as in existential philosophy, at least in its a-theistic varieties. The human agent may be derogated, instead;

the recognition of his limitations may be extended to a denial to him of all value or dignity; value may be displaced to the scene, which becomes the source of all value, the teacher of all wisdom. The all-powerful scene to which men are counseled to submit may be described in terms of God or Spirit, of History, or of a Nature independent of God or History. In any case, dignity is denied the human agent; his ability to choose, in this sense to be free, is discounted, his attempts to learn the wisdom necessary to participate in the determination of his destiny seen as arrogant pretensions and rationalizations.

When human agents are thus assimilated to the scene of action, human action ceases to be dramatistic in the full sense in which I defined it above. Action tends to become movement, devoid of dramatic meaning. Action and suffering just happen, and since the agent cannot learn from them or control them, there is no development within the action, no funding of experiences, no beginnings, climaxes, or consummations.

But drama is not easily excluded from human constructions, since it lies so near to the heart of the human. And, after all, materialisms, historical or otherwise, absolute spiritualisms, predestinarian theisms, or pantheisms, or doctrines of drift, are human constructions, whatever else they may be. So drama returns by the back door. The movement of History or of Absolute Spirit through the world may be conceived in terms of drama, as in Marx and Hegel. The timeless and necessary Being of God may be tortured with an engrafted temporal drama of salvation in which the happy ending, though delayed, is assured. The world of Robinson Jeffers' hawks—with unhappy, tortured, posturing, incestuous man eliminated—still has conflicts and cruel but orderly resolutions within its movement. The subdrama of human action, out of any of these illicit dramatizations of the scene, may be used to "symbolize" the "real" superhuman or subhuman drama. Man may write and enact plays with a purely didactic intent of communicating to men the wisdom of conforming to the movements of the scene, a wisdom which some men as votaries of the omnipotent scene have somehow learned. The developing human drama creates no new wisdom. It "imitates" and perhaps makes palatable a wisdom known by some other means from the beginning. Like the traditional recitation in schools, the teacher knew how the play would come out before it started, and the pupils, the docile ones at least, knew that the answers to the questions dealt with in the play were already known. Surrender to the scene may make of human action a morality play or a propaganda play. Its spirit and its working out may be edifyingly didactic to the devotee of an already known wisdom. Its spirit is certainly not the spirit of tragedy.

The endings of Euripides' *Medea* and of Jeffers' free adaptation of Euripides' play illustrate the difference in spirit which I am trying to suggest. We have already noted the ending of Euripides' play. The chorus chants: "The way men saw opened not / And a way was there which no man thought— / Thus hath it fallen here." The chorus has caught a glimpse of the way out of human misery and suffering which Medea and Jason did not find. They have learned through the drama.

In Jeffers' play, the gossipy human chorus is nowhere in sight at the end. Medea, the hawk in human plumage in Jeffers' characterization, speaks the last word to Jason as she carries off the pitiful bodies of their two children whom she has murdered.

> . . . now of all men
> You are utterly the most miserable. As I of

women. But I, a woman a foreigner alone
Against you and the might of Corinth—have
   met you threat for threat, evil for evil.
      Now I go forth
Under the cold eyes of the weakness-despising
   stars:—not me they scorn.[13]

The wisdom, not learned through men's actions and suffering but symbolized didactically by it, is, "Follow the heartless amorality of the stars." Surrender to the scene.

Where the surrender is to the immediate scene, to its conventional conditions and means, the resulting form of human action, at least to an observer, may become a kind of farce. Go about your business, follow the mode, though the heavens fall. Kenneth Fearing's "Dirge" suggests this dramatic alternative, not without a rudimentary comic irony.

And wow he died as wow he lived,
Going whop to the office and blooie home to
   sleep and biff got married and bam had
      children and oof got fired,
Zowie did he live and zowie did he die. . . .

Very much missed by the circulation staff of the
   New York Evening Post; deeply, deeply
      mourned by the B.M.T.,
Wham, Mr. Roosevelt; pow, Sears Roebuck; awk,
   big dipper; bop, summer rain;
Bong, Mr., bong, Mr., bong, Mr., bong.[14]

Surrender to the scene, with the variant forms of non-tragic action it may whelp, is very much with us in our world. Bred of the confusions and complexities of the scene which demand our judgment, of the vast power of only partly humanized agencies which demand our human control, born of a low estimate of human capability to assert the dignity of choice under those conditions, the counsel of surrender seems convincing to many. It may be a scene near or far to which we surrender or counsel others to surrender. The alternative forms of human action that follow from the surrender do not contribute to the learning of wisdom, whatever else they may yield.

3. THE LURE OF MELODRAMA

Melodrama is all around us, in fiction, on screen and radio, on the stage and in "real" life. Action is galvanized, alternatives sharply drawn, the hero and the villain sharply distinguished and delineated (or, more likely, in a collective world, heroic and villainous sides drawn up); suffering, when it is fully admitted as necessary and unavoidable, as it happens to the other side is suffering deserved, as it happens to our side is the fault of the other side and justifies the redoubling of our efforts to destroy the villain. What is fatal to the maintenance of this view is to recognize that the other side is also playing a melodrama with the roles reversed. For such a recognition brings the tragic (or perhaps comic) thought that both sides are right *and* wrong, and that somehow the action, with its conflict, unavoidable under the conditions, should be shaped to yield a painful common wisdom not identical with either the "good" or the "evil" of our melodrama but somehow partaking of both. Such a recognition is fatal to the wholehearted enactment of melodrama; so, by the devotees of melodramatic action, agents, critics and chorus alike, there is a constant temptation to suppress the recognition, to silence those who would coach agents toward such recognition.

If our first lure overstressed the isolated, individual agent and the second lure the scene, our third lure so concentrates upon agent and counteragent that balanced attempts to do justice to the complex factors that condition the outcomes of the drama are prejudiced and lost. Only *human* wisdom is an adequate wisdom from the tragic point of view; only efforts to learn a *human* wisdom, whatever committed action and suffering the learning may entail, can command the full allegiance of the tragic devotee. In our age of accentuated interracial, intergroup, interclass, international struggles, however attractive the tragic counsel, the melodramatic posture is easier to maintain. The power of its lure cannot be denied or, perhaps, resisted.

My earlier treatment of comedy was summary and perhaps disrespectful. If tragedy consists in a serious effort to define "the human," with supporting convictions that such definition requires committed choice and action and learning through suffering, comedy seeks to purchase its insight into the meaning of "the human" by a dialectic that falls short of a test in action and suffering. I do not wish to offer advice that would minimize the importance of verbal dialectic in the preparation for tragic action. To rush into choice and action, without seeking some verbal construction upon the issues, divisions, complexities and estimates, however shaky, of possible outcomes of acting this way or that, partakes more of the nature of melodrama, of farce, or of existential drama, perhaps, than it does of tragedy. The tragic agent is not likely to learn much from his action if he fails to bring to it some apparently just construction upon the major issues to which his action is addressed. Such a construction can be built by man in a time of troubles only as he plays ironically, comically, among the alternatives currently seen and proffered, the motivations and countermotivations that tend to divide him and his chorus, including his own favorite present constructions. What he knows further is that his constructions must be tested in the ordeal of action, that wisdom, though it does not come without the comic construction of a plan, does not come through the irony of thought and criticism alone.

I would endorse what I wrote on this point on another occasion, adding a caution at the end. It seems to me I was too much inclined to ingratiate Kenneth Burke and his advocacy of a comic approach to crisis, at the time I wrote it.

> I will close this essay with a half-hearted apology to Mr. Burke. It may seem a disservice to him to seek to enlist his *comic* approach to language, in which the actualities of language are related ironically to a free play among unactualized possibilities of language in the tragic cause of judgment as preparation for action. For it is in action that the agent evokes the passion of consequences and learns through the suffering of these. And this is the dialectic of tragedy. Yet the use of the resources of comedy as preparation for the tragedy of action seems to offer the best opportunity to men to learn through their suffering of consequences, if for no other reason than that it seems today to offer the best chance for human beings to survive the consequences of their action. After all, it was at the close of one of our supreme dramatic embodiments of dialectic, Plato's *Symposium,* that the master dialectician, Socrates, reached the conclusion that comedy and tragedy were eventually one and the same, a conclusion which unfortunately all of the other revelling dialecticians were too drunk to understand. So perhaps I don't owe Mr. Burke an apology after all.[15]

My caution is this. There is a difference between the use of verbal dialectic and the resources of comedy in shaping a plan for purposes of eventual action, and the use of verbal dialectic with the notion that it provides its own test of adequacy for the insights which it generates and the constructions with which it plays. The comic preparation needs to be chastened in its working out by anticipation of the ordeal which gives point and meaning to the preparation. Comedy in our time must be the hand-maiden rather than the partner of tragedy on my present view.

The next point is one that needs hardly to be mentioned. A tragedy needs comic even farcical relief in its effective working out. So does a tragic life. In a tragic life, all effort will not be focused upon the responsible pursuit of the wisdom which the crisis needs for its resolution. There will be side shows in the circus of life as well as a main tent. And, in the side shows, there may be room for comedy, farce, melodrama, morality plays and perhaps even for existential drama. The lures I have tried to resist are lures toward putting sub-, super-, or antihuman forms of action under the main tent of life or of education.

THIS ESSAY began with a major educational question in mind, "How educate for wisdom in an age of crisis?" Educational concerns have in a sense shaped the entire argument. Yet some pointing up of the argument in terms of the indicated deployment of professional resources and energies in our time may be useful. One caution needs to be given. I have been advocating a posture, an orientation, a mood, a form of attitude and action appropriate to contemporary human action and to the learning of wisdom from it. From a posture, a mood, an orientation or a form of action, one cannot sanely derive a program or even a detailed policy of education. What one can do is to point out educational affirmations and aversions, hopes and fears, emphases and de-emphases, consistent with the posture. And, while this is far from the whole story so far as educational program and policy are concerned, it may go a good bit further in suggesting the formal elements of a desirable philosophy of education.

1. Education must seek and use ways to induce in people a recognition and acceptance that we are living in an age of crisis. We must learn that the crisis penetrates every cranny of contemporary experience. Disorder threatens us at the level of interpersonal relations, at the social-political level, and at the level of basic norms which operate at the core of a culture and which regulate man's relations with the world and with other men. We must help people to recognize the presence of the larger crisis in all of the choices which they make. In a time when consensus on principles of order exists, at least among those people affected by our decisions, neglecting the fringe of irresponsibility that surrounds all decision may be a pardonable neglect. In a time of crisis this neglect becomes immoral. We cannot without help from each other become sensitive to the whole train of suffering to ourselves and others which follows from our decisions and action. Education must help to create such sensitivity.

The creation of sensitivity calls for breaking the old compartments that frequently divide ethical, political and religious concerns. For our choices, our tragic choices, require simultaneous attention to all of these concerns. This creation calls also for the development of ways of stating problems, methods of dealing with problems, ways of organizing instruction, which will permit the confrontation and interstimulation of ideas, insights, materials from the humanities *and* from the human sciences, disciplines now too frequently segregated and warring in university circles.

The practitioners of both sets of disciplines need to be reminded that they too are living in an age of human crisis. Collaboration between them is required by human problems which need all of the wisdom about man that we can focus and use. It seems to me that philosophers of education have a potentially important part to play here. It is easy to align ourselves with the "scientists" or the "humanists" and spin out endless melodramas. A tragic orientation to contemporary crisis indicates another role— a role both of mediation and of intellectual invention that will help both sets of partisans to see a common and important use for their special resources.

2. A tragic education must be focused on problems of contemporary choice. Man's most distinctively human function is that of choice. The central human discipline must be a discipline of choice. Whatever else choice involves, it involves value judgment. And we are caught as educators in all of the current uncertainties concerning the proper grounding of such judgments. These uncertainties are part of the current crisis in culture. The various positions urged in contemporary controversy concerning value judgments contain implicitly, if not explicitly, strategies for the resolution of the conflicts that beset modern society. These strategies need to be made explicit. As long as they remain implicit, we are tempted to try settling the question of how to ground value judgments on too narrow grounds—be they logical, grammatical,

ethical, sociological, psychological, political, esthetic, or what not. Somehow all of these resources have something to contribute to the clarification and settling of the question. Their contributions will not be made explicit until we see the question in its inclusively human setting, and this is a setting of practical judgment in which the question of what should we do must unavoidably be faced. Such advice may seem to lure philosophers of education away from the comfort of precision—a comfort which philosophers of education are apt to covet if not often to achieve. My position has at least this much precision in it—I distrust "abstract" solutions which are not oriented to, and explicitly concerned with, the flood of human suffering that follows the making of contemporary value judgments. Here is a field of study which philosophers of a tragic education cannot neglect. The disciplining of choices is a major goal of tragic education. The practitioners of such education need help in defining the character of the discipline.

3. I have insisted that there is a method of tragedy. I have sought to characterize it generally. I have tried to suggest its differences from and its similarities to the method of laboratory science and the method of comedy. I have also tried to suggest how the method of tragedy can come to include both other methods in guiding efforts to develop wisdom through experience. An education for tragedy must adopt the method of tragedy as its basic method.

4. Education must find ways of habituating learners in the charting and analysis of human motivations in all their scope, thickness, and depth. I have tried to use a dramatistic view of motivation to suggest the complexity

of factors that shape motivation. Human motivation is not narrowly psychological. Somehow we must escape the "psychologism" which haunts our thinking about motivation. In so far as the agent is a factor in motivation, psychological explanations are relevant. But as we include scene, purpose, agency and chorus as factors in action, the limitations of a psychological approach become apparent. The "subjectivism" which frequently haunts our attempts to chart and evaluate motives may be due in some large part to our thinking about motives in terms of psychology alone. It seems to me that a dramatistic view of motives is a first approximation to a more adequate view.

5. The barriers to the communication and common acceptance of a tragic approach to contemporary choices which I have named—and there are others—the alienation of the underground individual, the helplessness of the individual and his surrender of judgment to the scene, the hankering for moralistically oversimplified alternatives—present challenges to both educational philosophy and practice. There is no easy or painless path to wisdom here or elsewhere but these barriers suggest, however vaguely, areas of study where educational wisdom needs to be sought.

An age of crisis is an age of winter. The men who live in an age of winter must realize their humanity appropriately to such an age, if at all, for that is the only age in which they can learn to be men. Before we can think appropriately to such an age, we must feel the burden of suffering it puts upon us and other men. Before we can reason and choose adequately to such an age, we must learn to sing it. Education must be designed to help men to feel and sing an age of winter, even as it seeks to help them to choose and act more justly, more humanely

within it. Some such idea was working in me when I
wrote the following poem over ten years ago. I see no
reason to change it now.

> Teach me to sing of winter,
> Of night—
> (If particularly gay,
> Of twilight gray—
> Of artificial light
> That mocks the day
> Or memory of day.)
> And if my lips, remembering
> Spring,
> Murmuring nominate
> Dawn and day
> In tenderness verging on song,
> Open the western gate!
> Let winter night
> Teach them forgetfulness of spring
> For night is long.
>
> If after tutelage of night
> My lips sing on—
> Refusing winter song,
> Sing yet of spring and dawn—
> If, persistent in a dream
> With open eyes and without sight,
> I sing hopefully my song—
> Gay, fearless (all in shadows) seem
> Banishing night through loss of sleep—
> Teach me to sing of twilight
> For the night is deep.

Education in the
Quest for Identity

AMERICAN EDUCATION is, in a far from superficial sense, product and heir of the eighteenth-century Enlightenment. Its central faith is drawn from that tradition—a faith that through the liberation of individual minds the quality of both personal and collective life will be enhanced and improved. Its dominant mood was, in its beginnings and is today, a liberal-optimistic one.[1]

Among the assumptions that have sustained this mood and made it plausible is the notion that the will to be free and autonomous is somehow inherent in the nature of man. Boys and girls, men and women, do not have to learn or be taught the will to freedom. The responsibilities of educators, therefore, do not extend to the cultivation of this will, because, being "natural," its existence and operation can be taken for granted. In personal life, this means that individuals are impelled to make their own choices, to imprint their distinctive scheme of values and tastes upon the shape of their lives through the autonomous choices that they make. In civic life, it means that men and women inherently want to join with others, to participate in a rational community of deliberation and effort, in forging and executing the policies that are to govern their common lives.

Granted these assumptions, education can properly concentrate on the critical task of removing blocks to the fulfillment of this "natural" human impulsion toward freedom. The professed aim of education has thus remained the liberation of important individual potentialities. These have been identified, weighted, and "hierarchized" differently by various schools of educational thought, but the overarching aim has been more or less common to most schools of thought shaped in the American environment.

What are the main blocks to individual liberation which, assumedly, it is the task of education to remove? Ignorance, obviously, superstition, and commitment to crippling traditional authorities and restraints are the chief ones historically. And we have concentrated educationally on dispelling ignorance, on critically undercutting superstitions, and on loosening rationally the bonds of traditional authorities. We have tried to do so, at least where educators have been free from crippling pressures from the ignorant, superstitious, and totally committed elements in their publics and their profession.

True enough, proposals have been made from time to time in America to supplement or refocus this aim of education. These proposals have come from one of two moods alternative to liberal optimism—the therapeutic and the prophetic-revolutionary moods.[2] Those supporting the therapeutic mood have been impressed by the evidence of widespread failure of "natural" socialization processes to develop autonomous persons with a confident sense of identity and an effective will to be free. They have urged in various ways that emotional difficulties in maturation be brought from the periphery into the center of educational concern. Schools in which the validity of the claims of this mood has been admitted typically have continued to regard those with ego difficulties as abnormal exceptions and have relegated the management of their problems to specialists outside the main tent of the educational circus. The main show in most schools has continued to operate on liberal-optimistic assumptions.

Those who adopt the prophetic-revolutionary mood have been impressed by evidences of pathology in our institutions and their supporting ideologies. They have urged upon the schools direct responsibility for amelioration and reconstruction of these pathological social and cultural conditions. Their influence has been exorcised in "sound" education, except in periods of acute social stress, by anathemas upon their transgressions of the bounds of "legitimate" education, by their taking sides on controversial issues or their espousal of "indoctrination" —regarded as necessarily a chaining rather than a liberation of individual minds. Again, in most public schools, at all age levels, liberal-optimism has remained the dominant profession of educational faith.

The liberal-optimistic orientation has in it two related assumptions about the people who come to school to be educated; these are especially pertinent to a discussion of identity and community. This orientation assumes, first, that "natural" socialization processes are developing persons with a sense of personal identity, with an awareness and acceptance of who they are as persons, with a commitment and a will to become ever more fully free and autonomous. It assumes further that such persons have, in the nature of things, both will and opportunity to join with others in a rational determination of sound social policies, to become parts of a sustaining and rationally innovating community life. Personal identity and community, in and for those being educated, are assumptions, according to this point of view, not problems to be understood and dealt with educationally.

Yet scientific and artistic inquiries into the nature and condition of man, over more than two generations, have thrown serious doubt upon these basic assumptions of the liberal-optimistic faith. The impulse to freedom has come to be seen among students of man as, in some large part, a socially and culturally induced motivation, not necessarily inherent in man's biological and psychological nature. The will to freedom is a learned thing. Its prevalence among people in Western European civilization at the time of America's founding as a nation reflected more a particular set of social and cultural conditions which supported the learning of it than an evidence of man's inherent motivation.

More specifically, there has been growing evidence from studies of Western man, particularly of American man, that the conditions that foster the will to freedom can no longer be confidently assumed. Some studies have focused upon the vicissitudes of personalities, of selves as potential centers of autonomous thought and choice within the stresses and confusions precipitated by advancing industrialization. Men and women are widely alienated within contemporary society. They have lost traditional bases of identity as persons. They are seeking, where they have not given up the quest in despair, new bases of identity within the flux of a changing and conflict-ridden civilization.

Other studies have focused upon social disorganization and disruption, upon the decline and loss of traditional, common moral and institutional bases for collective decision and effort—in brief, upon the eclipse of community in modern life. Here too, those who have not surrendered the quest are seeking secure moral foundations for living their collective lives.

This accumulating evidence should have reminded educators that thoughtful and resolute attention to the psychological and social conditions of the will to freedom is a necessity, if our aim of using education to liberate human creativity and intelligence is to be realized in contemporary life. There have been prophetic voices speaking to the tragic condition of contemporary man, within and outside the educational profession, but their voices have been only faintly heard.

It has been more the impact of recent and dramatic historic events than evidence and inferences from studies of man which have led people to question the naïveté of our traditional formulas for achieving the liberation of individual potentialities. But, whatever the reasons, profound questions about the contemporary orientation and task of education are with us today. Let me suggest and comment upon a few of the historic events that have precipitated them.

We have seen people of whole nations, some as scientifically advanced as our own, acquiesce in and actively support the destruction of their political and social freedoms. In Nazism, for example, we observed a powerful drive to escape from freedom and the individual responsibilities that freedom puts upon its practitioners. And with this escape came the wholesale rejection of scientific and factual knowledge whenever it did not fit the official myth. We saw the manufacture and passionate defense of superstitions and the enlistment of the schools in their propagation. We observed a frantic commitment to wilfully manufactured "traditions" supporting an imposed national self-image.

We have felt the cold breath of a similar mass need and

response in our own country in movements like McCarthyism. And we are not at all sure, when we dare to think about it, that this impulse to escape from freedom is dead in the American people, and indeed in ourselves. A thoughtful response to such events raises the question of what is happening in current socialization, and in education as part of socialization, in relation to the commitment of Americans to freedom and individuality in themselves and others.

Another example is our response as Americans to the brainwashing experiences of prisoners under Chinese communists during the Korean War. Our feelings undoubtedly were mixed. In part there was anxiety about Chinese mastery of a new secret weapon; in part, perhaps, there was a guilty thought of its similarity to methods of re-education employed not infrequently in our own country. But, mixed with these reactions was, I think, a concern over a disproportionate percentage of American prisoners, as opposed to prisoners from our allied nations, succumbing to the technique. We asked ourselves such questions as these: Are our processes of socialization and education failing to develop a strong sense of American identity in our citizens? Do Americans know and feel strongly enough about what they stand for as Americans and as individuals? Again the more thoughtful question, mixed in with our anxiety responses, has focused attention on the adequacy of our current processes of socialization and education in helping people find confident objects of commitment and identification to sustain them in an intelligent struggle for freedom.

A last example is our response to being bested by the Soviet Union in the technological conquest of space. Traditionally, we have prided ourselves on our technological acumen and our organizational know-how. These

seem to us to be peculiarly American qualities and ex-
cellences. Being bested in these by an "enemy" raises
panicky doubts about the validity of our whole self-image.
The anxiety extends not only to our feelings of adequacy
as a nation but to our identity as a nation and as members
of a nation. Much of the anxiety released by this confrontation of ourselves, which shows the gap between our
reassuring ideal image and a dissonant actuality, has been
channeled into attacks, often rash and ill-considered, upon
the quality of socialization processes by which contemporary Americans are produced, and especially upon
schooling as the aspect of socialization that is most visible
and vulnerable to attack.

It seems to me that in the last two examples, there is
reason for doubt about the adequacy of our identity as
persons and members of a nation. In our response to both
the brainwashing and the Sputnik events, we ranked ourselves against other people in evaluating ourselves. What
was the Turkish score, for example, in giving in to brainwashing as against the American score? (It was "better,"
incidentally.) It is as if we had to compare ourselves with
someone else before we knew whether we were good or
not. This showed no great confidence in any inherent or
intrinsic values which furnish criteria for measuring our
own goodness or badness in this or in any other areas.
This, ironically, was the problem of our brainwashed
prisoners as well. In our reactions to Sputnik, we again
had to rank ourselves to find out whether we were good
or not. We were not sure ourselves. I will talk later about
this widespread substitution of status-ranking for thoughtful appraisal.

Now these precipitating events, of course, did not cause
the difficulties that are deeply imbedded in current socialization processes in America, and indeed in the whole

urbanized West. Rather they revealed them and brought them to public attention. They brought into public awareness what students of man have been observing and publishing during the past two generations and more.

Actually the two quests of modern man, for identity and for community, must be seen together if either is to be understood and pursued sanely. There has been some recent convergence of anthropological and sociological studies of community life with psychiatric, psychological, philosophical, and theological studies of the current identity crisis for individual persons. This is all to the good. I have chosen to distinguish the two for purposes of exposition. First, I will explore the identity crisis as it has been probed by ego-psychiatrists and psychologists and by existentialist-minded philosophers and theologians. Next I will look, more anthropologically and sociologically, at the eclipse of community in industrialized and urbanized societies, particularly in our own. In both cases I will be searching for the critical and reconstructive questions that these studies of person and community raise for the orientation and task of education. I will try to show how these questions about identity and community converge. My aim is not the megalomaniac one of answering the questions, but rather of trying to clarify them.

WHAT IS the contemporary identity crisis? I should like to begin by quoting Biff Loman, a young man in Arthur Miller's play, *Death of a Salesman*. At one point in the play, Biff says to his mother, "I just can't take hold, Mom. I can't take hold of some kind of life." Biff was showing, confessing if you will, an identity crisis. We need to look at many things about Biff Loman to explain his difficulty.

He had a father who was a salesman (and which Americans aren't salesmen?), who was more eager to be liked than to be respected or to respect himself; a man whose very livelihood depended upon putting on an appearance which would be pleasing and satisfying and, hopefully, sales-producing in terms of his potential customers; a con man who in the long run conned himself. Willy Loman had taught his son, "Don't worry too much about what you learn or what you think in school; learn to be liked by other people." The proudest day of his life was when Biff, playing in a high school football game in Brooklyn, made a touchdown and the whole crowd stood up and cheered.

Biff Loman had a mother who was not at all sure she wanted to be a wife or a mother. She was not sure whether her husband belonged to her or not. She was interested in ranking her son against other mothers' sons to find out if he were "abnormal" in any way that would reflect adversely on her adequacy as a mother, more interested in this than in helping little Biff Loman find out who he actually was and what he might become. Thus in his twenties, Biff finds himself saying, "I just can't take hold, Mom. I can't take hold of some kind of life."

All people with an identity crisis do not handle it in Biff Loman's way. His way is a good example of what Erik Erikson has called "identity diffusion." His identity was so diffused in all of the relationships he enacted with other people and groups of people—he was so desperately trying to be liked and accepted in all these different relationships —that the development of any kind of distinctive integrating scheme of personal values had been neglected and thwarted. Others might have seized on some totalistic view of life, some ideology, some church, some party, and thus shut out doubts about lack of fit between this ideology and other aspects of their experience. They would associate only with people who give validation to their position through echoing the desperately embraced creed. That is another way.

Biff Loman was asking questions which men in all ages must ask: Who am I? Where do I belong? What should I do with my life? What is the meaning of my life? These questions have acquired a new poignancy in our time, and convincing answers have become increasingly hard to come by.

A number of psychiatrists and psychologists of the ego and a social "characterologist," David Riesman, concerned with the vicissitudes of modern man, seem recently to have reached substantial agreement concerning man's difficulties in answering questions about his identity.[3] If they were to write a composite opinion, it might read like this: Along with the radical transformation in our technology have come equally radical transformations in our valuative life. Our former individualistic work-ethic is slipping away into an ethic of togetherness. Our former future time-orientation demanding strategic life goals is changing to a present time-orientation making possible only tactical expediences as life goals. We do not know where we are going next. Asking a young man what he is going to do after he completes his compulsory military service seems more and more like asking a silly question. What will the jobs be then, what kinds of abilities will they require, how will he feel at that time? We are saying, in effect, make tactical expediences into life goals. This shift in attitude shocks our former mode of future orientation. Our grandfathers, if they were middle class or aspired to become so, had the notion that a young man should set his career goals in early adolescence or perhaps that his father should do it for him even earlier, registering him at Harvard at the time of his birth. The attitude shift

shocks us, but the climate of opinion is changing to support the new orientation.

Personal autonomy is giving way to compliance. The
aim of development is not personal integrity but consensus, not rectitude but adjustment. Morality is becoming
a statistical, not an ethical concept. That is, we are confusing statistical norms with moral norms. To get a
statistical norm is to take a collection of responses to some
situation and find a central tendency. If you then go along
with the central tendency in your response, you are moral,
since the moral response is what the others think is moral.

> Having lost faith in religion, forsaken social
> causes, given up a sense of his own ultimate
> worth, modern man is spiritually a displaced per-
> son. He has suffered this loss in meaning . . .
> because he has suffered loss in identity. For iden-
> tity is the coherent sense of self, the awareness of
> who one is and what one is becoming, that pro-
> vides us with the sense of wholeness and integra-
> tion with the universe and makes conscious
> choices of right and wrong possible. It depends
> upon a stable set of values and upon the convic-
> tion that one's actions and values are harmoni-
> ously related.[4]

Thus might our imaginary composite read. As part of
his documentation for this view of the identity problem,
Allen Wheelis has reported the kinds of problems patients
are bringing to psychiatrists now as compared with the
kinds they brought to Freud and the early Freudians just
after the turn of the century.[5] When Freud set up shop
with his new technique and gathered a band of apostles
about him, people came for help with various kinds of
neurotic symptoms. These usually took the form of a feel-

ing on the patient's part of interference with himself and his life goals, which belonged distinctively to him. Inherent in these difficulties was a sense of self on the part of the patient. Patients wanted freedom to be more themselves than they were, in their difficulty, capable of being.

The problems patients bring now tend to be different. More of them are what the psychiatrists call "character disorders." Patients come asking the psychiatrist to help them get a scheme of values that will permit them to adjust more successfully to societal demands, not to try to see what blocks them in asserting individual self against social demands that prevent its autonomous functioning. The psychiatrist can no longer assume that people are coming to him with a self-identity; rather, they are coming to try to buy a comfortable and successful "identity." Their first thought might be, "Help me, Doctor, to get an identity that will assist me in rising in General Motors." Not—"Doctor, I am thwarted from achieving the kind of artistic or religious or spiritual or career goal *I* aspire to in my life. I am hampered by some kind of internalized or external restraints from functioning as the kind of person I am."

This attitude reinforces the notion that liberal-optimistic devotees of the liberation of man are going to have to pay direct attention to self-identity as a problem, not only in psychiatry but also in education. A viable sense of identity must be achieved and built before acquisition of the fruits and the methods of reason and intelligence can become important goods to any person, whether patient or student.

Now I would not take the ego-psychiatrists' or ego-psychologists' statement of the identity problem as gospel. They have projected a trend as they see it—one that cannot be dismissed lightly. Riesman, for example, collected data about man's use of his free time. He found that many people do not want their free time to be "free." They are not satisfied until their recreational life is as organized and scheduled as the collective life of the bureaucracy in which they work or the suburb in which they live. They guide their recreational lives by the television schedule. They are unhappy when their favorite program goes off the air or when anything interrupts this beautifully smooth but barren schedule which they are tending to impose upon technology's great gift of leisure time to modern man.[6]

But these specialists' picture of the identity crisis of modern man needs to be modified and filled in from other sources. They tend to assume too readily that the only pattern of individuality and identity available to man is one built on the traditional West European pattern. Identity has come through internalizing parental demands, which represent in effect the personally filtered demands of a compelling tradition. Having internalized these, men have a firm normative framework out of which they face novel demands emerging from the flux of life. Thus Allen Wheelis' book was subtitled "The Decline of the American Superego." The despair that the contemporary loss of identity is an ineluctable one comes from the quite realistic perception that we cannot rebuild a compelling superego in our changing and pluralistic society; we cannot coach young people unthinkingly to assume any tradition distilled out of the experience of a time earlier and different from our own. These students of man sense that there is functional rationality in modern man's discounting the superego and embracing some sort of consensual validation as a guide in the choices of life. But the doubt remains whether greater dependence on consensual validation necessarily means the loss of individuality and identity.

Helen Lynd's work on identity seems to offer an alternative approach to the problem.[7] She seems to think that ours may be changing from a guilt culture to a shame culture. Guilt comes to a person when some morally charged boundary is transgressed. It refers to the violation of an internalized code, not to a self-identified shortcoming in the self. Shame, on the contrary, involves a perceived injury to one's self-esteem. It may be induced by awareness of incongruity between one's self and his social situation. It indicates ordinarily some consciousness of having done something that falls short of one's idea of his own excellence. And this idea may be well or poorly articulated. Guilt marks violation of the superego; shame, some falling short from a nascent or articulated ego-ideal.

Identity and individuality may thus develop in the absence of a compelling superego. One may use shame as a mirror within the very processes of consensual validation to reflect the identity of the self. Facing these reflections may help men discover who they are and suggest who and what they may become. Shame, in this sense, revealing as it does incongruities between self and social situation, may define directions in which both self and society may be changed and need to be changed. Moreover, shame, if utilized reeducatively, may point beyond cultural relativism toward more universal human values. "Dreams need not be illusions." Realism we need, but "a realism that excludes the larger, enduring purposes of men and men's unrealized dreams is less than full realism." Mrs. Lynd's treatment of the identity problem begins where the diagnosis by the ego-psychiatrists also begins— with the personally corrosive ambiguity of man's life in a world of shifting and plural values. But she points to a possible resolution of the problem which, to a degree, eludes the other diagnosis.

Another source for deepening our grasp of contemporary man's identity crisis is the work of existentialist philosophers and theologians.[8] I will take as an example Paul Tillich's *The Courage to Be*. He notes contemporary man's widespread loss of "the courage to be." He notes the crumbling of a framework of assumed traditional values that once gave confident guidance to men in making their choices and helped them in making sense of their lives. Men are caught, thus, in the dislocations of a turning period in history—a transition from one era to another. So far his diagnosis differs little from those of the ego-psychiatrists and of Mrs. Lynd.

But when Tillich notes the peculiar quality of man's anxiety in our transitional era—the threat of emptiness and meaninglessness—he posits that this anxiety is rooted not alone in the historical but also in the cosmic condition of man. Man is again poignantly aware of death and nothingness as part of his existential condition. The faiths, secular and religious, which helped him to handle the anxiety inherent in this condition during the period of stable cultural synthesis no longer sustain him in answering satisfactorily the inevitably recurring questions about his identity.

Man is facing again, with few stable props, the ultimate question "Where do I stand in a universe in which death is for man the one sure thing?" He must work out a pattern for being in the presence of nothingness. Though Tillich does not develop the point as Jaspers does, it seems to me that the imminent possibility of the extinction of the entire human species in a nuclear war lends a new poignancy to this age-old question. Whether we think of it consciously or not, continuity in time for each of us is premised upon continuity in time of people, of societies, and of traditions that will endure beyond our own lives.

The imminent possibility of nuclear extinction of the species undercuts confidence in this continuity. A full clarification of the contemporary problem of identity demands, it would seem, a probing of it in its religious and historical dimensions, as well as in its psychological and sociological roots.

One familiar way of denying the contemporary pervasiveness of a critical identity problem is to attribute the identity crisis to the adolescent phase of human development—something that normal people naturally outgrow. Adults may say that questions and worries about "Who am I?" or "What shall I be?" or "What can I make of life?" are normal adolescent questions. But once a young man or woman gets "settled down" the questions will disappear because they will have found the answers.

It is certainly true that questions about identity are alive and potent at the time when an adolescent is undergoing the transition from a child to an adult. I think it is too easy to conclude that the questions will be answered adequately if we treat our adolescents right. It isn't that simple because socialization processes are not complete today with a man's or woman's transition from adolescence to adulthood. They continue throughout life. Beliefs and attitudes adopted in adolescence become obsolete as conditions of life change. Vocational choices have to be remade as occupations are radically redefined under the pressure of new knowledge, technology, and market demands. Moral and civic choices made in adolescence similarly become obsolete. The question of "Who am I?" must be continually raised and reanswered by anyone who is in meaningful contact with the world of events and of other men, whatever his age or status.

Since leaving Biff Loman, I have been discussing difficulties in achieving self-identity under contemporary conditions as if these difficulties were universal and not individualized. Actually, of course, the working answers to the identity questions are various, ideally as various as the individuals who contrive the responses. Yet the conditions under which the answers must be sought today have common characteristics which affect each individual's answer, if it is sane, however varied the answers may be. I would like to summarize these conditions, already implied, before moving on to the question: What are the criteria of an adequate resolution? I have mentioned continuing and accelerating change, which has rendered direction of life by fixed traditions untenable and dysfunctional, so far as either social or personal health and maturity are concerned. Contemporary answers to the problem of identity must be made in relation to continuing and disorienting changes in the required patterns of human life.

Mobility is a part of American life as it is increasingly a part of life in all industrialized cultures. A portion of this mobility is purely physical. Increasingly smaller numbers of people live a lifetime in the same neighborhoods in which they were born; frequent moves are the rule rather than the exception. One of the ways in which men and women once put meaningful boundaries around the question of who they were was by identification with the locality in which they lived. This areal location is increasingly denied to modern men. In other words, being part of a *local* community once set the stable framework in which answers to questions of personal identity could be worked out. This is no longer available to most men and women in urbanized and suburbanized America.

Even more destructive of traditional reference points for working out a pattern of personal identity is social mobility. This tends to deprive persons of identification with a family tradition. Men and women, committed to elevating their status beyond that of their parents must continually aspire to ways of life different from those of the family in which they lived as children. Pulling away from the values of one's parents is essential to finding higher status and validating one's self in the status achieved. This status may serve as a provisional answer to a person's doubts about himself and his worth. But status in contemporary communities is insecure, and once achieved, it often breeds new anxieties—"Will I be able to stay where I've arrived?" Social mobility thus may thwart people in their quest for discovery and fulfillment of themselves as individuals.

Our traditional liberal-optimistic world view has been deeply challenged by alternative moods. Some of its assumptions deserve to be challenged. But it is hard to locate self or others in any confident way within today's diffusion of ideologies. Locating one's self within an overarching ideology no longer gives rational support to a man in finding out who he is and what he stands for.

Finally, we live with the ever-present possibility of no future for man. This pushes our quest for identity to a deeper level. In our nuclear age, extermination of the human species is an inescapable threat, never far from our consciousness. Nonbeing, in these collective terms, has in it a threat of emptiness which the certainty of individual morality does not encompass. We must forge our pattern of being and live it in the very shadow of probable yet unpredictable extinction.

WHAT ARE the ways in which people are trying to solve the problem of identity? First, I will review what I call "pseudo-resolutions."[9] I would not talk about them if they were totally false or inadequate; I think each one has in it the grasp of a partial, but only partial, aspect of the problem. In reviewing these "pseudo-resolutions," we may uncover at least some of the dimensions which must be encompassed in any adequate resolution of the problem of identity under contemporary conditions.

The first "pseudo-resolution" is noninvolvement. One might say, "If I'm going to be hurt by the impact of change upon what I have identified myself with, I won't get mixed up with anybody or anything deeply. It's going to hurt too much when it ends, as end it must." How can a person build a rooted life when he won't risk pain and loss? He cannot, obviously, but that is what many people are trying to do today. This is, of course, no new scheme of life in the presence of certain but unpredictable change, when traditional community bonds have been severed. It is at least as old as the Epicureans of Hellenistic Greece and as new as the Beatniks. The weakness in this response lies in its atrophy of any moral development or growth for the individual. But its virtue lies in its stress on the need for detachment within the midst of involvement, for observation in the midst of participation. In the light of the changing conditions of life, I cannot see identity based on blind commitment as a virtue. A rational person must keep an observer's eye even as he is identifying or acting committedly.

Specialization is another favorite "pseudo-resolution," especially for learned men and women in our time. It seems too hard to be, or become, a man or woman in a general sense. Actually these sex roles are all mixed up today, and it is hard to define them. A person who uses this type of resolution might reason, "If I won't or can't be a complete man or woman, I may invest my libidinal energy in some specialist role, be it doctor, lawyer, merchant, chemist, social worker, or teacher. Within the confines of this role and its socially accepted and enforced prescriptions, I can master and defend myself somewhat against the threat of meaninglessness. I can shut out the larger darkness and ambiguity." Many people are, I think, overinvesting themselves in a professional or disciplinary role as a "pseudo-resolution" of the problem of identity. I do not think it makes them good teachers (or doctors, lawyers, or chemists either), since I suspect one cannot be a good teacher if he is not a person committed to actualizing his humanity through teaching and in other ways at the same time. One can master the proprieties, the language, and the techniques of the trade; but can one submerge self in any single role and still develop a viable self? There is a strength in specialization which should not be overlooked, because one does need confident role anchorage within the pattern of any kind of balanced personal life today. A person cannot go about being a fine person and doing his bit just as a person, because we live in a world in which people make their major impact upon the life around them through some set of specialized roles.

A third "pseudo-resolution" is to seek to live a complete life in fantasy. Like Thurber's Walter Mitty, a man can dream an image of self in which conflicts are resolved and made manageable, in which the surrounding world is made tractable to the acting out of his dream. The failure is in the self-defeating denial of realities which makes sustaining the fantasied image of self and the world impossible except through deeper and deeper self-obfuscations. But its strength lies in a recognition that any resolution of the identity problem today does demand creative imagination that goes beyond existing empirical realities in the interest of changing them. People who are afraid to imagine and feel possibilities and desirabilities beyond what is now empirically embodied, and who are trying to solve their problem of self-identity with a certain kind of hardheaded positivism, are forgetting something important. New patterns of identity have to be created. One has to go beyond what he now is in order to produce changes in himself. The place for the cultivation and discipline of imagination and fantasy in any adequate resolution of the identity problem should not be discounted.

I have already mentioned role diffusion as a "pseudo-resolution" in talking about Biff Loman. This consists of trying to be everything to everybody and succeeding only in being nobody. The danger lies in surrender of self as an autonomous center of integration, valuation, and choice. The partial value lies in emphasizing the realistic diversity of social demands upon anyone living in the world today and the corresponding need for adaptability within the quest for identity.

The last "pseudo-resolution" that I will discuss is totalism—a term which Robert Lifton used in his study of thought reform in Red China.[10] Many people find totalism attractive when the pressures of determining who one really is and what he stands for become difficult and onerous because of a lack of effective interpersonal and social support. Men and women are always under temptation to identify totally with some ideological formulation, and usually with the group, organization, or institution which embodies and promotes this ideology. The organization may be a church, party, cult, or state. Inclusion and exclusion tend to be sharply polarized, both in terms of beliefs and of persons with whom the totally committed will associate. Totalism might cause one to say, "These things I will not think about because they are wrong. These people I will not associate with because they haven't been washed or blessed or cleared. You cannot come into our life unless you believe and practice life as we do. If you persist in your differences, you become a threat to us."

A person who accepts the totalistic response to ambiguity and confusion has foreclosed his quest for identity by surrendering the responsibility for working out a personal identity for himself. Parts of his unreconstructed self are excluded from the totalistic belief system. His tendency is to project these against the evil outsiders. If I am deeply anxious about being aggressive in my ideology, for example, then I find that it's the other fellow who is really being aggressive, forcing me to fight. Unreality thus pervades the lifespace of the "totalist."

For me this is the "pseudo-resolution" in which it is hardest to find a partial good. I think it points, at least logically, to the need for wholeness of response in any adequate identity. Wholeness of response is part of what people are looking for in order to avoid identity diffusion and noninvolvement, to bring the resources of the whole person to bear upon some area of crucial choice.

Wholeness of response, on the surface, may sound like a totalistic response, yet psychologically it is quite different. Its principle of operation is inclusion rather than exclusion. The inclusion is not uncritical or indiscriminate. Differences are recognized, not denied; they are shared and examined. Mutual learning and growth through personal encounter with those who differ is the prize sought. Autonomy of self is encouraged and maintained, even in the midst of the remaking of the self as a result of new encounters. Boundaries between the parts of the self or between the self and others are actual and important but not impermeable. Free movement across these boundaries is permitted and encouraged so long as respect for differences is maintained.

Thus it seems to me that the idea and practice of wholeness of response is psychologically quite different from what I have called the totalistic response. The goal of wholeness in response to difference is a valid goal in the sane quest for identity in a world of differences. Totalism seems to me a surrender or a foreclosure of the quest.

The dimensions of an ideally adequate resolution of the identity problem under contemporary conditions have been implied in this critique of more or less attractive "pseudo-resolutions." The quest for identity is a continuing one which persists throughout the course of a man's lifetime. It cannot sanely be denied or foreclosed. It is a quest that requires participation with others for its consummation, and self-revealing and self-strengthening participation involves significant confrontation of differences between self and others. Autonomy must be developed and sustained in relation to such confrontations which challenge it even as they induce it. Autonomy thus requires commitment to a distinctive personal scheme of values and an investment of intelligent effort in its development. It requires cultivation of detachment and self-observation in the midst of participation. It involves a discipline and use of creative imagination which goes beyond the empirical conditions of living, even while one recognizes and accepts these as conditions to be both utilized and changed. It involves specialization of effort and skill, even as this specialization is kept in perspective in relation to other specializations and to a constantly refocused ideal of whole, human response to confronting situations. Wholeness of response is an achievement, not a gift; it is a prize continually sought but never fully achieved. It requires zest in the confrontation of differences; it welcomes encounter rather than merely formal interchange with other persons and gladly risks the destruction of previously cherished values—a risk which such encounter always involves—in the interest of a fuller and more valid realization of self. It faces death and accepts it as a part of life. To learn to live well must include concern with learning to die well.

This is a general statement, and necessarily so, since, by its own premises, it must encompass a vast variety of uniquely personal questings and arrivals. And each of these questings must be autonomously reshaped again and again in relation to a developing and changing experience of self and others and situations. But its generality does not deprive it of meaning or directive power in defining the conditions of the sane pursuit of the identity to which it beckons. Has education a part to play in providing the conditions necessary for this quest?

If educators are not to forsake their traditional aim of liberating the potentialities of individual persons, they can hardly avoid some sort of responsibility for enlisting students in a search for identity or in seeking to support and discipline students in such a search. This is true even for educators and schools committed primarily to promoting intellectual excellence. A person deeply involved in working on the problem of his identity will hardly be able to focus his energies on acquiring the tools, skills, and disciplines of intelligence which intellectual liberation requires. And a person who is caught in one of the "pseudo-resolutions," who, in a sense, is seeking to foreclose or deny his quest for identity, has also forsaken the quest for autonomous intellectual development, at least in certain areas of life. To stimulate the latter quest is to open up the former by helping the person see and accept his inadequate "resolution" as a "pseudo-resolution." This seems true of all the "pseudo-resolutions" noted earlier except "specialization." And, even here, pursuit of intellectual excellence in a specialization, to the exclusion of other areas of intellectual excellence, develops more of the truncated and merely technical intelligences, whose multiplication has already gone far to destroy any genuine community of learning in our academic and professional life today.

If those who limit the school's or college's central concern to the students' intellectual liberation must grant the necessity of extending its responsibility into finding ways of furthering the personal quest for identity in the interest of this concern, those who see the school or college as committed to the moral, civic, and esthetic, as well as the intellectual, development of students must grant this responsibility even more willingly and fully. But what does this extension of responsibility entail?

No doubt thousands of specific questions about a school's effects on students' handling of their identity problems would be raised by a thoroughgoing appraisal of current educational policies and programs with this criterion in mind. I do not pretend to know what all these questions might be. But two areas of inquiry seem to me especially important.

First, what attention does the educational program pay to the significant relationships of students both as conditions and elements of the teaching-learning process? Those who have practiced and studied ways of helping persons with their identity problems in psychiatric or counseling settings would, I believe, agree on one point, whatever the school of thought to which they belong: that is the importance of the relationship between the helper and the client in facilitating or hindering the reeducative process. Teachers have given relatively little attention to significant relationships—between teacher and students, between student and student—as these hinder or facilitate the teaching-learning process. Nor have they typically sought to focus conscious attention on understanding and changing these relationships as a significant part of learning. This relative neglect may not be serious where the acquisition of "external" information and skill is the goal of instruction. (Teaching machines may guide many such learnings better for an individual student than a teacher and other students can do.) But where the goal includes helping a person find who he is and who he wants to become, neglect of relationships in the teaching-learning transaction is a well-nigh fatal neglect.

A person's confusions and conflicts about himself show up in the relationships he seeks, avoids, enacts, and sustains, as do stable patterns of personal operation which he has thoughtfully or, more typically, unconsciously or preconsciously acquired. The question is, do and can teachers help a student become aware of what is revealed about himself in these behaviors?

I am not advocating that we eliminate subject matter from instruction and teach persons instead. This cliché foolishly denies that *teach* is a verb with a double object. One always teaches *people something*. But it is equally foolish to ignore the "people" in a presumptively hard-headed interest in getting *something* across. While learning, people relate to, identify with, or separate themselves from the subject matter (where it invites any investment or projection of the self) as well as other people in the teaching-learning situation. It is in these relationships to subject matter and to other people that important potential content about the self in its conflicts, aversions, preferences, and aspirations is provided, if it can be objectified and analyzed reflectively.

Suppose a group of students are studying *Hamlet*. One identifies strongly with Claudius or Gertrude; another shows sharp aversion to either or both. The students are revealing something about themselves in these relationships. It may be something they are not very clear about, something they are fighting against recognizing, something they are ashamed of. Yet these meaningful points of identification or aversion are places where the self of each student in its identities and conflicts is being potentially revealed. These ways of relating to subject matter usually have their analogues in the way the student relates to the teacher or to other students. A real confrontation of student with student may occur in seeking to understand their different reactions to *Hamlet* and to each other. If schools and colleges are concerned with helping students become more aware of themselves, can they neglect using these revealing relationships and to help students recognize and learn from them?

One additional note about the choice of subject matter is perhaps in order. Our liberal optimism gives us a preference for stories with a happy ending. Our exclusion of pain and death from conscious focal attention in both life and study deprives students, and teachers too, of bringing their relationships with their own finiteness and mortality into the range of responsible expression, analysis, and reflection. The anxieties about individual and collective extinction, which dog all of us at some level of consciousness today, tend to remain below the surface of conscious attention and responsibility. A sense of unreality thus pervades the desperately cheerful picture of life presented by the typical choice of projective materials for study and discussion. We are so afraid of morbidity that we fail to achieve a reality-oriented vision of health. If death, loss, and failure are excluded from educative attention and responsibility, life fails to be viewed with any completeness or depth.

The reaction of the teacher to such propositions as these

may be that this is not the business of the school. But it is this very question—what is the business of the school?—that we are reexamining in the light of the current problems of identity that have been thrust on all of us today. "But," you may say, "are you giving to education a therapeutic dimension?" I would reply, "I am not giving such a dimension to what goes on in the classroom—it is already there, preconsciously if not consciously. The question is rather how well and constructively is it now being handled? And how can it be handled to better effect?"

I am not asking teachers to become psychiatrists. I am saying rather that one way of helping students work responsibly on questions about their identity is for teachers to learn to help them work on their significant relationships—to a teacher, to other students, to subject matter—as a part of the expected and accepted program of the school. For it is in these relationships that the strengths, weaknesses, confusions, and conflicts of the self are revealed. The task is to use what is there but what is normally not used educationally. And it is in building relationships that support students in developing their unique and distinctive responses to people and events, to loss and failure as well as to success, that the often stultifying effects of conformity processes in "natural" groupings can be offset and overcome.

My second area of inquiry concerns the responsibility assumed by the school or college for helping students develop distinctive personal schemes and systems of values. Schools often swing between a "value-neutral" position, trying to teach "factual" information with no bias, and an attempt to impose certain official values on students—patriotism, brotherhood, democracy, free enterprise, and so forth. Neither approach is calculated to make value questions a matter of continuing, reflective, responsible concern to students along with involvement in factual and theoretical questions. Yet all who study the problem of identity agree that development of a personal scheme of values is an important part of the development of personal identity.

Whatever methodological faults Jacob's report of studies of the effects of higher education upon students' values may have had, his major conclusion is probably correct.[11] Most colleges have little effect upon the values of the students passing through them. The exceptions seem to occur in colleges where there are significant numbers of faculty members who are actively concerned with value issues and who communicate this concern to their students in their teaching. And again the exceptions occur where there is a more than ordinary development of a community of inquiry and of responsibility for managing the learning environment on the part of students and teachers in the college. What most colleges are doing, where they have any lasting effect at all on students (outside of technical briefing for jobs in industrial and governmental bureaucracies), is simply reinforcing the value orientations, or lack of them, induced by life in nonacademic culture.

We may well question whether studies of the impact of formal education upon students' values at elementary and secondary school levels might not reveal quite comparable results.[12] Where responsible inquiry is not pushed into the areas where the bases of choice, personal and collective, with respect to live issues are revealed and examined, effects of education upon students' evaluations and upon their habits, methodologies, and strategies of evaluation are likely to be fortuitous and incidental. Community membership always has a potent effect on the values of its members. Where community is not developed in an educational situation—a community of inquiry and of responsible management of the learning environment jointly by students and teachers—the impact of the educational experience upon value orientations is again likely to be minimal. Schools concerned with supporting students in their quest for identity must assess to what extent conditions prevail that make the stimulation of student concern with responsible inquiry into personal and social values an expected and prized outcome of the educational experience.

David Riesman ends his review of the Jacob report on a realistic note which provides a bridge to discussion of the condition of contemporary community life:

> Professor Jacob and I can agree that we do not want colleges to polish people for corporate or professional success as Alphas in a Brave New World, nor do we want universities to become ganglia in the chain of communication in a Garrison State. But suppose, perchance, we can escape both fates; what then? Is it not possible that the wry, resonant, and deflated quality of some of the most gifted and sensitive students . . . reflects a malaise no single institution can greatly affect.[13]

I have been suggesting that schools develop an internal community of mutual concern with the self-development of all its members. It would be a community of inquiry not only into the external world but also into the internal world through attention to the self-revelatory potentialities of significant relationships and sustained concern with the enhancement of the quality of these relationships as supports to autonomous personal development. It would be a community of inquiry which did not stop with matters of information and skill but pushed its way into a reflective probing of the bases of current choices and decisions, personal and collective. And all of this in the interest of encouraging and supporting adequate rather than "pseudo-resolutions" of the identity problem. But schools are parts of wider communities. And how far can one institution create a regenerative internal community within the wilderness of contemporary community life?

Education in the
Quest for Community

MEN HAVE built a vast society in the modern world. The
fortunes, good or ill, of each man are now inextricably
bound up with the fortunes of all men everywhere. We
are bound together by bonds of interdependence, visible
and invisible, into mechanical associations, whether these
be friendly or hostile, degrading or ennobling, liberating
or enslaving.[1]

Historically we link the building of this complex society
with the industrial revolution and all it implies concerning
changed and changing conditions of human livelihood;
this revolution has been triumphantly under way in virtually all parts of the earth, from its early and continuing
exploitation of chemical and electrical energies to its
fumbling with the release and use of nuclear energies and
the conquest of space. In building a vast society in the
West, we have shattered traditional bases of community—
local, agrarian, and economically self-sufficient—and have
failed to build new bases for the community which hopefully should grow out of and into the vast society in
which we now live.

Social interdependence is a necessary condition of community life, but it is far from a sufficient condition. For a
community requires, in addition, shared beliefs, ideas, and

values, and what is probably just as important, shared ways and methods of meeting the crises, of effecting the adaptations which are inescapable in the contingent and conflict-ridden lives of people and societies. Most basically, a community looks to the conditions and processes of its continuity and perpetuation in time. This means that any community is and must be a pedagogical enterprise. Most accounts of primitive cultures indicate a widespread sharing of pedagogical functions by adults in the induction of their young into adult membership in community life. In the West we have specialized the pedagogical function. One of the points I shall make later is that we are despecializing it again, often without knowing that we are or without assuming full responsibility for the unanticipated effects of this despecialization.

A society becomes a community only as it becomes a common, moral, and consciously pedagogical enterprise as well as a circle of mechanical interdependence. It is in the processes of building community into and out of the great society in which we are now enmeshed that the free and full-bodied communication of alternative ideas and values becomes desperately important. For without the widespread communication, testing, and reconstruction of ideas and values that are relevant to us, to others, and to our vastly expanded environment, viable community cannot be built today. This communication must somehow cross the strongly defended boundaries of caste, class, race, culture and subculture, age groups, differing professions and specializations, faith, and nationality, if viable community life is to be built and sustained, if stable and free persons are to become the normal product of community life. What barriers stand in the way of such free communication among people?

Traditional bases of common valuation have been eroded and shattered in all industrialized and urbanized societies. Men cannot call upon common value-orientations; they cannot depend upon them, as they move out of their protective circle of normal and regular communication, into interchange with men huddling in other protective circles of limited communication. The effect is to narrow the range of those with whom we regularly communicate to people who already think as we do about important matters. David Daiches testifies to this fact out of his examination of contemporary literature:

> One of the most outstanding features of Western civilization in the twentieth century . . . has been the drying-up of traditional sources of value and the consequent decay of uniform belief. Just as in the two great dry patches in European culture . . . the general background of belief crumpled up and created a new kind of gap between every man and his neighbor . . . so that same phenomenon has arisen in our own time. . . .
>
> In a stable civilization . . . the artist . . . does not need to answer the general question, "What is significant?" though of course an infinite variety of personal interpretations of the answer agreed on by his age is possible for him.
>
> .   .   .   .
>
> [In the twentieth century] each writer has his own personal schematization of reality, and he will feel impelled to select character and incident on the view of the significant which that schematization yields. Or he may have no view of his own at all and thus be faced with an even more difficult problem. . . . to make convincing [in his work] a personal standard of his own. . . .[2]

Daiches has described, as he has studied modern literature, some of the responses to this "crumpling up" of a common basis of valuation to which the literary artist can appeal or which he can assume in his efforts to communicate his distinctive views of the world. One way is to give up the task of trying to communicate to people who differ markedly from one's self. This usually results in the artist developing or joining a cult or a coterie and justifying his own efforts within it. The danger is that the artist may mistake the echo of this group's acclaim for a wider validation of the significance of what he is doing and saying. I think we find a similar process in academic and nonacademic circles. Some of the appeal of specialization is just this. If men cannot speak meaningfully to a general audience, they will specialize, form exclusive associations, develop their own language, read only esoteric journals published by their own cult, and rest uneasily secure in the validation this limited consensus brings.

In this process, basic challenges to assumptions tend to be lost. Opportunities for growth into new and possibly more viable assumptions and orientations fail to appear or are rejected when they do.

According to Daiches, other artists not certain of their normative content, develop a vast virtuosity of methodology and technique. A Gertrude Stein or a James Joyce can be understood partially in that way. The writer makes up for lack of common normative content by dazzling his readers with pyrotechnics in the use of language. I think this practice has not been absent entirely from the study of education and other academic and nonacademic subjects. The less sure we are of how important the content that we have to communicate is, the more we try to make up for it by becoming ingenious methodologically in "validating" and communicating it. What we are communicating comes to seem less important than the correctness or the impressiveness of our methods of communication.

Daiches noticed that the artist may also respond to this loss of a basis for valuation by giving up the aspiration of speaking to universal and important human themes: he finds a kind of common denominator that everybody knows about and he writes, teaches, and talks about that. In the process the artist has given up the pursuit of common basic valuations or even of significant personal schematizations of value. This is what happens in mass communications and in education when an attempt is made to communicate only what the mass audience is prepared to listen to without being troubled or thrown into conflict. We play it safe and popular; we avoid the frontier issues.

These responses are very understandable but fatal to the serious quest for a new normative basis for community life where consensus has been lost. To assume that it has not been lost when it obviously has been is downright immoral. To assume that "everybody really agrees with us" is not only ineffective and boring; it is also immoral. Our attention somehow needs to be focused on the fact of clash and on ways to marshal resources of honest communication at the points of maximum strain and conflict. When we think of individual educators in this respect, the problem of identity reappears. Where will men get the inner strength to raise the conflict-laden questions and to explore the clashing orientations, if they are not sure of their own identities and need to draw some semblance of security out of a pseudo-agreement, if they are not able to risk significant encounter and conflict with other people around them? But the problem of community comes in at the same point. How can men build communities of deliberation where support and reward are given to raising honest doubts about majority opinions, to engaging in significant encounter, intellectual and moral-political, with those around them? These are complementary approaches to the same problem.

I have suggested that many people do not leave a gap in allegiance when the normative basis of an inclusive community is lost to them. Many attach the allegiance, which was once attached to a more inclusive circle of life, to the particular segment of the community into which they are born or in which they work.[3] There again, the processes of validating one's self consensually against some type of association—some type of meaningful human response—tend more and more to be limited to testing one's self against one segment or one part of the society. All men are aware of the cacophony of the voices of competing groups when issues are raised on any kind of public question. This is potentially good if the voices can be orchestrated intelligently.

But how do men find or build new bases for consensual validation that cut across the lines of the segmental groups, formal and informal, which for many have taken the place of a community? Certainly, many mass communication studies have shown that people tend to pick out of communications those parts that fit the scheme of reality which they already hold. The aim of using mass communications and education to open up issues within peoples' minds tends to be effectively blocked because what people hear is what squares with and reinforces their own present sense of reality. They reject the communication as subversive and to be distrusted if it cannot fit into the limited scheme of reality which their particular group identifications provide. Perhaps building new alternative and significant associations, dedicated to exploring ambiguities and to framing and considering issues, is part of the answer. Where belonging is problematic, educators do not get far by undercutting beliefs on which the maintenance of present belonging depends. The better strategy may be to build new, significant bases of belonging in which beliefs can be studied and weighed and rebuilt, while the prop to identity which lies in significant group memberships is not withdrawn.

A third barrier to communication which, if eliminated, might restore alienated individuals to responsible participation in building and sustaining common life is a sense of powerlessness. A person who feels helpless to affect the major policies and decisions that influence his life tends to adopt a stance of noninvolvement or futile protest toward events around him. Can he be helped to find or build associations which will enable him to make decisions and exert influence without being subjected to the demand that he take a totalist response to the purposes and program of the association and so cease to become an individual person?

The suburb has become an increasingly prominent part of the social geography of our time. It offers a window from which to view the aspirational lives of those who would move into its way of life as well as of those who have succumbed to its lures. Does it provide a viable answer to the eclipse of community which once shaped the characters and outlooks of American men and women —a community that provided the basic pedagogy, if you will, which the school depended upon, refined, and embroidered? Maurice Stein has commented eloquently on the condition of life in the contemporary suburb, especially on the high place which status striving and status defense hold there:

> The social structure of the prosperous suburb is strangely paradoxical. On the one hand it arranges matters so that the daily life of the individual, no matter what his age or sex, is divided into many compelling tasks that leave little or no time for freely chosen activity. Like modern industrial employment, which it fundamentally resembles, the suburb is frantically devoted to the rhythm of keeping busy. Even the playtime of the children is routinized and many families find that the separate schedules of the various members leave no time for intimate moments with one another. On the other hand, while people are so desperately busy, they do not know or have forgotten how to perform some of the most elemental human tasks. . . .
>
> We face a curious and probably unprecedented situation . . . a society of material comfort and apparent security in which the most fundamental of human relationships—that between mother and child—has become at the very least problematical. . . . mothers regard suburban children as cases" the moment they lag behind the formalized routine accomplishments of their peers or, still worse, show signs of distinctive individuality. The paradox between busyness and helplessness, between outer bustle and inner chaos, may now become easier to explain: "Keeping on the go" is the prime way for the suburbanite to avoid facing the vacuum in which he lives. . . . it is an unusual mother who really knows her own child.
>
> For that matter, no one in the suburb really has to know anyone else as long as appearances

are kept up. Housewives, taught to desire careers, are trapped in the home. Husbands, trapped in careers which drain their best energies, must look forward to a fate that has become as dreaded as death—that of retirement and free time. Looking ahead to their own prospective life cycles, the children soon learn to submerge the specter of a life that lacks rooted values and creative meanings by throwing themselves into the struggle for status. . . . Not to perform these [expected roles in expected ways] . . . is to lose one's place but, sadly enough, performing them can never give one a place.[4]

Stein admits that this is a somewhat jaundiced, though generally true, view based upon suburban studies. He does not claim that all suburban families are like this and that all suburban children are preoccupied primarily with where they rank in relation to their peers rather than with what they are really interested in and desire to create. He grants the exceptions and says these too must be studied to modify the general picture of the quality of human life in the suburb. But the picture should not be rejected because it is a caricature; there is often stark truth in a caricature.

Suburban life lacks community, by almost any definition of the term. It is not a common moral enterprise. It does not involve persons in meeting the challenges that life presents to their own values. It is rather a way of life that in effect presses people to avoid the agony and pain and victory of formulating their own distinctive values and trying to live by them. It substitutes success in the bustle of the status rat race for thoughtful appraisal of the meaning or basis of life and of what is good in that life for the particular individual. It is not surprising that suburban schools are pressed to substitute the ranking of students as a measure of their worth for our professed assumption of the worth of all individuals. Such ranking tends to distort processes of self-appraisal designed to reveal each student's aspirations and needs, strengths and weaknesses. It imports the personnel department of the factory into the semirural fields of the suburb.

I sometimes think of the suburban movement, along with whatever positive things have attracted people to it, as a general and continuous role playing. We still have with us in our fantasy life the notion of the village. We carry around a nostalgia for the village, where people were neighborly and friendly and cared for one another as persons. Much of that has been lost in actuality. But it is possible to engage in role playing while living in a traditional neighborhood, even though the economic, political, and social conditions which once sustained it are now gone. Continual role playing on a collective scale leads to continual individual role playing of a life that is necessarily different from what it purports to be. In the process, a firm sense of reality, personal and collective, tends to be lost.[5]

These, then, are some of the barriers to establishing the communication of ideas and values necessary for building and rebuilding community under contemporary conditions of life. Are there no strengths in the situation? Is the quest for community a forlorn one? I do not think that it is. One strength is the undeniable fact of social interdependence which presses home the counsel of "communicate or perish." Learn to communicate in more significant and common ways or perish—this is the message that comes to us when we are rational enough to hear it. "Reality" counsels the building of a more reality-oriented and person-supporting community life. Facing current reality may be frightening, but one of our educational tasks is to help people to do so, since facing a reality is the first step in moving rationally toward changing it.

A second strength lies in the intricate facilities of communication which modern science and engineering have given us. They have been weakly and unimaginatively used up to now, from an educational standpoint. But they may be used, in conjunction with personal interchange, in helping people face the realities and frame the alternatives that confront all of us. The facilities of mass communication, if we can learn to mesh them effectively with indispensable processes of face-to-face communication, can be a great strength in building community. They are weak, however, when they are used by themselves and for commercial purposes which cannot risk offending anyone and, therefore, usually succeed in challenging no one.

A third strength is a vast supply of tested and partly tested ideas and beliefs, relevant to the intelligent reconstruction of our common social life. Students of society and of man have not labored and are not laboring in vain. Refined and developed methods for testing and validating ideas, beliefs, institutions, and relationships with some objectivity are just as important as tested ideas, if we can work them into the fabric of personal and collective choices and methods of choice. They are no substitute for processes of consensual validation which people are going to use anyway, but they can become tools and aids in making it more valid.[6]

Fourth, we have available demonstrations of the use of group associations to strengthen personal identities even as they help persons establish significant communication about situations of common concern. I am thinking here of group psychotherapy, where there is a deliberate use of association, not for destroying personal identity, nor for

walling people off from facing themselves or from significant encounter with others, but ideally for equipping
them for these very tasks. I am thinking also of some of
the extensions of psychotherapy, which have been worked
into processes of training and reeducation in human relations. Unfortunately, these processes have made greater
headway so far in noneducational institutions—industries,
governmental bureaucracies, health agencies—than in institutions devoted primarily to education.[7]

In judging the possibilities of building community into
the fabric of our fragmented and suburbanized society,
we find strengths as well as formidable weaknesses in the
current situation. Out of many possible approaches to
assessing what part education can play in reinforcing the
strengths and minimizing the weaknesses, two seem to me
strategically important. The first of these has to do with
the improvement of current processes of consensual validation. The second focuses on the complex and confusing
dispersion of educational functions in contemporary society.

Consensual validation seems inescapable in the life of
man. Apart from the controverted issue as to whether
the validation of factual statements is ultimately consensual in character, there is little doubt that men always
validate themselves, their life orientations, and their self-
images against the standards of some significant group or
person. Self emerges originally in the process of interaction and interchange with others. There is a continuing
reference of self to others in the maintenance and revali-
dation of the human person, as long as life lasts. Of
course, the reference is not always to concrete historical
groups in which a person has contemporary membership,
though his ways of management of significant memberships, where these put dissonant or contradictory require-

ments upon his thought and action, are necessarily major factors in the quality of self-maintenance, self-adaptation, and self-validation which he achieves and sustains. In validating their own character and worth, persons also refer their behavior to internalized reference groups which have been introjected from the actual and ideal social and cultural environment. (Value systems are part of the internal society of the person, as distinguished from his unarticulated attitudes.) Each person, therefore, operates within an internal and an external society with all degrees of consonance and dissonance, harmony and conflict, between the two and among the parts of both. It is in relating and reconciling, comparing and contrasting, elevating and suppressing the various demands and expectations of the parts of his internal and his external society that the drama of self-development or self-deterioration is acted out.

The processes of consensual validation which characterize social life thus have much to do with the quality both of the personal and of the community development achieved within that life. To improve ongoing processes of consensual validation in a society is to support both the quests for identity and community. If the standards of an association support and reward likeness and uniformity in the behaviors and beliefs (at least those that are overtly expressed) of their members, and the appearance of harmony among members at all costs, its effects upon those to whom the association is significant will be to foreclose, thwart, and make difficult their quest for personal identity. If, on the other hand, the standards of a group elicit and reward honest individual self-expression and self-searching by its members and meaningful encounters and conflicts among members, its effect upon those to whom the group is important will be to support their quest for identity.

The latter kind of group supports also the development of community within the range of its influence. Martin Buber's distinction between "collectivity" and "community" may help to make this point clear:

> Collectivity is not a binding but a bundling together; individuals packed together, armed and equipped in common, with only as much life from man to man as will inflame the marching step. But community . . . is the being no longer side by side but *with* one another of a multitude of persons. And this multitude, though it also moves towards one goal, yet experiences everywhere a turning to, a dynamic facing of, the other, a flowing from *I* to *Thou*. . . . Collectivity is based on an organized atrophy of personal existence, community on its increase and confirmation in life lived towards one another.[8]

Let us look the other way round at the problem of building community by improving, not by attempting to supplant, processes of consensual validation. Persons who deny their problems of identity, who falter in or seek to foreclose the quest for identity, will try to give the associations of their lives the quality of collectivities rather than communities. Or they will strive to maintain their associations as collectivities when they find this character already in them. Persons resolute and skilled in the quest for identity will seek to give to the associations in which they take part the character of communities.

Improving the quality of consensual validation in contemporary social life, therefore, opens an important way in which education can serve both quests of contemporary man. But what does improvement mean? Part of the answer has already been suggested. It means building standards into the life of any and all associations that elicit and reward personal growth as well as commitment to definition and pursuit of the objective task for which the association was formed. It means including significantly different interests and orientations within each association, both for the challenge to personal growth that differences provide and for the greater reality and validity in the consensually validated beliefs and orientations which the association comes to represent externally and to reinforce internally. It means equipping persons with the understandings, sensitivities, and skills that will enable them to welcome conflict and confrontation in their group life. It means learning to face value difficulties, along with the need for facts, in the choices that are made in and by an association; it means extending objectivity into the area of commitment and commitment into the exercise and extension of objectivity. It means building associations in which the stultifying dualism between individual and social is in fact, as well as in idea, undercut and bridged in the thought and action of the association.

Such associations are in fact educative in a normative sense of that term. The task is to make more and more of the associations of contemporary society educative. The place for schools to begin is perhaps with the sociotherapy of their own institutional life, building community there, where now only collectivity may exist. But schools cannot stop at this point. For more and more institutions and professions of contemporary society have become deliberately educative in intent, toward both children and adults. And these, along with the school, must come to see their educational aims and effects as supportive of individual efforts to achieve identity and of collective efforts to achieve community, if the impact of the society, in the basic sense of a pedagogical community, is not to remain sporadic, confused, and halfhearted.

This brings us to a second basic consideration. School people who focus on the formal education of children and youth still frequently tend to think of the school as the principal agency of education in contemporary society. Educators of adults have found good reason to realize that this is no longer the case. Many professions and institutions are now taking part in the educational act. More are entering it and those already in it are intensifying their efforts. This involves more than the familiar platitude of elementary educational sociology, which identifies "education" in the broad sense to include all of the incidental shaping influences of life in the institutions of a society—in this sense it becomes synonymous with "enculturation" or "socialization." The platitude goes on to distinguish between "education" in this sense and "education" as a deliberate attempt, consciously and selectively, to shape and discipline the thinking and conduct of the young of a society. In the latter sense, it tends to become synonymous with "schooling."

This distinction no longer holds true. Various professions are consciously, deliberately, and selectively seeking to influence and change the thinking and conduct of adults and, increasingly so, the thinking and conduct of children. In the health field, health educators, doctors, social workers, nurses, and podiatricians—and in the mental health field, psychiatrists, clinical psychologists, nurses, and social workers are very much in the educational act. The recreationist now thinks of himself as an educator, and camping rivals schooling both in its physical outlay and budget and probably also in its educational impact. The story is similar in welfare, agriculture, industry, organized labor, and organized religion.

A dispersion of the deliberate educational function has occurred in the modern "community." This is all to the good when we do not look at it in detail. It means that the community, in its various professions and institutions, is again recognizing and exercising its basic educational responsibility and function.

But, looked at more closely, the picture is too largely one of organized chaos and disorganized competition. Laurence K. Frank has noted the many professions that give advice and tutelage to the contemporary family:[9] in the school, teachers and counselors; and in other institutional relationships, social workers, pediatricians, mental health workers, church workers, and recreationists—not to mention program makers in the mass media. Amid this barrage of advice, it is surprising that more families do not reject professional help altogether and rely instead upon the astrologer or upon their untutored "common sense." No doubt all this advice deepens the anxiety of the harried suburban housewives and mothers whom Stein has described.

The chaos is not bad primarily because of its inefficiency or because of the multiplicity of the various voices offering advice. Some overlapping responsibility is potentially good from the standpoint of generalization of ideas and values from one area of life to another and from the standpoint of reinforcement of learnings in one context by reemphasis in another. And the variety of viewpoints is certainly not bad *if the conflicting voices speak in a context of cooperative inquiry and deliberation.* But this condition does not ordinarily exist. The chaos is bad because it reflects a variety of competing "collective" efforts to educate and not a "community" of diverse educational efforts. In this respect, professional life in its educative function now parallels the life of action in our fragmented society.

No common view of human nature, of its potentialities

and dynamics, now permeates these diverse efforts. No common commitment to helping individuals and groups deliberate and decide for themselves in processes of re-education suffuses the various pedagogical enterprises. No sense of common cause in the task of public enlightenment and of rebuilding community out of collectivity typically characterizes these diverse attempts to influence socialization processes.

Yet this very condition does offer a unique opportunity for an important educative impact upon larger processes of community building and rebuilding. Community of orientation and effort will not come through the development of coordinating councils of all of those interested in education. Such councils tend to become arenas for testing and exposing the power and weaknesses of the various combatants and for working out mechanical compromises among unexamined extant interests. Such has been the story of most attempts to build a community of pedagogical effort through adult-education councils. What is needed instead is the establishment of widespread occasions and opportunities for mutual encounter and re-education across professional lines, through joint studies of conditions and needs and through interpersonal and interprofessional confrontation in a consciously developed atmosphere of mutual trust. These occasions will not come easily or automatically. Professionals who have "solved" their problems of personal identity through overidentification with their professional role will perceive personal attack in challenges to their professional assumptions and orientations from members of other professions, and they will resist accordingly. Therapeutic-educational environments must be built in which persons can come out of their professional shells and explore man's crisis, which is their crisis too, seriously and objectively. Until this happens, the clients served—children and young people or "culturally deprived" adults—will tend to remain, in some degree, counters and pawns in professional status-seeking games played among educational workers in health and welfare agencies, churches, and schools.

A leadership which is at once prophetic and therapeutic must work to build and utilize opportunities for developing community of thinking, planning, and action across the lines of entrenched and irrationally defended professional and institutional interests. The stakes of leadership are high. The remaking of collective life in the image of community requires professional leadership, if the fruits and methods of learning and intelligence from research and scholarship are to find their way significantly into personal and collective decisions about our social future. The task of leadership is difficult. Is it too much to believe that members of the teaching profession can come to exercise such leadership? I think not. But the reorientation required within the teaching profession, if such leadership in educational collaboration for the building of an educative community is to come to pass, is a major one.

I HAVE tried to show that modern man's quests for identity and community grow out of a common human plight. Educators, caught in the liberal-optimistic mood that has historically shaped their outlook and enterprise, must move beyond this mood if its central value-affirmation is to be realized under contemporary conditions. The commitment to utilize education to liberate and discipline distinctive individual potentialities and to enlighten the processes of rational community deliberation and effort still remains, for me, a valid commitment. But examination of the plight of the contemporary psyche in its search for personal identity or in its desperate and baffled temptations to foreclose the quest has indicated that this educational commitment requires the building of a responsible therapeutic dimension within the educative process. This dimension must be built integrally into the process, not assigned to specialists outside while policies and practices of ongoing teaching and learning remain untinctured by awareness of this grave responsibility.

The danger of a therapeutic orientation is that, without a simultaneously quickened awareness of the pathologies of extant social institutions and ideologies, it may unwittingly be made an agent of adjustment to social conditions as they are. An examination of the conditions of social life, from the standpoint of the criterion of community shows that the pathological condition of contemporary human relationships and institutions is part and parcel of the problem of personal identity. Education must seek prophetically to change contemporary collectivities in the image of community. A prophetic-revolutionary dimension must, therefore, also be incorporated into our traditional liberal-optimistic mood. The temptation of the prophetic-revolutionary mood is to conceive and pursue changes in institutional conditions by means that thwart the development of persons who can intelligently and collaboratively operate the new institutions envisioned in the prophecy.

Can such fusion of moods be accomplished in reeducation of the teaching profession and in reorientation of the policies and practices of schools and colleges? Not easily, of course. Perhaps a first step is for school and college people to appreciate how the quest for identity and the quest for community operate in their own lives, as well as in the lives of those they would try to help. We of the educational profession share the tragic plight of modern man. Perhaps, as we launch our own quest for adequate resolutions for ourselves, our profession, and our institutions, we will begin to see and to build traversable avenues into the larger educational task.

The Uses of Fraternity

MANY PEOPLE find it a contradiction to emphasize group experience as a condition of eliciting and stabilizing individuality in members of our mass society. Such an emphasis often evokes defensive responses against both "groups" and "conformity." The anxiety seems deepest in those intellectuals most committed to the battle for individualism and freedom, who see a radical disjunction, if not a downright contradiction between "group" and "individual," between "fraternity" and "freedom." As the cohorts of a specious "togetherness" grow stronger and more vocal, anxiety is transmuted into despair. Yet this despair-engendering disjunction is not a valid one, although it disturbs many democratic minded American intellectuals.

Clarification of the meaning and uses of "fraternity" may help. The traditional literature of democracy gives us relatively little aid. Liberty and equality have been extensively compared and contrasted, analyzed, berated and defended, but fraternity has remained neglected. Connoting the relations of siblings, and by extension any peer relation, fraternity has stood in Western minds under the shadow of parent-child relations and, by extension, of leader-follower or, in bureaucratic forms, superior-subordinate relations.

The normative orientation of our democratic culture, including its qualified commitment to "brotherhood," was shaped within a Hebraic-Christian religious heritage. In this heritage, the ideal relation, in the first instance, is between parent and child—the relation of God to man—and, only secondarily, a peer relation—the relation of man to man. In the former, the themes of dependence and counter-dependence, often posturing as independence, predominate. As the Bible enjoins man to function in the image of God, personal maturity is conceived in terms of independence, autonomy, self-sufficiency. It is difficult to keep in focus the alternative ideal of maturity—the ability to function autonomously, creatively, and productively in interdependence—an ideal more consonant with the democratic value of fraternity. The second lacks the "reality" of the first, not only in the secular thinking about processes of maturation and socialization by psychotherapists and teachers, by parents and publicists, but also in the religious thinking of priests and rabbis.

In contemporary scientific studies of human development, their main line, as inspired by Freud, is for the most part firmly within this religiously shaped tradition. In Freudian thought the "representative anecdote" (to use Kenneth Burke's term) for characterizing the agony of maturation is the Oedipus myth. In this view, both the central problem and the dynamism of personal maturation remain within the parent-child relation and the various surrogates of this relation. Freud might have evolved a different version of the process of human development had he instead taken the parable of Joseph and his brethren as "representative anecdote." If he had, the place of peer relations in man's development would have been illuminated. The values and dis-values of peer group membership in eliciting a man's talents and stabilizing his orientations would have moved from the periphery to the center of our awareness. Joseph's relations with Jacob and Rachel would still have been important, but equally so would his peer relations.

Our traditional thinking on human relations has developed a vast literature on leadership but only a tiny one on membership. "Members" tend to dissolve into a faceless host of followers, and are not studied in their own right. Nor is it surprising that thinking about an individual's socialization has been dominated by parent-child and teacher-pupil relations. Correspondingly, it has neglected the problems of peer relations within the processes of education and socialization. This imbalance of attention is no accident, and it represents more than a cognitive difficulty, one that goes considerably deeper into the values of our culture. Before it can be overcome, Americans will have to do more than acquire additional concepts and knowledge of groups and peer group relations. Yet the relative emphasis on the influence of parents (or parent surrogates) and peer groups in the processes of socialization seems to be undergoing a fundamental change within our increasingly bureaucratized and suburbanized culture.

David Riesman has observed in the adult community of our culture a continued habit of mind once considered characteristic of adolescence. Possessed of no inner convictions, or torn by pulls and counter-pulls as to right orientations, many adults, when faced with alternatives, turn to their peers in determining what opinions to hold, what conduct to adopt. "Other-directedness" replaces "inner-directedness." The "normal" takes the place of the "normative." The peer group has become, and tends to remain, the principal arbiter of adult choices and evaluations.[1]

William H. Whyte has dissected the governing values of the managerial elites and subelites in our suburbs and exurbs.[2] He, too, notes a decline of inner direction. The chief aim of life is to satisfy the demands of the organization, its Kafkaesque internal needs, and its needs in public relations, which are often contradictory. Organizational policies (more and more determined by group processes) are elevated to the status once occupied in the Protestants' system of values by theology and the ways of the fathers.

These changes in the guiding values of adults are bound to bring correlative changes in the rearing of children. Indeed, shifts in these patterns must have been occurring far earlier in order to have made the alleged changes in character patterns noted in many contemporary adults. One theme runs through much of the already large and growing literature on the patterns of early socialization in American culture. The influence of peer groups in adolescent attitudes, orientations, and the criteria of taste and morality (always a strong one) is being accentuated in contemporary teenage culture. And the role of the peer group, as against the family group, in validating the self seems to be gaining ground in children below the age of adolescence.

The purveyors of the instruments of enculturation—popular music, magazines, comic books, television programs—are well aware of the emergence of a distinctive youth market and are exploiting it. They realize that the peer group has gained as an arbiter of youthful taste and conduct. Even a casual examination of the products prepared for this market indicates a new image of hero and heroine, for whom the peer group, not the adult, is the source of criteria for self-validation, for determining success or failure. Youthful heroes and heroines accept the authoritative limits to their actions set by their parents

more to humor or conciliate them than through any conviction that they may be right. Nor do they respect such
limits in a spirit of healthy rebellion that projects an
alternative rightness.

A favorite approach by young people in persuading
parents as to a new idea about clothing, recreation, or
privileges is that all the others in their age group now
possess and enjoy whatever they are asking for. It is hard
for parents to resist this appeal, since their own choices
of what is needed in a good home are made on the same
consensual basis. One story shows a convergence in the
process of consensual validation on the part of two generations. The parents in a suburban town were widely
entreated by their fifth grade children to extend bedtime
on the basis that all other fifth graders were enjoying this
new freedom. The parents got together and adopted a
common standard for negotiating with their children. It
is difficult to say how typical this way of dealing with a
"value-issue" between children and parents actually is.
Probably its main atypicality lies in the highly conscious
way in which parents employed the processes of consensual validation.

The trends in our culture seem to elevate the peer group
as an influence in both early and continuing socialization
and to diminish both the influence of parents and parental
surrogates in early socialization and also that of internalized parent figures (in the form of superego and ego ideal)
on continuing processes of socialization in adults. Whether
the effects of these trends are admirable or not, they
respond to a social reality—the fact of pervasive change,
which moves all men away from a reliance upon fixed traditions as the validators of choice and conduct.

Today, socialization and resocialization are not complete, in any sense of the word, at the end of adolescence.

Adults are pressed by a changing reality to make and remake major choices as to career, outlook on the world, or political and ethical orientations. Previous choices are being upset continually. Adults who do not avoid the reality of the choices confronting them, though they frequently do so, turn for guidance to some source other than fixed traditions. Consensual validation by some group or groups of peers is a realistic adjustment to this situation. It is not something that can be abolished by preaching against it.

If we accept the trend as actual and in some measure based on reality, that does not, however, support the near despair of many democratic intellectuals; the values of individuality or of liberty, in a positive rather than a negative sense, need not fall prey to the trend. Stripped of its sophistications, the claim that they must runs like this. If in early experience peer group influences become a socializing force with a much greater influence than they once had, the values of individuality and freedom in our culture are doomed. The argument assumes that peer group influences cannot be utilized to elicit, strengthen, and develop individual resourcefulness and talent. It assumes also the triumph of "equality in mediocrity." In this degraded sense, equality is stripped of its normative meaning of uninhibited access to resources for various patterns of individual or subgroup development, and becomes instead a uniformity or sameness among people.

These assumptions bring our attention back to the relation of fraternity to liberty and equality. The part fraternity has played within the traditional drama of socialization may help to explain the fixation which impels many people to oppose peer group influences to "individuality" and "equality."

In traditional patterns of socialization, peer group influences have been related dialectically to those of parents or parent surrogates—that is, they have been assumed to operate in opposition to the legitimate influences of parents. Ideally, if the dialectic were completed, out of the conflict there should come a synthesis, in which children could become the productive partners of their parents or teachers. The normative orientation of our culture and the dominant social organization which has fostered it have so far operated against the completion of this dialectic.

Peer groups among siblings within a family are often formed to resist objectionable parental directives or influences. The normal rivalry for parental approval is then suppressed to present a united front. Any group with the primary goal of defense against authority develops rigid codes of loyalty and standards of uniform behavior. The range of individual variation among its members is narrowed. Their distrust of deviations from group codes is augmented when, outside the defensive or offensive alliance, the members are rivals. There is something clandestine in the affairs of such associations; vows of secrecy are enforced rigidly. Thus, the function of fraternity in its earliest manifestations within a traditional family has been to reward the standardization of its members and to punish individual variations.

In this respect, the situation is not different in the nonfamilial adolescent peer group, which also functions both offensively and defensively in the dialectical process of transferring authority away from the family. Again, the function of fraternity traditionally has been identified with group standards that punish individual variations and that tend to reward conformity to a type. The enemy here is not only powerful: it carries with it legitimacy, which in part the rebels themselves accept. Mechanisms for handling guilt get involved with this brave banding together to defy authority.

The profusion of adult peer groups, or voluntary associations, has likewise served both offensive and defensive purposes in resisting the pressures of the dominant society, such as the purposes of immigrants striving to maintain the ethnic patterns of the old country against the pressures of the dominant Anglo-Saxon, white, Protestant culture. Groups like the religious denominations within a religiously pluralistic society have traditionally been enrolled for attack and defense, however ambivalent their professed ethnic of brotherhood may have made them in recognizing this motivation. Upwardly mobile vocational groupings—labor unions, for example—have developed a semimilitary internal organization in their struggles to heighten the social and economic status of their members.

In the light of these experiences, it is hardly surprising that peer group solidarity and loyalty should be considered as inherently opposed to individual variations in taste, thought, or conduct. The uses of fraternity that we know first and best have been to reduce and narrow, rather than to widen and enhance, the range of members' individual variations in expression and development. Fraternity in this view *is* opposed to liberty, and peer group to individuality.

But this opposition is neither inherent nor necessary in peer group experience. Cohesion and the suppression of individual variations are not inevitable concomitants in the life of a group. A group organized for purposes other than simple offense or defense against authority develops an internal division of labor, the better to achieve its common purpose. Differences in ability and talent lend strength to a group, if the talents complement one another in relation to its goal. A good baseball team cannot be made up entirely of pitchers; it requires a variety of abilities, in the interest of the game. The emphasis is on achievement, not on defense or offense against authority.

Where the accepted goal of a group requires complementary and variegated abilities, variations in individual behavior are rewarded rather than punished, encouraged rather than condemned.

The principle of complementarity among members has forced itself upon the attention of students of group life. The rationalization of life that has accompanied the bureaucratization of work, of health and social services, and of education has necessitated the deliberate formation of groups—in contrast with families, agrarian neighborhoods, or guilds, which were not consciously built. This process has made objective studies of the formation and operation of groups both possible and necessary. Men who are to build groups must know something about how they work; they cannot depend on traditions.

Study has drawn attention to some characteristics of groups other than those related to early socialization and has focused on groups in which the engrossing drama of counterdependence and dependence is not so focal or so deep. A comparison of the operation of authority-subordinate relations with that of peer relations in the lives of various groups is now possible.

It is easy to see in problem-solving and activity groups—as in all those formed for achieving a task—that group processes may be applied to elicit, reward, and develop differing abilities for whatever the goal requires. But this observation about the operation of task groups falls far short of answering questions about peer group experiences in releasing individual talent. The effects of group participation on the value systems and life orientations of the members are also important. Many peer group influences on children and adults in contemporary organizations with a well-rationalized task are now working toward destroying individuality rather than developing distinctive styles

and talents. Contemporary group experiences often educate members against a value system which would lead
them to continue to develop their own abilities. The
functional rationalization of society has often led to an
increase in the irrationality of its members. If teachers or
other group leaders focus primarily or solely on rationaliz-
ing the task or problem-solving aspects of group life, they
may fail to recognize the deeply "miseducative" effects of
these group experiences on their members.[3]

Peer group experiences, however, cannot only help
members to work more effectively with others but also to
develop the basic attitudes and values that aid the growth
of an autonomous and rational individual. Some of these
values are: an awareness and acceptance of self in its
limitations and uniqueness; a validation of self as capable
(within limits) of creative accomplishment; a commitment
to build and maintain an interdependence with others, in
which help can be both given and received; and a positive
appraisal of the differences and conflicts among members
as potentially productive of growth and progress. These
values are either absent or are being destroyed in many
natural processes of socialization today. Yet the peer
group, which is rising in importance as a means of early
and continuing socialization, can strengthen a value system that supports creative individuality, the practice of
liberty, and genuine equality.

People learn value systems, in the first instance, as they
form relations with others. These relations in turn develop
norms, with corresponding rationales, which the individual then internalizes. If people, young or old, can
build groups with standards that reward and strengthen
honest self-expression and self-acceptance, creativity,
mutual helpfulness, and the capacity to cope with conflicts
(within the self or with others), then the members of such

groups will assimilate these values as conditions of membership.

Conformity is not necessarily stultifying; in itself, it does not define the standards of a group. To understand the power of conformity is to become aware of the wide range of purposes, for good or bad, this power can serve. Thoreau, the advocate of individuality and civil disobedience, learned his values in association with others. He found them through his conforming to certain values within his family and in the New England culture of his day. His own values were shared by many of the Unitarians of his time, and were certainly not unknown to his own peer group in Concord. In short, he had group support for recognizing, respecting, articulating, and asserting his individuality.

The pressures for conformity need not suppress individuality unless the standards of the group reward its suppression and punish its expression. Fraternity can either destroy or build the personal values and orientations necessary for the practice of liberty and equality. Theoretically, there is no essential incompatibility, therefore, between peer group influences and the development of individual potentialities. These influences can build the basic values in individuals that are necessary for the social nurture of unique potentialities, and the major obstacles are practical ones that can be overcome.

Since 1947, I, together with an increasing number of university colleagues, have tried to help people build training groups that to some degree embody growth-releasing and growth-sustaining standards. The members of such a group are asked to construct their own miniature society, the only requirement being that they jointly observe and analyze and jointly seek to learn from their experiences. The training leader helps the group to carry out this requirement. Such groups succeed—though often painfully—in constructing a peer group which to some degree embodies the standards discussed above, and some members do acquire values consonant with these standards. The degree of cohesion and individual involvement often is higher in training groups than in other kinds of associations to which the members have belonged. Training groups demonstrate that, at least under special circumstances, the practical difficulties of making fraternity serve the disciplines of liberty and equality can be overcome.

What are some of these practical difficulties? Groups must develop trust in the honesty and helpful intention of the training environment and its leader. Peer groups normally unite (defensively or offensively) against the symbols of authority, and from this fact flow the identity-destroying effects of the group on its members, its punishment of individual variations, its exaltation of uniformity. In training groups, the members must resolve their normal resistance to authority if the group is to relax that defensiveness and support a wide range of individual variations. In this process the dominant normative orientations of our culture toward authority-subordinate relations and toward peer relations are reviewed and revised by the members. The authority figure must also be disciplined to accept the rigorous testing he must undergo in order to earn trust. As the group overcomes its distrust and works out its relation with him, its defensiveness relaxes, and there develop not only a toleration of individual differences but also the active encouragement to express them creatively.

Group members must struggle through and beyond the habit of stereotyping one another, to develop a mode of perceiving one another in all the bewildering and fascinating multiplicity that personalities freed from stereotyping present. The behavioral correlate is the achievement of a sense of real encounter. Members make at least a little progress beyond the bloodless interchanges that characterize so many of our relations with others, and move toward the often frightening but growth-releasing encounter of person with person. Conflict as well as agreement characterize this new level of human relations. Members come to see the microcosmic world they are building and also the larger social world as inherently ambiguous and paradoxical; but the ambiguities and paradoxes are now faced in a setting of mutual trust and security. For the realistic acceptance of conflict and ambiguity is one condition of creative response to environment. Some of the members of training groups learn this fundamental truth.

I have worked with a number of training groups of managers from industrial and governmental bureaucracies. The conflicts with which such organization men struggle are not essentially different from those of teachers, social workers, priests, and psychiatrists, though their roles may differ. One experience from a training group of industrial managers may give the flavor of conversation in such a group, and will illustrate a problem with which the organization man must often contend.

A member confessed to the group that he was not actually interested in getting ahead in his company and had to hide this from his colleagues, so he would not be considered queer. At first, this confession produced a punishing response from other members; on the surface, they had accepted the normal assumption that the road to self-validation was to rise in the bureaucratic structure, and to question it appeared somehow subversive. As some members began to take the side of the deviant one, conflict developed and subgroups formed; these argued over the proper hierarchy of values for a manager who was also a person. In time, it became clear that the real focus of the conflict was within each person and that it concerned the legitimacy of the organizational demands as related to their own unique needs. Various conflicts in personal values were brought out and clarified, and differing strategies for changing the system were discussed. The man who opened the discussion discovered he was not so much of a deviate among managers as he had believed.

It is not surprising that in many of the quandaries brought out in such a training group the members should regress to an adolescent attitude, for it is in adolescence that nonfamilial peer group identifications first gain their power. Though they are not necessarily valid ones, choices made then are now thrust up into consciousness again and reviewed. Such choices might be concerned with career, outlook on life and the world, the falsities in the adult world, or the identity and adequacy of self. These are questions that are normally of great concern to many adolescents, but adults in training groups revive them with a new earnestness.

A training group of adults thus provides a lens for examining the true nature of the fateful choices which our culture has led people to make in their adolescence. Contemporary adolescents might raise different questions in a training group, for the world has changed. In a group of middle-aged adults, however, the results of some of the stresses and strains of our culture that were operative in their adolescence can be observed.

Many crippling constructions of a self-image are revealed, reviewed, and revised in training groups. Among them are those masculine self-images that deny and suppress feminine components in the male, and female self-images that deny and suppress correlative male components. One of the most stultifying effects of our culture comes from the stereotyping that forces people to deny parts of themselves. These false constructions make for a waste of energy in the defense of an invalid self-image before one's self and the world. Abraham Maslow has said that the acceptance of one's total nature is one of the most dependable criteria of a creative personality.[4] It is a plausible hypothesis that today both peer groupings and families support this form of crippling self-rejection.

The training group, of course, is only one example of the current attempts to use peer group experience to support a valid self-acceptance and the acceptance of one's individual limitations and potentialities. The group is perhaps a unique attempt to foster a value system that supports continuing realization of these potentialities, an experimental attempt to apply fraternity in an unorthodox manner and for unorthodox ends.

An example of a similar use of fraternity is the reported effort of detached group workers to establish rehabilitating relations with youth gangs.[5] This process presents difficulties like those encountered by the trainer in a training group. The worker, like the trainer, does not try to deny the importance of peer group experience in the personal lives of the gang members. He recognizes that it has a value, even under the constricting and stultifying form of the gang. He must begin by affirming the personal value of fraternity. By implication, he does not affirm a priori the adequacy of the values of the adult environment, against which the gang is in revolt. He comes in, not to break up the gang, but to gain a special kind of membership in it that will enable him to work with it toward remaking its standards in patterns that release growth. This is the same problem that the training group leader faces in struggling toward a mutual and reciprocal relationship with the training group. In both situations, trust of the authoritative adult environment, or of the leader as surrogate of that environment, must be achieved before the group can give up its fixation on primitive offensive or defensive goals and its slavish reliance on standards that inhibit the growth of its individual members.

A closely related example comes from the experimental efforts of social workers in Boston to construct neighborhood peer groups around physically or emotionally handicapped youngsters.[6] One criterion in choosing the peers is the nature of the boy's or girl's handicap. These workers are trying to learn more about how to construct and utilize peer groups as part of the rehabilitation of handicapped persons in general. Equally important are some of the reported effects on normal children who work with the handicapped ones in peer relations. The workers consciously endeavor not only to assist the rehabilitation of the handicapped member but also to help the other members to grow in the process. Growth comes from acquiring a new shared outlook of acceptance of their differences. In a sense, the handicapped person dramatizes the differences and deviations that are inherent in every individual, though in more subtle forms.

In a boys' group, for example, the boys are expected to show tenderness as well as robustness. This is a hard but important thing for male children in our culture to learn to do. As members work through the dramatic differences between themselves and the handicapped member, other differences, not so dramatic, in themselves and others tend to be accepted also. The adult worker is needed to help the group accomplish these new insights, but he must work with the group in such a way as not to destroy its peer character. Again, a new and difficult role for the authority figure in socializing processes is indicated. He must exert a reeducative influence within a group, without destroying the group's peer character, on which its reeducative value depends.

Thus the practical difficulties in utilizing fraternity to develop the disciplines of liberty and equality can be overcome, at least in specially created settings. True, the experimental demonstrations of this fact have accomplished little when measured against the magnitude of the social problem to be solved, but their results have been encouraging enough to warrant extended effort along analogous lines. It is important that the experimentation not be limited in the future to the educational, semitherapeutic and therapeutic contexts to which it has thus far been confined. Our society has drifted into patterns of early and continuing socialization which elevate peer group influences to a new prominence. In this drift, values of individuality, of liberty and equality, have been eroded and in some cases lost. Our inherited normative orientation and our unanalyzed experiences with peer groups in our own socialization frequently block us from seeing that the best hope for maintaining, strengthening, and extending these eroded values may well lie in transforming the quality of peer group experiences.[7]

To make peer group experiences serve individuality, leaders in socialization must reanalyze and reevaluate the normative orientations of our culture toward valid processes of socialization and valid ideals of personal maturity. They must achieve an understanding of the uses and abuses of fraternity.

Relations with authority will never disappear from work and citizenship or from early and continuing processes of socialization. However, the role of authority in socialization must be reconceived. Authority figures must learn a new respect for peer group processes as potentialities for either growth or stultification. Like training group leaders and detached group workers, authority figures must translate this respect into actions appropriate to the social affiliations they control and direct. This translation will require the relatively novel utilization of authority to enhance the normative content of peer group life without destroying its essential character. The first step in endowing group life with creative responsibilities may well be a realistic revaluation, both cognitive and affective, of the uses and abuses of fraternity.

Man and Moloch

THE LIVES of most contemporary men are lived on the sufferance of some bureaucratic organization or another. This is true, in the first instance, of a man's vocational life. His talents are employed, or not employed, by some bureaucracy in advancing its goals or enhancing its image. If employed, he is provided by the organization in turn with means to draw on the products of other bureaucratic organizations in sustaining him in the rest of his life. Bureaucratic organizations are thus primary factors in contemporary man's employment as worker. Increasingly, he must reckon also with bureaucracies in his nonworker roles—as citizen, as student, and as client in quest of health, recreational and welfare services as well.

Moreover, the organizations which environ his life are endowed with earthly immortality as legally corporate persons—an immortality to which biologic man cannot reasonably aspire. They are made up of men but possess a continuity and character which extend beyond the life spans of any or all of the men who for a time occupy positions within their pyramidal structures. Being pyramidal in structure, to men living on their middle or lower slopes, the decisions of the organization—decisions which affect fundamentally their employment or nonemployment, their status as workers or nonworkers, indeed, as men—are shrouded in mystery. Perhaps the mystery enshrouds those on their utmost pinnacles as well.

It is not surprising that these corporate persons—these quasi-human giants on whom our lives basically depend—have received increasing attention by scientific students of man and society over the past three generations of mortal men. But it may be doubted whether these studies have plumbed the mysteries of corporate organizations. Nor is it surprising that temples, schools of administration and management, have developed to instruct men in manipulating, if not always in comprehending, these mysteries. Polemic writings of justification and attack upon bureaucracy are vast in bulk but only meagerly enlightening.

Some writers of imaginative literature too have attempted to assay the inner reactions of men to organizations which make a more or less total demand upon their lives. The most insightful literature has been written from the standpoint of men dependent upon but in some degree estranged from a bureaucratic system.

FRANZ KAFKA's *The Castle* is a study of a man (K.), bound up with, yet fundamentally estranged from, a bureaucracy. Most interpreters and critics move, too quickly as I see it, to the ontological and theological significances of Kafka's work. These significances are undeniable. Any deep examination of contemporary man and organization involves the examiner in ontological and theological questions. But to allegorize too quickly K.'s organizational involvements may rob Kafka's work of its power to illuminate the social plight of contemporary man.

Kafka's hero, K., finds himself in a village huddled near the Castle which is the principal employer of people in the village and the determiner, usually by indirection, of the life patterns of the village people. K. has been employed by the Castle to serve as land surveyor in the village. He has come to receive instructions concerning his work and legitimation of his status. The action of the novel is taken up completely with K.'s abortive and frustrated attempts to find some authorized representative of the Castle who can clarify his task and recognize and validate his status as a Castle employee. The action moves in a dream sequence, from one conspiracy by K. to make contact with the Castle to another conspiracy, from one frustration to another. The "rational" content of K.'s conspiracies—trying to clarify his job assignment—diminishes as the nightmare "progresses." The content of seeking contact—any contact—with those on whom he fundamentally depends, who presumably have him, his interests and his future in mind, becomes more prominent in K.'s plotting. The increasingly desperate purpose of contact with the Castle is to validate his status. And his status in the Castle comes to coincide more and more with his very existence as a man. Nonacceptance by the Castle becomes equivalent to Nothingness. Assurance of his acceptance by someone in the Castle becomes a very condition of personal existence and self-acceptance.

The novel as Kafka left it is incomplete. As it stands, it ends with K.'s complete isolation from human contact. Frieda, to whom for a time K. had given conditional love and from whom he has received anxious love in return, has rejected him and turned to Jeremiah, one of his dismissed assistants from the Castle, whom she is nursing in her room at the inn—"within it seemed to be bright and warm, a few whispers were audible, probably loving cajolements to get Jeremiah to bed, then the door was closed." According to Max Brod, Kafka's confidant and literary executor, Kafka planned a concluding chapter which he did not live to write. As Brod describes the plan—"He (K.) was not to relax in his struggle, but was to die worn out by it. Round his deathbed the villagers were to assemble and from the Castle itself the word was to come that though K.'s legal claim to live in the village was not valid, yet, taking certain auxiliary circumstances into account, he was to be permitted to live and work there." Kafka had apparently seen no resolution of K.'s struggle for unconditional acceptance by the organizational power that controlled his life, unless death be taken as resolution.

When the dynamics of K.'s relationships with the Castle and with other people in the village are probed more deeply, several aspects of K.'s plight are thrown into sharp relief. The demand of the Castle upon him, though nominally a vocational demand, becomes a total demand, at least as K. perceives it. The demands of the organization upon K. frustrate and distort his aspirations, choices, and actions throughout the range of his life. This is true, even though these demands are unclear. That the demand is total lends desperate importance to the quest for its clarification. And, because the demand is seen as total, the quest for clarification becomes an agonized quest by K. for the meaning of his life and for ultimate validation of himself as a person.

K. is quite aware of the desperate anxiety with which the clouded yet total demand of the Castle infuses his life.

> In this life it might easily happen, if he were not always on his guard, that one day or other, in spite of the amiability of the authorities and the

scrupulous fulfillment of all his exaggeratedly
light duties, he might—deceived by the apparent
favor shown him—conduct himself so impru-
dently that he might get a fall; and the authorities still ever mild and friendly, and as it were
against their will, but in the name of some public regulation unknown to him, might have to
come and clear him out of the way. And what
was it, this other life to which he was consigned?
Never yet had K. seen vocation and life so interlaced as here, so interlaced that sometimes one
might think they had exchanged places. What
importance, for example, had the power, merely
formal up till now, which Klamm exercised over
K.'s services, compared with the very real power
which Klamm possessed in K.'s bedroom? [Klamm
was K.'s superior in the Castle who had written
him vague messages commending him for work
he had not done. K. had taken Klamm's mistress,
Frieda, into his own bed as one of his strategies
for winning an encounter with Klamm, a *bona
fide* representative of the Castle.] So it came
about that while a light and frivolous bearing . . .
was sufficient when one came in direct contact
with the authorities, one needed in everything
else the greatest caution, and had to look around
on every side before one made a single step.

In effect, K. deifies the system of the Castle. The graded
ranks of the Castle's personnel become avenues toward
the godhead which, by assumption, resided in the Castle's
upper reaches. One's nearness to the top becomes a
measure of one's reality and one's worth. It is not that K.
is unaware of the bureaucratic stupidities and mistakes
which seem empirically to mark the Castle's mode of
operation. But awareness of these only deepen the mys-

tery which clouds the "real" motives and plans which faith in the deity force him to believe are available, if he might only encounter those nearer to the top of the system.

Yet the system operates consistently to frustrate his quest for contact with those who might reveal the concern of the Castle for him and its plans for him. Alienation becomes a way of life for K. And heightening alienation only augments the vigor of his efforts for encounter with personifications of the system which puts him under some total demand for service to purposes of which he is unaware.

All of K.'s life activities become operations to reduce the anxieties of his alienated state. The usual antidotes to alienation do not work for him. Thus the joys of sex and companionship with Frieda are always subsidiary to her possible usefulness in effecting for him a face-to-face encounter with Klamm, her former lover. Sex and companionship cannot reduce his alienation since it is rooted deeply in his estrangement from the Castle. Similarly, his other peer relationships in the village have in them no solace for him. For these relationships are all undertaken for their possible instrumental value in facilitating his upward movement in the system.

Nor do K.'s frequent, vivid, frank and logical analyses of his own motivations and condition help him toward a management of his alienation through understanding it better. His verbal catharses lead to no relief because the "right" persons are not available to hear his confessions. His logical analyses lead to no insight. They serve merely to vary the pattern and augment the intensity of his persistent struggle to meet the determiners of his destiny face to face.

Deep resentment is mixed with K.'s adulation of the

Castle, a resentment which he scarcely dares acknowledge to himself. The amiability of the Castle serves only to augment this resentment. As Kafka puts it—

> By the fact that they had at once amply met his wishes in all unimportant matters—and hitherto only unimportant matters had come up—they robbed him of the possibility of light and easy victories, and with that of the satisfaction which must accompany them and the well-grounded confidence for further and greater struggles, which must result from them. Instead, they let K. go anywhere he liked—of course only within the village—and thus pampered and enervated him, ruled out all possibility of conflict, and transposed him to an unofficial, totally unrecognized, troubled and alien existence.

His very manhood is threatened by the blandishments of the Castle. He seeks encounter, challenge and conflict. He is taken care of with a bland, impersonal kindness which meets his creature needs but fails to honor his deeper needs to be taken seriously as a man. He is taken as a manipulable instrument of the Castle's purpose just as K. takes the villagers in his abortive associations in the village.

This resentment is most clearly portrayed in his treatment of the assistants, Arthur and Jeremiah, with whom the Castle has provided him. It may be flattering to have assistants. But the provision of the assistants for work that has not been defined is a frustration to a man compelled to prove himself and "make good." Moreover, Arthur and Jeremiah behave as clowns, seeking always to cajole and entertain him. But K.'s plight is a serious matter to him. And the clowning of his assistants only underlines his doubts about his adequacy, about his status and about himself. It is small wonder that he beats his assistants, and shuts them out in the cold. When he dismisses them finally, Jeremiah, freed from the inhibitions of his former role relationship—one never speaks openly with his boss—is able to tell K. that his and Arthur's instructions from the Castle have been to get K. to take himself less seriously, and presumably as a result to accept his amiable management by a kindly bureaucracy without question or challenge.

K.'s central quest is to validate himself as a man and a person. He seeks this validation through rising into the Castle to confront those (or perhaps the One) who, he continues to believe, command the bases for an adequate validation. The more vigorously he seeks the critical encounter, the more effectively it is denied him. In his resulting alienation from the system on which he still depends for his life, his desperate attempts to reduce alienation pervert his human relationships in sex and companionship, distort the fruits of his logic and self-analysis, divert his energies from productive work, and leave him in complete isolation from himself and from other people. So ends K.'s unequal struggle with the Moloch who lives in his Castle.

THE ORGANIZATIONAL world portrayed by Joseph Heller in his *Catch-22* seems, at first glance, a vastly different place from Kafka's *Castle*. And so it is in many respects. It is peopled by Americans rather than Europeans. It is filled with a riotous, farcical abundance and variety of action where the actions in *The Castle* are marked by a somnambulistic sameness. The occupants of the upper reaches of Heller's bureaucracy are on open and frequent public display where Kafka's castellans are seen only momentarily and dimly.

Yet Heller's Yossarian seems no nearer to a resolution of his struggles with the total institution which dominates his life than is Kafka's K. with his Castle. The universe of Heller's *Catch-22* is a bomber squadron based on a mythical Mediterranean island during World War II. Yossarian is a captain and a bombardier who is malingering in the squadron hospital as the novel begins. Yossarian's struggle with the bureaucracy in which his life is imbedded—a struggle which persists throughout the novel—is to leave it. He has flown a number of missions well above the number required for home leave in most squadrons of the 27th Air Force of which his squadron is a part. But Colonel Cathcart, the commanding officer of this squadron, in his efforts to impress the generals above him, moved by an unwavering yen to become a general himself, keeps raising the number of missions required by personnel in his squadron. Yossarian's ineffectual attempts to bend the system to his individual purpose provides the central thread of the novel on which its numerous and varied demonstrations of the inanities of military organization are strung.

Where Kafka's K. assumed a lucid and rational plan which guided the affairs of the Castle, however inaccessible this plan might be to him, Yossarian (and Heller too) makes no such assumption about his Air Force. (It is fair, I think, to assume an identification between the author and Yossarian.) As a matter of fact, he has "seen through" the system. The functional rationality with which its operations are publicly presented and justified offers no barrier to Yossarian in seeing the deep and unrelieved irrationality which permeates the organization and motivates those vested with responsibility for its decisions.

The treatment of Colonel Cathcart may be used as an example.

> Colonel Cathcart was a slick, successful, slipshod, unhappy man of thirty-six who lumbered when he walked and wanted to be a general. He was dashing and dejected, poised and chagrined. He was complacent and insecure, daring in the administrative stratagems he employed to bring himself to the attention of his superiors and craven in his concern that his schemes might all backfire. . . . Colonel Cathcart was conceited because he was a full colonel with a combat command at the age of only thirty-six; and Colonel Cathcart was dejected because although he was already thirty-six he was still only a full colonel.

This scheme of motivation is carried through the portrayal of Colonel Cathcart's decisions and actions throughout *Catch-22*. He has accepted the system of his bureaucracy as reality, with its rules, formal and informal, and the validation which upward mobility provides to persons in the system. His primary effort is to manipulate the system in service of his own upward mobility. He gives no serious thought to the task purposes of the organization except to use its stated patriotic purposes to justify publicly decisions taken on quite other grounds. Colonel Cathcart's motivation is typical of nearly all of the "leaders" within the system as Heller portrays and Yossarian envisages them.

Examination of these "leaders" will show the variations on the basic motivational theme which Colonel Cathcart so clearly, stupidly, and anxiously exemplifies. A major expenditure of libidinal energy by General Dreedle, operational wing commander of the 27th Air Force, is designed to offset the efforts of General Peckem to dilute or to take over his organizational power. General Peckem is ostensibly in command of services to troops—bringing U.S.O. entertainers to them and cajoling or threatening them to attend the entertainments which he has arranged. His real efforts are devoted to augmenting his power by seeking to make operational command organizationally subsidiary to his department of services to the troops. His chief weapon in his prolix struggle with General Dreedle is his unrelenting devotion to enhancing the public image of the air force by making it to seem more patriotic or to be more photogenic. (General Dreedle is more appealing to the reader since he is partly moved by a passion not derived from the status game of the organization—his implacable hatred of his son-in-law and aide, Colonel Moodus.)

Once incident in the unrelenting struggle between the two generals may be useful both in illustrating their differing styles of "leadership" and in introducing the Wintergreen theme.

> The U.S.O. troops were sent by General P. P. Peckem, who had moved his headquarters up to Rome and had nothing better to do while he schemed against General Dreedle. General Peckem was a general with whom neatness definitely counted. He was a spry, suave and very precise general who knew the circumference of the equator and always wrote "enhanced" when he meant "increased." He was a prick, and no one knew this better than General Dreedle, who was incensed by General Peckem's recent directive requiring all tents in the Mediterranean theater to be pitched along parallel lines with entrances facing back proudly toward the Washington Monument. To General Dreedle, who ran a

fighting outfit, it seemed a lot of crap. Further-
more it was none of General Peckem's goddam
business how the tents in General Dreedle's wing
were pitched. There then followed a hectic juris-
dictional dispute between these overlords that
was decided in General Dreedle's favor by ex-
P.F.C. Wintergreen, mail clerk at Twenty-Seventh
Air Force Headquarters. Wintergreen determined the outcome by throwing all communications from General Peckem into the wastebasket.
He found them too prolix. General Dreedle's
views, expressed in less pretentious literary style,
pleased ex-P.F.C. Wintergreen and were sped
along by him in zealous observance of regulations. General Dreedle was victorious by default.

The power of ex-P.F.C. Wintergreen which is manifested here and at other junctures in *Catch-22* is borrowed
from his location at a control point within the flow of
paper exchanges which furnishes a nervous system to the
bureaucratic giant for whose entertainment and edification the drama of *Catch-22* is enacted. Wintergreen is
always running afoul of the system. His almost continual
ex-P.F.C. or ex-Corporal status attests to this. He is thus
free from the status motivation which keeps most of the
movers and shakers of the system active. In spite of,
perhaps because of, this, he can occasionally offset the
schemes of the movers and shakers. His decisions to
beat the system are undertaken on private grounds—in
this case, it is his literary taste that moves him, in others,
his concern for a black market deal. But his existence
provides a needed inspiration for all the others, lowly
and estranged within the organization. He reenforces a
hope, necessary for their psychological survival, that the
system can be beaten without enslaving one's self in the

status elevation-and-maintenance game which preoccupies those on the upper slopes of its slippery pyramid.

Yossarian is no less estranged within the system in which his life is involved than is K. in his system. Yet, where K. idealizes his system and continues to seek the rational purpose which operates, he believes, at its core, Yossarian has lost the idealism and surrendered the quest. In fact, Yossarian seems to believe that the quest is complete. He has seen through the antics of the denizens of his air force. He has explained to himself, like a "good clinician," their individual antics by radically separating their public statements and posturings from their private motivations. The latter are taken as real, the former as phony. "Seeing through" the system in this way has helped him to rationalize his unshakable desire to leave it. Yet it has not explained the hold of the system over him and others—the dependence which makes leaving it so difficult, which makes his very struggle with the system meaningful for him. Explaining, in personality terms, the antics of Cathcart, Dreedle, Peckem, or Wintergreen in seeking to manipulate the power of the system for sub-jective and irrational purposes does not explain the power of the system over them or over Yossarian. Moloch is only partly unmasked. Nor is his power diminished by this attempt at unmasking. What is accomplished rather is a vision of power that is diabolic rather than divine, malev-olent rather than mysteriously beneficent. This trans-valuation permits Yossarian to render his efforts to escape the system moral rather than immoral, to make his malingering within the system seem meritorious rather than guilt producing.

Actually, Yossarian projects no alternative image of the divine or the human to bolster his resistance to Moloch. The grounds of his resistance, as he expresses these, are as individual, subjective and private as are Colonel Cathcart's grounds of anxious affirmation. He doesn't want to die; he is afraid of dying. These professed grounds for wanting to escape, being private and individual, defeat in advance the formation of any collective action to contravene the demands of the system, to build joint power against the power of the system where it is seen as unjust. (His professed grounds of wanting to leave also provide the novel with its title. Being emotionally incapacitated is adequate ground for leave, according to air force regulations. But not wanting to die is evidence that Yossarian is eminently sane. Therefore, his very efforts to plea his need for home leave furnish justification that the regulation does not apply to him. This is a prime example of the catch—the use of organizational regulations to contravene their ostensible purpose.) In fact, words with a collective reference for justifying actions, words like "justice," are forsworn in Yossarian's vocabulary (he has debunked such terms as "public relations" lies in himself as well as in others), just as collective concepts are eschewed by him and individual concepts used exclusively in explaining the behavior of persons within the system. If defense of his wish to live were to be attempted, Yossarian would probably claim that it is "natural" in some primitive and biologic sense. Yossarian's vision of the "natural" place to which he might go in escaping from the air force is not developed—he is mainly trying to get away not to go anywhere—but insofar as his mythic "Sweden" is portrayed, it is a Rousseauistic place of nature with girls to make love to and sun to bask in, all free of charge.

Actually, it is doubtful that Yossarian's analyses of his own motivations and values are more accurate than his explanations of the behavior of others in his institution.

For example, he is a loving man. The first words of the novel, along with many others of his actions throughout the novel, support this aspect of his character. "It was love at first sight. The first time Yossarian saw the chaplain he fell madly in love with him." Yet life within the system led him to curtail his love. The curtailment grew in part from his desire to save himself from grief, to preserve himself from the loss of loved ones, which death —and his air force was dedicated to death as were the opposing military forces also—would be bound to bring him. If Yossarian must curtail his love within the system of which he is a part, so must he curtail his other interpersonally generated feelings and emotions—hate and awe and respect. This outrage to the feelings of being a loving man creates protest reactions in him—sitting naked in a tree during the military funeral of a friend, receiving a military decoration in the ranks but also in the nude, pretending illnesses he doesn't have. But these protests are not direct or authentic expressions of his feeling. They are as much posturings, as much shot through with public relations lies and role playing, as are Cathcart's shows of the hardness and decisiveness befitting a general, Peckem's patriotism, or the protested devotion of Milo Minderbinder—the nonpareil black-marketeer posing as mess officer—to free enterprise. It is the direct meeting, the encounter, of person with person, which Moloch denies to Yossarian as he moves among his fellow men. And he is as much Moloch's victim in his efforts to escape as Cathcart is in his efforts to curry favor and move upward. The difference lies in Yossarian's refusal to sacrifice the humanity within himself to Moloch's world of pervasive make-believe.

Yossarian resists becoming a cell in the environing tissue of lived lies which surrounds him, a tissue of lies which makes truth or even the idea of truth problematic and unreal. His great temptation came in an offer from Cathcart that he join the production line of lies by going home to do public relations work for the air force and, thereby, to gain his proposed aim of escape from his squadron and its mortal missions. It is interesting that his temptation came after his dead friend Nateley's whore had stabbed him in outraged grief—a genuine interpersonal emotion. Part of his lie would have been to convert the stabbing verbally into the deed of a Nazi assassin. Yossarian resisted the temptation, after temporarily agreeing to the plan, and decides at last to desert.

Part of Yossarian's ineffectuality arises from his denial of the love that was within him with all of the pains of grief that love given would have brought to him. For denial of love is also a refusal to develop a valid counter-collectivity to resist the antihuman thrust of Moloch's power. Another psychological factor militated against the growth of any effective resistance around Yossarian's protests within the system. Life in Moloch's presence is life shorn of time perspective. Life is lived from mission to mission, from leave to leave. No firmly envisaged human future grows to become a focus of resistance to the dehumanization of persons with which the system threatens its inmates. An abbreviated time perspective, a debunking of all ideals including his own, and a denial of love combine to make Yossarian's protest against Moloch ineffectual and to render escape to some dimly envisaged other place, where hopefully but doubtfully Moloch is absent, the only way out for him.

Catch-22, since it portrays reactions to an institution dedicated to death, leaves us in some doubt as to how far

Yossarian's relations with his institution derive from its mortal purpose and how far they stem from other aspects of its avid and all-encompassing organization of human life and effort. Bernard Malamud's *A New Life* provides a study of the effects upon an instructor of total organization in a college, the avowed purpose of which is to augment rather than to destroy life—for its students at any rate, if not its faculty.

Actually, Malamud provides a setting more like Kafka's Castle than Heller's *Catch-22*. Malamud's Castle, a state college in the Pacific Northwest, has its village in the small town in which the college is located. (Heller's "village" is almost completely a whorehouse for the personnel of the air force.) In *A New Life*, S. Levin, thirty years of age, has come from New York City as an instructor in the English Department of the state college. He has sought to leave behind him a period of alcoholism which marked his unsuccessful earlier attempt to cope with the stresses of urban living. His graduate study of English after his breakdown had brought him a modest vision of a new life as a college teacher of English and a professed idealism concerning humanistic studies as an ingredient in the maintenance of a free and democratic society. Success in his new college post is thus important for him both as a way of living down the failure of his past and as a way of serving his educational ideal.

Levin wears a beard when he comes to the college. In the beginning it serves him as a physical symbol of the new status he hopes he has attained. It becomes within the college also a symbol of the estrangement from its collective life that he is both unable and unwilling to overcome. From what factors does Levin's estrangement stem? In part his estrangement arises from the bureaucratic organization of the life of the college and its extension into the village life surrounding it. In part, it stems also from the character structure which Levin has brought to his new assignment.

We may look first at the college. It is an institution dedicated to producing the technical competences in prospective agricultural, engineering, and scientific personnel which employing organizations are willing to hire. English, like the other humanities, has become a service department to the core technical departments of the college. The main courses taught are required courses in Freshman English. Grammar and composition furnish the main content. The "literature" read has mainly to do with scientific and technological matters.

Gilley is the professor in charge of Freshman composition and Levin's immediate superior. Gilley has accepted fully the values and regulations of the college and of the function of the English department as defined by the powers that be. He has laid out the work in "Comp" like a good bureaucratic manager in a way to make minimum demands upon the intellectual powers of the instructors. He works assiduously in keeping the departmental machine running smoothly. He is kindly, amiable and paternalistic toward "his people." His chief aim in life is to become head of the English department—a post which is being vacated at the end of Levin's first year by the retirement of Professor Fairchild. This promotion will shore up his shaky self-esteem against feelings of inadequacy in his roles of husband and scholar.

Levin has been fully informed of the department's expectations concerning its employees' behavior by Professor Fairchild in an orientation interview after his arrival. Students should learn *The Elements*, Fairchild's frequently revised textbook in English grammar. But, just as important as teaching what they are supposed to teach, in-

structors should not "upset the applecart" of the system
—in the college or in the village. Sexual improprieties are
very serious. But just as serious are revolutionary or unusual ideas and teaching practices. Duffy, one of Levin's
predecessors, was used by Fairchild as a terrible example
of the latter. Before his well-deserved dismissal—which
was called not exactly a dismissal by Fairchild in bureaucratic soft-talk—he had been unpunctual, he had graded
papers on the floor of his office, he had used *The Commu-
nist Manifesto* as reading material in his classes. His
sexual peccadilloes were only hinted. Fairchild's well-
intentioned warnings did not save Levin from being drawn
into struggle with the college.

Levin's ineffectual encounters with the system center
on two issues. One is the selection of a new department
head. The other has to do with an affair which developed
between Levin and Gilley's wife. In both, Levin finds
himself in opposition to Gilley who becomes for him a
personification of the system against which he is compelled, not primarily through his own volition, to assert
his not-too-robust ego.

It is mainly Levin's vision of the importance of scholarship in the humanities which leads him to espouse, cautiously and after much soul-searching, the candidacy of
Professor Fabrikant against Gilley for the leadership of
the department. Fabrikant leads the life of a hermit
within the department and college, continuing to write
and publish scholarly papers, even though these activities
are not highly prized by the officials of the institution.
There is no evidence that Levin has understood, valued or
even read Fabrikant's writings. He does value the fact of
Fabrikant's persistence without support in his scholarly
activities. Levin rejects Gilley's indifference to scholarship. Scholarship has personal importance for Levin as

an ideal if not as a practice. But he also rejects Gilley's kindly paternalism. Levin sees this, rightly no doubt, as related to Gilley's wish to gain the headship of the department. It is hard for the reader to assess Levin's motivations fully. Levin is as confused as the reader concerning the persistent and continuing well-springs of his conduct. His actions seem to flow out of segmented responses to immediate situations with little deliberate attention to other parts of himself or to consequences.

His affair with Gilley's wife, Pauline, stems in part from sexual hunger and her availability. But it stems also from his growing enrollment against Gilley and the system which Gilley symbolizes for him. The picture of Levin driving away from the college and the village at the end of the novel in his antiquated Hudson with a pregnant Pauline and the two adopted Gilley children (Gilley was as sterile in bed as in scholarship) represents a sardonic victory of the system over a rather passive Levin whom the system has elevated to the status of an active rebel against it. The burden of proof for winning the new life he sought has been placed entirely upon Levin with new obstacles to the achievement heaped upon him. Gilley has become head of the English department. President Labhart of the college has terminated Levin's services "as of today, in the public interest, for good and sufficient cause of a moral nature." The president refers to his former instructor in justifying his own action, as a "frustrated Union Square radical."

Actually, Levin was frustrated but was not by choice a radical. The character brought to his unequal combat with the college system was one foredoomed to failure. Levin begins and ends his career as an "existentialist" hero, always on eager and naive lookout for changes in his experience. His hopes in such changes are not for actual changes in the conditions and overt patterns of his life which frustrate his professed ideals. His hopes begin and end with fresh perceptions and evaluations of himself and his situation. He is not identified with any regulations of society. In fact, he seems incapable of unqualified and sustained identification with any collectivity beyond himself, indeed with himself. (It is difficult to see Levin as a devoted family man. Many of his doubts about union with Pauline stem from a realistic acceptance by Levin of this defect in himself and remain with him as he drives away with her and the children into an unknown future.)

Levin's real concern is with his socially nonconforming and existential self. It is this concern that brings him into predictable conflict with the college and department which has no regard for Levin's self or that of any other employee, and with the system's perceived representative, Gilley. Since Levin seeks only changed perceptions—he has learned before coming to the college to regard hope beyond such inner change as dangerous and unrealistic— he can never hope to find any permanent solution to his problems. The fate assigned him was that of an observer of psychological reality drawn into the responsible role of rebel, not by his volition but by the need of the system to sacrifice those who do not respect the regulations on which its authority rests in the maintenance and continuation of its power.

The importance of regulations in the maintenance of the college system is illustrated at many points in *A New Life*. An example is that of one of Levin's students who is suspected of having cribbed a theme. Gilley is moved to zestful search, along with Levin and other colleagues, to locate the source from which the student's theme was copied. This assumed breach of regulations releases far more ingenuity and research on the part of the members of the department than do the problems of their teaching or, most certainly, the lures of their scholarship. Catching the delinquent student is identified with maintenance of high standards. The standards of conduct of a student (or a faculty member) with respect to institutional regulations are vastly more important than standards of excellence in teaching or scholarship in assessing his worth. Gilley is disappointed when Levin gives up the search after a few days and decides to give the student an A for his theme. Gilley later transfers the student from Levin's class, on the student's request, on the grounds that good teacher-student relationships are very important in teaching.

Levin's mode of adapting passively to the shifting and immediate demands of life makes robust encounter with the stultifying effects of Moloch on education impossible for Levin to choose and to will. He is drawn into unequal combat with the system in his efforts to play on the edges of struggle. If Moloch has no robust opponents to devour, he must take his meal from such human material as is available to him.

LEVIN DID not choose to achieve heroism and risk a rebel's punishment. These laurels were thrust upon him by the Castle and village of the college which had called him to a new life. His unwilled rebellion served to strengthen the power of the system. It is doubtful that his experience augmented his own wisdom and stature as a man. Nor did others around Levin gain clarification through vicarious participation in his drama.

McMurphy's heroism and rebellion are of a different quality in *One Flew Over the Cuckoo's Nest*. In Ken Kesey's novel McMurphy, weary of work on a penal farm where he has been serving a jail sentence, wangles commitment to a state mental hospital as a putative psychopath. Like the state college in which Levin sought his new life, the scene of McMurphy's crucifixion is also in the Pacific Northwest. The personification of the bureaucratic system of the hospital is Nurse Ratched, known to her patients as Big Nurse. McMurphy swaggers into the well-lubricated social system of Miss Ratched's ward—an over-masculine hedonist, a gambler and a con man.

McMurphy is, at the beginning, a man who plays life for the kicks it may provide. He is a tall talker, accustomed to use his wits and eloquence to draw from people around him the means to support him in his amiable vagrancy. McMurphy finds his fellow inmates docilely resigned to playing the role of "patient" assigned them by the organizational system of the hospital. They are varied in personal make-up, in physique and temperament, in the illusions and rationalizations with which they present their psychic wounds to the world or seek to conceal them. But they are alike in their lack of hope, in the futility with which they view the future, and in their conviction that they can do nothing to shape their environment to their individual or collective purposes.

McMurphy likes laughs. He finds himself among persons unable to laugh. McMurphy has an exaggerated view of his ability to fight and talk his way out of any situation. He finds himself with people in despair. His efforts to change the system of the ward to accommodate and support him in his hedonic life become, not without hesitation and struggle on his part, increasingly a life commitment. Since he cannot change the social system of the ward without changing the people in it toward greater self respect and greater belief in life and its potential victories, McMurphy's mission becomes a therapeutic enterprise.

His therapeutic mission inevitably counters the official therapeutic program of the hospital. He is drawn into deepening conflict with Big Nurse, maintainer of the hospital's system of services, routines, and regulations. This conflict, moving inexorably toward McMurphy's destruction—a decimation accomplished in the name of ministering to his madness—defines the central theme of the novel.

The author tells his story through the person of one of the patients, Chief Bromden. Bromden is a tall and powerful Indian—actually a half-breed. His white mother had vitiated the strength of his father, a tribal chief, to resist efforts of the white "Combine" to buy the land of his tribe. With the tribe's loss of place had come destruction of their way of life. Bromden has been a personal casualty in this collective death. He finds evidence of the "Combine" and its clever will to destroy men within the organization of the hospital. To Bromden, the hospital is literally a machine designed to make men little and weak, to reduce their self-assertion against whatever opposes their way of life, to tame them into shadow men. Bromden has for many years sought to protect himself against this debilitation by feigning deafness and dumbness. This cover has permitted him to move invisibly among both patients and staff, hearing and observing both acutely and distortedly.

The use of Bromden's eyes and ears and voice by the author lends a hallucinatory quality to the whole novel. The reader must discount the credibility of the narrative even as he is led to identify deeply with Bromden and with McMurphy, Bromden's hero and savior. Yet the author's device permits the reader to see the ways in which efforts by those in charge of the hospital to maintain its system and reputation run counter at critical points to the therapeutic aims and intentions of its leadership. The rules and regulations of the organization come to be identified with, at any rate indistinguishable from, therapy. Those who question the rules and regulations are seen, automatically and no doubt quite honestly, as resisting therapy themselves and endangering the therapeutic process for others.

There is a deep horror in the self-government sessions of the patients as described in the novel. Big Nurse maneuvers "group" decisions into the service of organizational efficiency and smoothness of operation. The professed therapeutic aim of increasing the ego strength of the individual patients through responsible participation is thwarted by these decisions and by the processes through which the decisions are reached. Big Nurse is unable to see the conflict between the two aims. The horror is enhanced by her unctuous use of therapeutic jargon and values to justify her actions undertaken in service of organizational efficiency and reputation. She seems unable to distinguish her role as priestess of Moloch from her role as minister to patients in quest of healing.

The author seems uncertain about how to treat the motivations of Big Nurse. At times, her sense of responsibility to maintain the smooth operation of the organization with which her life and career are identified seems to be recognized as a powerful factor in her struggle with McMurphy, the "troublemaker" in the system. At other times, her actions are interpreted primarily as personal power operations or as the "surgical" moves of a castrating female against a potent male. (Perhaps the author's use of Chief Bromden as his mouthpiece gets in his way here.) As the components of organizational loyalty and responsibility in her motivation are stressed, Big Nurse becomes a tragic figure along with her antagonist, McMurphy, con man turned prophet of humanity and crucified savior. When her personal motivations are emphasized, the struggle tends to become a meaningless melodrama with Big Nurse on the side of the bad guys and McMurphy on the side of the good.

McMurphy gets hooked into the role of therapist to his comrades and rebel against the total therapeutic organization, just as Levin had the role of rebel thrust upon him. The difference lies in the conscious volition which enters into McMurphy's decision to make the role his own, contrasting with Levin's passive drifting into it. When he makes his choice, McMurphy is well aware of the fate which lies before him. He has been drawn reluctantly into a fight with the hospital orderlies. His fighting is no longer as assertion of his individual rights or interests against the system. He is defending an old patient, whose dignity as he sees it, the orderlies are demeaning. Chief Bromden moves out of his self-imposed isolation to join McMurphy in the battle. Both are diagnosed as in need of "help" and given a series of electric shock treatments. When McMurphy returns from his treatment to Nurse Ratched's ward, he accepts fully the role of a leader in rebellion against the system for the good of all the patients who have drawn hope and self-respect from him.

His final act of rebellion includes bringing a whore into the hospital to help a buddy uncertain of his sexual identity. This is a more serious offense than any of his former rebellions, since publicity was unavoidable and the public image of the hospital was at stake. The treatment prescribed for his illness now is a lobotomy. Bromden cannot endure the thought of his hero, a vital and self-loving man, living the life of a vegetable. With a pillow he smothers McMurphy in his sleep. The Chief, a man again, tall and self-respecting, escapes the hospital and moves to build a new life, after touching earth again at the place where once his tribe had lived.

McMurphy, like Yossarian, was a loving man. He made the discovery only as his responsibility to the other patients for the hope that he had kindled in them came home to him. Unlike Yossarian, McMurphy did not deny his love. He acted on it, fully aware of the fate that might well follow from the action.

There is more hope in McMurphy's struggle with Moloch than in the struggles of K., Yossarian, or Levin. We know that McMurphy gained stature as a man. We know also that Chief Bromden achieved rebirth through the sacrifice of his hero. Perhaps other patients too were helped on their way to recovery of manhood. Unfortunately, Kesey's novel does not give us any insight into the effects of McMurphy's sacrifice upon the system of the hospital, including its chief protagonist, Nurse Ratched. We may be certain that Moloch has not been routed. We do know that one victim escaped his power.

THERE ARE few, if any, firm conclusions that my analysis of these four imaginative probings of man and organization supports. The most nearly firm conclusions, at least to me, are meta-scientific rather than scientific in character. This does not mean that they are, therefore, of small concern either to scientific students or to practitioners of organizational life. For these meta-scientific conclusions point to assumptions which underlie the definition of the priority problems of organizational behavior to be studied and to be solved and to the definition of criteria by which the adequacy of solutions may be judged. And the bases of their definitions are frequently the least probed elements in the thinking of scientists and practitioners alike.

Operating within the relations of men with bureaucratic organization is a demonic power which I have called

Moloch in this essay. This power rests on two claims that organizations tend to make upon the men within them. The first is an overwhelming claim to the total allegiance of member men. When the perpetuity and success of an organization are taken as ultimate goods, this claim acquires rational plausibility. The second claim of the organization is that it provides an adequate validation of the worth of a man in it. Success in the system is taken as a measure of the personal value of the system's members.

Both of these claims are tempting to men in our historical period. Total allegiance is attractive to men torn by multiple and conflicting loyalties, not the least galling of which is loyalty to one's self and to the potential humanity that lies within that self. By its usual definition, the relationships within a bureaucracy are impersonal and "business-like." When men accept as valid, consciously or unconsciously, the claims of an organization to serve as an object of total allegiance and to provide validation of their personal worth by criteria of success within the organization, men are alienated from themselves. To pledge oneself to an impersonal existence is to forswear human existence. For it is the genius of human life to live personally and interpersonally—to love, to hate, to aspire to a more than arbitrary meaning in life, to grow according to the pattern of one's unique potentialities. And it is this genius of his life from which the devotee of Moloch has alienated himself. (It should be noted that Moloch's total demand also perverts the functional impersonality and rationality of bureaucratic relationships.)

A life of alienation from one's self, achieved through deification of any human organization, is a life of despair, of self-destroying frustration, and of poisoned interpersonal relations. Kafka's K. provides a classic demonstration of this truth. A more shallow K., who has accepted the organization's claims without question or questing, lives in perpetual ambivalence and anxiety upon the surface of life. Colonel Cathcart in *Catch-22* is a K. who has not undertaken or has forsworn a quest for *his* identity and for the meaning of *his* life. The temptations of Moloch are particularly insidious for some members of the helping professions. Latter-day K.'s like Professor Gilley and Nurse Ratched may mask from themselves their desperate attempts to find self-validation and self-fulfillment in their organizational careers, in the guise of helping others—students or patients—an enterprise which connotes interpersonal encounter and exchange. But their helping efforts are perverted into a kind of role playing—a role playing designed to shut out from themselves the despair that infuses their personal lives as they remain true to Moloch.

Levin's attempt to shield himself from encounter with the demonic powers of organized life through living within the circumference of his personal sensibilities proved forlorn. Such attempts must fail unless those who try to live in this way forswear a life of action in bureaucratized society. Men and women with a desperate and anxious investment in the regulations of an organization must victimize those who live among them and remain indifferent to the rules. Indifference to a system is a greater threat to its devotees than rebellion. For rebellion acknowledges even as it challenges the importance which indifference denies. Yossarian's rebellious attempts to escape his organization rest on an acknowledgment of the futility of any or all attempts to change a dehumanized system. This acknowledgment is also an acknowledgment of Moloch's unimpeachable power. Its lack of realism derives from its failure to recognize that bureaucratic organization has

become a universal way of life in contemporary civilizations. No mythic places of nature to which one may
escape exist except in the imaginations of civilized pseudo-
primitives.

McMurphy's rebellion in love is the most hopeful response examined in this analysis. It is hopeful because it
faces and does not deny Moloch's dehumanizing power,
though his power operates beneath the mask of giving
help. McMurphy's response is hopeful because it is based
on an acceptance of the human potentiality and need for
love, for interpersonal encounter, for fraternity which live
and move within himself. It is these human potentialities
and needs which both those committed to Moloch and
those who would individually escape his power, in their
different ways, deny or discount. McMurphy's rebellion is
hopeful because it recognizes that a collective power,
organized to fulfill deep human potentialities and needs,
is required to counter the power of Moloch, a power
organized to curtail and frustrate these very potentialities
and needs. To counter the power of Moloch in one
organization with the power of another organization based
on Moloch's dehumanizing claims is still to serve Moloch.
And it is to reject the possibility of rehumanizing man's
corporate life.

Both scientific students and practitioners of organizational life might well review the assumptions which shape
their definitions of the problems they seek to understand
and to solve. Should they find that they are enlisted unwittingly in the service of Moloch, they might well ask
themselves what McMurphy would do in their place.

The Re-education of Persons in Their Human Relationships

LET ME begin this essay by stating two basic assumptions which underlie its development. The essay assumes with Aristotle that man is by nature a "community animal."[1] Men achieve the good life, if at all, through membership in various associations. To learn to be human is to learn responsible membership in some inclusive round of human associations. It is in human relationships that men, if they are apt for the learning, learn individuality, creativity, and dissent as well as conformity, discipline in traditional orientations, and consent. Man in either his educative or his miseducative development is a community animal, and neither the goals nor the strategies of his education and reeducation can be determined sanely without analysis of the conditions of community life in and through which he lives.

Second, the essay assumes with Plato that man is, at least potentially, a rational animal. It locates the instruments of his rationality in his inclusive symbolic resources, linguistic and nonlinguistic. The fullness, accuracy, and adequacy of his use of available symbolic resources in guiding the choices that confront him, individually and collectively, define the measure of his rationality. In his very potentiality for rational behavior, which involves transcendence in idea and in ideal of the factual conditions of his choices and actions, lie also the possibilities of error and irrationality. The focus of responsible educative and reeducative efforts is to help men achieve a discipline in the use and transformation of his symbolic resources in keeping with some tested, ideal image of rationality.

Man then, in the viewpoint of this essay, is basically and potentially a rational, community animal. It is in attempting to diagnose and to treat the problems of man's contemporary group and community life and the problems of contemporary rationality and irrationality *together*, rather than to see and to treat them separately, that the distinctive contribution of a "human relations" approach to education lies.

WHY DOES the contemporary situation require the continuing reeducation of men and women in their values, understandings, and practices of human relationships?

Let a philosopher, A. N. Whitehead, speak first to this question.

> Our sociological theories, our political philosophy, our practical maxims of business, our political economy, and our doctrines of education are derived from an unbroken tradition and practical examples from the age of Plato . . . to the end of the last century. The whole of this tradition is warped by the vicious assumption that each generation will substantially live amid the conditions governing the lives of their fathers and will transmit these conditions to mold with equal force the lives of its children. We are living in the first period of human history for which this assumption is false.[2]

Let an artist-architect and critic of the arts speak next to the question.

> Our time, there is no doubt, must be characterized as a period of crisis. The fundamental change of economic conditions taking place under the insignia of industrialization and mechanization has shaken social order to its foundations. A complete transformation of life is taking place. Wherever we look, at the state or the people, at economics or society, at science or art, fundamental changes are in process. A world of obsolete forms and institutions is coming to an end, another slowly struggles into existence. With violent concussions, that everlasting spectacle of dying and growing is taking place again on the stage of the world. With combat and convulsion the old forms of order are broken to pieces. With intense resistance the emancipation from traditional habits of law is carried through; emancipation from forms that once were original and full of life, but which in the course of historical evolution have lost their primary meaning and their relationship to life. Reluctantly, but at last, the discussion is opened on the changed reality that forms our environment. . . .
>
> Whether regular or irregular, static or dynamic, all form is a final result of the desire for order. To build is to make a plan. To plan is to follow a definite concept of order.
>
> In building we find . . . two different principles of order: one that takes the structure as an organism; growing on its own according to the proper and immutable law of its individual existence; adapted to its function and environment, as a plant or any other living organism grows, developing itself in its proper life-space. Then,

in contrast to this principle, we find another idea of order taking the structure as mechanism, composed of various elements put into order according to the immutable law of a system *a priori*. Viewing these two different concepts of the problem of structure, we speak of organic order as opposed to mechanical order. . . .

The disastrous conditions into which an excessive rationalism and a humiliating mechanism have forced our rational existence have awakened a new . . . desire to be nearer to the sources of life. A complete reversal of outlook on life is taking place in these times: we see another approach of man to nature, this time however, not in the sentimental spirit of a Rousseau, but in accordance with the strict teachings of science and technique which have revealed the idea of organism, and have opened to us, in this way, the wonder of creation and life anew.[3]

A sociologist, a wise man in industrial affairs and a pioneer in human relations research and education, Elton Mayo, adds another dimension to the question.[4] Mayo pointed out that Western societies have shifted and are shifting from an "established" to an "adaptive culture." Traditional groups and associations in an "established culture"—families, clubs, guilds, family-controlled businesses, industries, and farms, neighborhoods, and churches—tended to operate in established, customary ways. Where these ways embodied "reason" in their patterns and relationships it was the "reason" of time-tested, historically selected, and validated "common sense." Members of groups adjusted to customary ways and requirements. Men did not seek consciously and planfully to adjust these ways to the changing purposes, insights, and needs of members. Changes in group patterns and relationships in "established culture" were slow and often surreptitious and unacknowledged as well.

In "adaptive culture," men pass into and out of groups and organizations, they construct and reconstruct them, as technology, human needs, knowledges, and purposes, and accompanying social, political and economic relationships change. Conscious, planful management of organizational life and its continued remaking has become an unavoidable demand in groups closest to changing industrial processes, to changing sciences, and to the merging and melding of cultures underway nationally and internationally.

Traditional associations—families, churches, schools, neighborhoods—are changing too, though often with greater reluctance and resistance. Leaders in traditional groups and organizations, as well as in "new" ones, are increasingly recognizing the need for conscious, deliberate, planful management of changing human relationships because of the both terrifying and hopeful breakdown of customary patterns of control and of customary rationalizations for these.

Let one more voice speak to the question addressed to our contemporary situation. In 1941 I sought to examine the present status and the enduring basis of pedagogical authority.[5] Finding this basis in the idea and practice of "community," I could not avoid analyses of contemporary community life such as those which Whitehead, Behrendt, and Mayo have undertaken. What I found there was a growing alienation of persons and groups from the constructive and reconstructive communication and participation which characterize "healthy" and productive community life, particularly in an "adaptive culture."

Induction of the chronologically immature into established community life has traditionally been the overall task of pedagogy. This task remains, complicated though the location may be of defensible and dependable bases of authority in a crisis culture. But the pedagogical task of induction and reinduction of alienated persons and groups into processes of significant communication and participation with their fellows, is, I argued, the inadequately met task of contemporary education which stretches from cradle to grave.

The "reduction of alienation" points toward the problems of offsetting and transmuting into rationality the surges of irrationality, individual and collective, which always accompany alienation. It points at the same time toward the problems of building and developing a dynamic, yet secure, community life in full recognition of the puzzling contemporary paradox of unprecedented interdependence and of increasing social fragmentation and noncommunication both in the life of knowledge and in the life of action and practice.[6]

WHAT PROBLEM or, better, problems does the contemporary human relations situation, as delineated above, set for education?

One general problem for educators, suggested by all of the commentators on the human situation cited above is: How do we teach when the answers to the questions about which we seek to guide the learning of others are not known? To fail to accept this problem as genuine is to make the "vicious assumption" which Whitehead warned us against. It is also to vote against the building of an organic order out of the confused and conflicting materials of contemporary experience which Behrendt identifies as the emerging new spirit of our times.

Failure to accept the challenge of this problem is failure

to face the realities of the "adaptive culture" into which, according to Mayo, we have moved and are moving. It is to seek the reduction of alienation by imposing the specious "certainties" of the favored solutions of some segment of our fragmented society upon other segments whose experience breeds and reinforces other and often conflicting specious "certainties" of solution.

Acceptance of the problem means that educators must learn to make their teaching-learning efforts into cooperative inquiries into areas of experience which are today genuinely confused and problematic. But to will that teacher and students engage in cooperative inquiries without helping to build conditions of mutual trust and confidence among the inquirers in holding up the specious "certainties" of their partial perspectives to joint, public criticism and amendment, is to will a desirable end without willing the means to achieve it. Building the social and psychological conditions of cooperation in inquiry calls for *conscious* understanding and deliberate control of self and others, of interpersonal relations and conflicts, and of processes of participation, organization, and communication which cut beneath the conventional norms of roles and relationships that characterize any now established subculture or culture, be it that of middle-class America, of Western civilization, of industrial management, of labor, of Jew or Christian or Mohammedan.

Educators must seek understanding and control of *human* processes of association, of *universal* problems of membership, if they are to help release effective communication across the strongly defended barriers of nationality, caste, race, class, religion, specialization, and age, which characterize personal and group living in contemporary society. This does not, of course, rule out the importance of accurate materials—information, ideas and systems of ideas—for adequate instruction. It does mean that the best materials in the world will not inform and stimulate creative and cooperative learning under adverse social-psychological conditions.

This necessity in education for shifting from the maintenance of socially inherited, customary patterns of relationship in the teaching-learning situation to conscious and planful analysis, invention, and testing of patterns that fit the needs of learning in relation to changing goals, functions, and conditions of life has become a necessity in all areas of our associational life, not just in formal education.

Learning how to plan and to institute conditions which release and sustain cooperative and creative learning and action in changing situations is the basic learning for all men and women in an adaptive culture, if all men and women are to have any share in shaping that culture to the growth requirements of their individual lives. This is the basic learning which educators must acquire if they are to help others to acquire it.

Many educators cling to the notion that their task is to make relevant and accurate ideas, information, and skills available to people with respect to the problems of adaptation and adjustment that confront them. On this view, the attitudes and values of people which help to determine the uses they make of their information are no valid concern of the educator. No one in his right mind would deny the importance of communicating relevant and accurate ideas and information to people who need them. But the contemporary crisis in human relations, if our commentators are right, has penetrated beneath the level of cognition and overt behavior into the inner areas of emotions, attitudes, and values.

Inclusion of alienated persons and groups in a viable

community life means that they must make choices among, and must integrate discrepant value orientations, as well as acquire "new" knowledge and more apt and effective behavioral skills. If choices among value alternatives and integration of discrepant value orientations are to be in any sense a rational process, reeducation in human relations must, at one and the same time, take responsibility for guiding the value choices and integrations of those learning as well as communicating more adequate information and more apt and effective skills.

This cannot and should not mean an imposition of some arbitrarily selected value orientation upon learners in areas of value conflict, personal or collective. Answers to our value quandaries are no more settled in many areas of contemporary experience than are answers to our knowledge and skill questions. What is needed is an experimental discipline of thought and judgment which extends to problems of valuation and goal determination as well as to questions of fact and means.

To fail to achieve such an extension of method is to leave education geared to the communication of more effective means toward goals and in the service of values which were acquired through early habituation in some fragment of a fragmented culture and which remain unexamined in relation to alternative goals and values which others espouse, to changed and changing conditions of life, to changed and changing knowledge, and to changed and changing behavioral requirements. This way lies further deepening of contemporary alienation and community disruption.

Whatever else the acquisition and communication of such an inclusive discipline of judgment may require of educators, it does demand a degree of objectification of self and of our culture which moves educative efforts over the traditional lines of "education" into practices once reserved for "therapeutic" treatment of persons and groups radically alienated from the main streams of community life. But the requirement seems valid for an education that is committed to the rational reduction of alienation in contemporary life.

The title phrase, *"reeducation* of persons in their human relationships," has not been idly chosen. For the process must be one of reeducation, not of education afresh. The persons now being taught have been learning how to deal with other human beings since their infancy. And many of the basic attitudes and strategies that determine the quality, character, and limits of their relationships are deeply imbedded in their personality structures and function as parts of their system of security as "selves." To ask persons even to consider alternatives to some of these attitudes and strategies is, therefore, deeply threatening. Yet effective change and reeducation depend on helping learners to entertain alternatives with respect to deeply defended patterns of interpersonal relationships which, under confronting conditions, thwart effectiveness and growth.

This emphasizes for educators the requirement that they learn to build groups of learners: groups that embody satisfying and secure patterns of relationship which contrast at points with patterns now held by their members. Only in this way can alternative ways of relating to authority figures, to peers and to subordinates, to strangers and strangeness, come alive for those who are seeking to learn new and better ways of relating which can be genuinely internalized and applied.

This problem of *reeducation* again emphasizes the requirement that educators acquire a high degree of objectivity toward themselves and their own cultural conditionings, as well as skill and motivation to invent and create conditions and methods that make possible rational dealing with emotionally charged experiential content as an integral part of the teaching-learning process.

The fragmentation in contemporary social practice and action extends also to the contemporary life of research and scholarship. The knowledges and the methods relevant to the rational resolution of contemporary conflicts are now scattered among many specialized disciplines. Those who profess these various disciplines are independently organized, achieve only fitful communication with each other, and engage not infrequently in unproductive competition and conflict. A discipline of "human relations," which is to become also a core discipline for education, must seek and find ways of achieving fuller community among men of research and scholarship as well as among men of action and practice.

The road to fuller community in either area of experience does not lie in leveling, destroying, or suppressing specialization and difference. These have functional values for the society as well as personal value for those who live in and by these specializations. The road lies rather in the achievement by the "specialists" of some degree of common orientation toward the confronting problems of man in our society, of commitment to participation in the solution of these problems out of the resources of their specialties, and of some common discipline in evaluating relative importances and desirabilities in the use and application of knowledge in human affairs. Leadership in such achievement belongs to educators who accept reeducation of persons in human relations as a central and continuing concern.

SPECIFIC EDUCATIONAL strategies for the extension and reenforcement of rationality and community in contemporary life vary widely from locality to locality, from region to region, and from nation to nation. This is as it should be. People must face and diagnose the particular conditions in which they find themselves, must invent and test plans and programs appropriate to the diagnosis, if they are to modify these effectively toward fuller rationality and community in choice and action. Canned programs, canned materials, canned methods are suspect if movement toward a more organic order of life and mind is to be the goal of educational effort.

Yet such specificity of strategies in creative programing, far from precluding, actually demands common lines of "grand" strategy, in view of the world interdependence which has become a fact of contemporary experience.

1. Educators should seek to build groups with membership drawn from across major lines of social division in our society. Such groups must be built in a way to invest them with deep personal significance for their members in order that more inclusive, alternative bases of consensual validation of ideas, values, and beliefs become available to people from different social classes, different races, different religions, different occupations, different specializations, different nationalities and different age groups. If people continue to validate their ideas and values consensually only against the modal opinions of their partial segment of society, barriers to communication with others are maintained and reenforced. The building and development of personally significant learning, planning, and action groups which bridge these barriers provide a force toward rational community in our segmented society.

2. It is not enough that "cross-cultural" groups be built more widely than at present. It is important that these groups develop standards which elicit and reward creative thinking by individual members, which support positive evaluation of individual variety in outlook as a *resource,* not a blemish, and which maintain a decent respect for members' areas of privacy and specialization.

The discipline that binds such groups together must be a rational discipline which permits an honest and secure facing of conflicting social "realities" and supports the weaving of a variety of *discrepant* outlooks and beliefs into significantly new syntheses of orientation and commitment. Such a discipline is a requirement for mature functioning in a divided society that is at the same time pledged to the creative use of conflict.

3. There is potentially available in contemporary culture a vast unused supply of tested and partly tested ideas and beliefs relevant to the rational reconstruction of our common life and, what is perhaps more important, a growing repertoire of refined and developed methods for validating ideas and beliefs. Research and scholarship are developed to a degree never before achieved.

Many relevant ideas, tested through research and scholarship, are available for application and use in action and practice, if barriers to their effective communication and practical adaptation can be overcome. Moreover, methods for testing and validating ideas and beliefs, developed first in the university and the laboratory, can be adapted for use by practical men in constructing and validating the ideals, ideas, and information needed in making their decisions and in ordering their lives.

Educators must find ways of bridging the barriers of specialization which fragment research and scholarship and of creatively connecting scholarly and scientific resources of knowledge and methods on the one hand with the life of action and practice on the other, if the bases of rational community are to be extended in our time.

4. Traditionally, the main medium of *social development* for persons has been a local community which incorporated the necessary variety of specializations into a commonly perceived and accepted *round* of life. These communities tended to be *static* in their assumptions and patterns and often violently resistant to changes induced by dissatisfied persons or groups within or by social movements and trends from the outside.

These static communities have been shattered by forces stemming from industrialization, social mobility, and intercultural mixing. It is doubtful if full sanity of functioning and development can be effected by and for individuals without some social-psychological equivalent of local community within the fabric of the larger society. Yet such local community will not develop naturally today. It must be planned and replanned in relation to changing patterns of production, communication, and social control.

A major task of educators is to develop a "local" community life, which is dynamic rather than static, ready for the consideration of demands for change from within and from without, and open rather than closed to currents of thought and opinion, especially to thought stemming from centers of scholarship and research.

Such are the grand lines of strategy for educators who have accepted the reeducation of persons in human relationships as a major demand upon their resources and their ingenuities.

From Polarization to Paradox

IN SEVERAL earlier essays in this volume, while probing various aspects of the plight of modern man, I have tried to show the need for innovations in the education and reeducation of contemporary persons. The purpose of this essay is to discuss in detail one such innovation which I, along with colleagues from disciplines other than my own, helped to create twenty years ago. This innovation has undergone many changes and refinements since its beginnings, as thousands of men and women of action and men and women of knowledge have joined with its originators to test it, to improve it, and to extend its use into various academic and nonacademic settings.[1]

This innovation has been called the laboratory method of human relations training. And one of the central formats used in the laboratory approach to teaching and learning is the training group, or T Group as it has come widely to be called. In the laboratory approach, learners are asked to create a "learning laboratory" for themselves, in which they function simultaneously or alternately as experimenters and as subjects in the study of their own behavior and relationships. They are asked to enact and to integrate roles that are typically segregated in contemporary experience—the role of "actionist," the role of "educator," and the role of "researcher." The teacher or "trainer" functions in relation to the laboratory group not to tell them "the answers" to their questions or the results of his own or others' investigations but to help them organize, conduct, and evaluate their own projects of action-education-research.

Since learners in training laboratories are seeking to learn validly and reconstructively about their own ways of observing, interpreting, and handling social and interpersonal events, groups become the laboratory's principal media of reeducation. A group is a microcosm of larger social systems of various sorts. In a face-to-face group members encounter, enact, and experience, on a directly observable scale, the principal difficulties and conflicts of contemporary society and culture. Members learn to help each other in diagnosing these difficulties and conflicts, in assessing their involvements in these, and in developing clarified commitments toward investing themselves reconstructively in dealing with comparable difficulties and conflicts in the world outside the laboratory.

The group which persons study in laboratory fashion— for personal learning and for group redevelopment—may be a "natural" group in which members function outside the laboratory—a work group, a community council, a family. Or it may be a group with no previous history before and no prospective career beyond the ending of the laboratory—a temporary social system developed by learners to accomplish learning about themselves and about their interpersonal and social relationships. The T Group discussed in this essay is of the latter sort—a temporary system.

In laboratory learning, a T Group is designed to serve two sets of interrelated functions for its members. It is designed to support members in reeducating themselves toward greater personal integrity, toward deeper understanding of themselves, of their potentialities and limitations, and toward enhanced skill in diagnosing and modifying the social determinants of their patterns of conduct. It is designed also to help its members discover and test ways in which they can help to change the collective structures on which their lives depend toward greater community of aspiration and effort.

The task of the T Group is easy to state but difficult to achieve. Members, in effect, are asked to develop their group toward a community which will optimally support the personal growth and learning of each member and to learn about themselves, about others, about groups, organizations, and societies, through analyzing and evaluating the human events that occur in this process of development. No agenda, no rules of procedure, no leaders are prescribed in advance for the group in its venture. The trainer seeks to find and enact ways of facilitating the development of the group and the personal learning of group members in a manner that will augment, rather than diminish, the freedom and responsibility of members in shaping their own learning enterprise.

The remarks which follow are clinical comments based on experience with some eighty T Groups in which I have functioned as trainer during the past twenty years. The comments are hung around a framework of eight selected aspects of T Group development and functioning. The first three of these are "sociological" aspects, in the sense that they isolate various social system characteristics, or member-relationship patternings, that can be accurately noted and described from time to time but ordinarily change observably during the course of a T Group's career. The remaining five are "cultural" aspects of group life, in the sense of "normative," "ideological," or "world-outlook" elements that crystallize out of the history of the group and function with varying changeability to give meaning, value, and control to the experiences of the group and of its members.

These comments frequently fall into the form of a statement of some polarization which group members encounter as they seek to bring order out of the initial chaos of T Group life. The discussion goes on to show how further experience in the group tends to convert the polarization into a paradox which can be handled creatively by the group, if not always eliminated. The movement of T Group life, when it is successful, seems to be from polarization to paradox, from melodrama to tragedy, from collectivity to community.

THE MOST obvious characteristic of a T Group is the absence of any prearranged or externally assigned task. If we were to interview members of a T Group during its early sessions concerning the goal of the group, we would find two modal perceptions. One is a perception of goallessness. The other is that the goal is what a few members have stated it should be and that most of the other members are aimlessly (or willfully) wandering from this goal.

If, on the other hand, we think of the goal as that which an observer might see to be the focal direction of member efforts and energies during any unit of time, the T Group is never devoid of a goal. For the efforts and energies of the members are channeled by the situational requirements confronting the people in the collectivity. And these requirements in the early stages of the T Group are common, however differently they may be seen, interpreted, or handled behaviorally by different individuals in the group. The "realities" of the situation which require response inhere in the *ambiguities* and *uncertainties* of an unformed group. These include not only, or primarily, indefiniteness in the verbally stated task or goal of the group. They extend to role definitions of "member" and of "trainer," to standards of appropriate and inappropriate participation, including emotional expression as well as work contributions, to authority and power relations in the group, and to procedures and criteria for consensually validating or invalidating (judging) member and group choices and decisions. The resultant group goal, the direction in which effort is actually channeled, is toward the dispelling of these uncertainties.

The goal, on this view, is to give form to an unformed group of people. And as one observes with detachment the early behavior of a T Group, or as the group subsequently, from the vantage point of comfort if not paradise regained, reconstructs its early history, there is seen to be goal direction in even the earliest overtures to participation, however chaotic or arbitrary these overtures may have seemed consciously to most members living through the throes of community formation.

But the problem of goals in the group is still more complex and paradoxical than the above discussion indicates. The ideal goal of the T Group, in the minds of those who organized it and of those who have paid tuition to take part in it, is to help members learn about processes and problems of community formation and functioning and about themselves as members of groups. Nor is it enough for them to learn their "way around" in this particular group. Rather, learning that generalizes reliably and validly to other groups and to themselves in other social situations defines the rational purpose for participation in the T Group. The central goal of the T Group is, therefore, not the more or less conscious contriving of work products—verbalized public conclusions growing out of consecutive discussion of agenda items or written-down policies and decisions. *Yet the T Group must do work in order to accomplish its learning goal.* Nor is the central goal to build and maintain a group—to construct a social system in which members can participate with comfort and growth. *Yet the members must build, maintain, and rebuild a social system if they are to learn about group building and maintenance and about their participation as members in these processes.* So problems of work and problems of group formation and re-formation do set complex goals which become engrossing to group members, though rationally they are always instrumental to the overall goal of learning.

It is my custom as a trainer to state at the beginning of the first session what I believe to be the "contract" between me and the group.[2] The ideal goal of learning about groups and self is reviewed. A general definition of my role as helper to the group and to group members in finding ways of learning from their experience is stated. The two sources of data for learning which are available to the group are noted: (1) the pooling and analysis of knowledge about and experience with groups other than this one which members bring to it; and (2) the observation and clarification of behavioral events, and the relationships that emerge in this group as we deal with one another. It is proposed that my special function as a trainer in the group is primarily to help the group collect, interpret, and use the second kind of data for member learning. Special responsibilities of the trainer for setting the direction of work or for organizing the group for work or for prescribing the forms or patterns of group life are denied.

This early, general delineation of the role of the trainer

is not normally understood or accepted fully by group members. Yet the early statement of it seems important for two reasons. It serves as a point of reference in later struggles by the group to give concrete shape and definition to the role of the trainer. It helps also to differentiate the complexities actually inherent in the goal structure of the T Group and the co-related complexities in member responsibilities for contributing to these goals.

This discussion of the goals of the T Group underlines what seems to be a fact. Its goals are complicated, diverse, and not always capable of easy integration. One way of seeing "maturation" in the T Group is in terms of progressive differentiation and integration of these various kinds of goals—conscious work production, group formation and re-formation, and learning. The early tendency in many groups is, in effect, to select one of these as *the* goal and to attempt to deny the others. Of course, such "abstract" selection of one facet of the concrete group "reality" will not work for long. For the fiction involved leaves whole areas of the experiences and the goal systems of members unattended to and uncontrolled. Such abstraction falsifies the reality which the group and its members must somehow recognize, negotiate, control, live with, or reconstruct, and so is unviable—cognitively, esthetically, and practically.

These unviable abstractions concerning *the purpose* of the group frequently maintain themselves for some time when they become slogans and platforms in the power struggles of factions in the group. One faction may become a "production" faction. They will try to treat the group as if it were really a work group, with work to get done and a brief time in which to do it. They may seek to impose well-defined agenda upon the group, with well-defined management offices and working procedures to match. Another faction may emerge as a "feeling" or "process" faction. They will resist agenda, officials, and defined procedures. They may wish only to probe member feelings and interpersonal relations. Often they resist going beyond the expression of feelings and perceptions, since the selection or development of a system of concepts for sorting, relating, and interpreting feelings and perceptions is seen as structure, and as such is seen on the side of the "production" faction. These untenable positions about what the goal of the group really is or should be may persist, because the viewpoints involved and the rationalizations of them are functioning as weapons in struggles to impose a partisan control over the group's thought and action.

In such struggles, other members may point out the untenability of both production and feeling slogans and platforms. They may point out the common basis in reality out of which both polarized abstractions emerge— the lack of form and legitimacy within the life of the group—with one faction seeking to impose a familiar but inadequate form upon this formlessness, and the other faction resisting any effort to invent and test forms for managing the group's life. Or they may point out the common forms that are emerging in the group willy-nilly in the very struggle between "familiar form" versus "no form."

The task of training leadership is to support efforts to bring the group to accept and to understand the concrete realities in which their struggles are set. It is only as the group comes to work in a way which incorporates as relevant data the expression and exploration of member feelings and relationships that workable common goals will emerge. It is only as the group comes to combine such work with clarification and interpretation of what is happening to the group and its members now, and of how this is related to what has happened before and to what may happen next, that the group can learn how to handle paradoxes with respect to its complex goals. The purposes of work, of group formation, and of learning can be furthered best through realistic recognition, clarification, and interpretation of the situational plight of the group and of its members. Only through such realism can unworkable polarizations about goals and goallessness be converted into manageable paradoxes about goal complexities.

IN ANOTHER connection, I wrote of the dialectic of competing authorities during crises in group life. This dialectic seems well illustrated in the struggle of the T Group to achieve a workable basis of legitimacy in the control of its life and career. Basic group instability "is marked by attempts on the part of each of various competing 'parties' to capture the dominant authority symbols of a social group for its own use in control of that group. In the stress of the conflict, confirmed partisan constructions on 'proper' authority tend to grow fixed and dogmatic. The 'masses' of the group membership tend to grow confused and insecure as various partisan 'authorities' compete for control of their minds and hearts, for the 'legitimacy' which, in the long run, only popular acceptance can give. An ever-present danger in such competition of 'authorities' is that the social group will seek to purchase a restored clarity and security too cheaply by accepting the control of some 'strong man' or 'strong party' which promises security through the imposition of order and the suppression of conflict. A clearheaded understanding by people of the nature of authority, its virtues and limitations, might help to offset this danger."[3]

Certainly, the refusal of the trainer to act as authority

figure in the traditional pedagogical mode throws the group into an authority vacuum. Early unsuccessful efforts to impose authoritative patterns which have functioned legitimately in back-home groups only underline the fact of this vacuum. As insecurity mounts, various attempts are made to seduce the trainer into acting as a familiar authority figure. Usually these attempts are countered by other members who resent domination by any and all authority figures. Sometimes, though not invariably, the earliest factionalism in the T Group swings around this issue. Typically, both parties refuse to believe that the trainer is actually rejecting the functions of authority in setting goals for the group or in determining its social organization, whatever his statements and deeds may imply to the contrary. Frequently, elaborate myths about the mysterious and omnipotent manipulation exercised by the trainer in controlling the group are projected into the situation by partisans both of authority and of freedom. Members more affectively neutral toward problems of leadership and authority are often unheard by others as they point out the irreality in many of these projections. And the trainer's attempts similarly to clarify the situation are frequently twisted into a pattern of partisan support or attack on the side of freedom or of authority.

Within this struggle, various contrived authorities may be accepted temporarily by the group. Elaborate agenda may be rammed through by one faction. Officers may be selected who are followed slavishly for a time by some and sooner or later ignored or attacked by others. Elaborate sets of rules or laws may be adopted temporarily in the search for legitimate order. Usually, none of these makeshift authorities lasts long. More workable patterns of relationship and control typically get hammered out under the surface within the very partisan struggles that occur. These patterns give some measure of security out of which the authority problem in the group can be recognized and diagnosed by the members. Such clarification often becomes possible when new alignments or factions form on a more realistic basis of common and conflicting interests.

Recognition by a group of the unviable character of opposing authority in general to freedom in general does not solve automatically all the concrete problems of authority and freedom which group life presents more or less recurrently. But it does permit the working out of provisional compromises, whether in terms of acceptable standards, procedures, or offices, or in terms of consensus about permissible and valuable areas of member spontaneity, variation, and change within these patterns of control. It does permit assessment of specific patterns of conscious control and of free member spontaneity and the experimental testing of proposed changes in such arrangements. As a group becomes more mature, patterns that permit the interpenetration of specific authorities and freedoms tend to become the rule rather than the exception.

No other issue in the group taxes the personal stability or the ingenuity of the trainer more heavily than the issue of freedom and authority. For the trainer becomes inescapably the personal symbol of authority for many members of the group. He is simultaneously attacked, whatever his behavior, both for being dominant and for being derelict in his proper duties. Some members find less need than others to project distorted perceptions on the trainer. They are able to point out what the behavior of the trainer actually is. The trainer's job is to reinforce the reality elements in the perceptions of members and, at the same time, to help those who are distorting the situation to recognize the character and source of the twisted perceptions that thrive under conditions of no legitimate order within the group. It is easy for him, when he is attacked for what he is not doing or thinking, to become defensive and by his defensiveness to reinforce distorted perceptions and to suppress rather than to bring up for conscious examination the assumptions and conceptions of authority and freedom which bolster and rationalize these distorted perceptions.

Nondefensiveness is the attitude which the trainer attempts to achieve. Does this mean that he remains impassive and enigmatic, intervening only to clarify and question, but not to join the fray? At times this seems the best strategy. Members will detect their own projections better if the trainer maintains his objective clarifying role under threat either of seduction or attack. However, if there are few nonconflicted members in the group or if they are not strong enough to be heard, the interventions of the trainer may have to be more direct, whatever the risks involved. He may share his own feelings of discomfort, anger, uncertainty, and helplessness with the group. This means that the group is challenged to deal with him as a person as well as a symbol and a role. The main risk is that the challenge will be too great and that unproductive flight from the authority problem will ensue. The advantage is that the reality elements in the perceptions of less-conflicted members will come to be expressed openly, as the trainer has expressed his own, and that the authority problem can then be clarified.

THE T GROUP is a species of the genus, learning group. Its distinctive characteristic is the degree to which it uses clarification and interpretation of events in the group's own ongoing experiences as data for learning and as part of the dynamism of learning. This presupposes, of course, that the *primary* subject matter of learning in the training group is social and interpersonal relations.

Clarification of the group's own experiences calls for more or less objectified, or at least publicly checkable, sources of observational data about what actually takes place in the group, as well as a common language system, more or less impersonal and disinterested, for classifying and interrelating the observations.

The problems encountered in adopting and adapting a commonly acceptable and usable language of interpretation will be discussed later. It may be enough here to say that the requirements upon this language of interpretation are complex, partaking of the required characteristics of the language of social science, the language of art, and the language of social policy. For the uses of data interpretations in a T Group are not alone to verify or disverify hypotheses formed independently of (but relevantly to) the value choices or actions of the group or to make post hoc sense of historic events in group life. Interpretations serve also to clarify and guide the current choices of action policies and of procedures in and by the group. It is only as interpretations are translated into action policies and tried out by the group that they are effectively tested, corrected, and qualified in the minds and experiences of T Group members.

These combined functions of post hoc reconstruction of events, of prediction, and of action planning served by data that are fed back, organized, and interpreted by the T Group help to illuminate some of the paradoxes which the goal of learning through personal experience introduces into the life and career of the group. If primary stress is placed upon the immediate usefulness of observation and feedback in confronting problems of maintenance or work, "moral" and "political" considerations will narrow the scope of learning achieved and so prejudice the probability of its generalization to other situations. Yet, without some such practical reference in the selection and interpretation of observations, motivation to use data from personal experience is reduced, at least initially, and the habit of observing and analyzing one's own experience is not reinforced.

On the other hand, if primary stress is placed upon elegant and convincing post hoc reconstructions of group history, the danger is that the esthetic satisfactions of plausible, clever, and relief-giving verbal dramatizations of past frustrating and painful events will override considerations both of "practicality" and of "truth" in the meanings that are lifted out of and built back into the group's ongoing experience. However, without "artistic" reconstruction of its past, the group develops no common self-image, no mythology, no unique conscious ethos and character—in brief, no living culture. Finally, if the group were to become completely "scientific" in its self-observations, concerned only with verifiable statements about groups and group membership, it would dry up its sources of data drawn from its own actions and decisions. Conversely, a T Group that fails to put important emphasis on striving for "truth-value" in its statements about itself likely will leave its members with little *validly* generalizable knowledge.

None of these abstract alternatives is likely to occur in pure form in a training group, and certainly not throughout its career. But I have seen training groups attempt to approximate each of them for limited periods. Different T Groups do emphasize different aspects of self-interpretation and attain different characters in the process: the practical group, which maneuvers adroitly and circumspectly through its difficulties with little imagination or deep introspection; the esthetic group, which builds a rich and flavorful mythology out of its successes and failures; and the scientific group, cautious, even awkward, in its choices and movement, sparse in imaginative constructions upon its experiences, but ever hygienic and tight in its manipulations of language and observation. The more mature group cultivates a balance among the three modes of interpreting its experiences and, in the most happy instances, achieves some degree of synthesis among the three.

Part of this process of maturation comes through increasing assumption of responsibility for observation and interpretation by more and more of its members. The spread of training responsibilities is seldom, if ever, mechanically even among the members. Perhaps, too, the group achieves a balance through some informal allocation of practical, esthetic, and scientific interpretations to different members. A mature group may need to develop more or less specialized "managers and politicians," "poet laureates," and "research scientists" among its membership, as well as a common language and orientation.

Much has been written about the resistance of group members to observation and interpretation of their behavior. This resistance has been attributed to defensiveness of members toward exposing feelings and motives to others who, it is feared, may use such knowledge to hurt and destroy. The disarming of such resistances is believed, on this view, to come from the development of nonjudgmental attitudes by members toward themselves and toward other members and by the development of a climate of mutual trust among the members. There is no doubt a considerable truth in this prescription. Some members want to "judge" adversely, whether justly and rationally or not. Some members are highly uncomfortable in a climate of trust. Also, a group which chooses among alternative actions and alternative standards of conduct must make judgments and apply sanctions. In order to grow, a group must make action choices and develop criteria for choosing and acting. In order to reduce irrational resistances to accurate self-observation and interpretation, a standard of accepting and encouraging members in expressing and enacting their individualities must become one of the powerful standards in an effective T Group. Nevertheless, the group must judge ideas and behavior and develop standards to guide such judgments in the course of its development.

This principle, however, hardly goes the whole way in explaining either the motivation toward self-observation and self-interpretation in a training group, or the resistances to them. All members want to achieve greater consistency and integrity in their own behavior and in their group environment, even as they resist exposure that is perceived as painful and destructive to self and/or to the group as currently maintained. It is this strain toward greater consistency and integrity of behavior and perception that training leadership supports as it helps the group to face and accept and understand the empirical realities of their experiences. At least some of the resistances to observations and interpretations attempted by the training leader or by others may come, not from personal defensiveness primarily, but rather from inappropriateness of the interpretation attempted to the need of the group for interpretation and clarification at the time. Perhaps the three functions of interpretation already distinguished—practical, esthetic, and scientific—give some mindhold toward locating and identifying the group's changing needs for self-clarification from time to time.

THE CULTURE of the small group is a relatively neglected study. Cultural anthropologists generally have kept their eyes on the life patternings of larger social units. The social psychologists and sociologists who have preempted the small group field typically have not raised anthropological questions about the groups they have researched. So the discussion here probably will move farther beyond the pale of academic respectability than my sociological discussion which, whatever its possible appearance to the contrary, was written with the growing body of small group research in mind.

The T Group begins its career with a life expectancy of ten to forty hours. The fact that the group is foredoomed to early extinction plays an important part in the economy of its cultural development. The certainty that the association will not be prolonged lends to members a freedom of expression and sharing that is harder to achieve in a group where the tenure of continued association is indefinite.

This initial time perspective lends a related quality to the association—a motivation to live the association intensively with some relaxation of anxieties for the consequences. As members begin to realize positive values in their T Group experience, a resolution to actualize to the full its unique potential becomes a spoken or unspoken assumption in their participations.

These effects of predated group death facilitate in some measure the purposes of the T Group. But they also present problems with respect to the development of robust learnings which will transfer out of the T Group into the continuities of life. Associations on a shipboard excursion, while often marked by unwonted intimacy and intensity, are notorious for leaving little imprint. The lasting impress is a faded memory, framed in lavender (or perhaps in purple) and reviewed only covertly in moments of sentimental escape and unguarded fantasy, or perhaps more overtly on other week-end excursions. How can the T Group use the "advantages" of predated death and yet help members achieve learnings which will tincture and alter their "real" associations?

The answer seems to lie in the development of a time perspective, alternative to that of calendar time, within the associations of the T Group—a time perspective which comes to rival in "reality" that of everyday life, and, in some sense, comes to intermesh with the time which stretches beyond the dissolution of the group. The achievement of such an alternative time perspective seems to be related to the accumulation and formulation by the T Group of its own distinctive, meaningful culture and to the internalization of this culture by its members.

To save this broad generalization from an aura of mysticism, let me try to illustrate more concretely what this accumulation of a group culture means.

A T Group, meeting indoors during the twenty mornings of a summer laboratory session, began, during its seventh meeting, to attach great symbolic significance to the question of whether they should move the table into the outdoor sunlight and continue to meet there. This choice gathered into it several current ambiguities about the development of the group. The stilted politeness of their early honeymoon period had grown thin and was becoming a burden. The inability to reach a conscious decision which carried the group continuously through any extended period of activity had become a matter of concern to several members. The question of moving the table had come up originally as a way of testing the trainer's willingness to let the group make its own decisions. His refusal to rule *ex cathedra* had made his relationship to the members a matter of general concern among them. No one could quite believe in his acceptance of his role as described to them—as helper to the group in clarifying and diagnosing the processes of its own development and functioning. Some members had adopted the attitude that the T Group was a pawn within an assumed master plan. Members variously feared, hoped for, and resented the idea that they were powerless to modify the larger laboratory environment.

When the table was actually moved outdoors, many aspects of their group life up to that time fell into a new shape. Members became freer and more confident—to express their feelings about the trainer and his role, to look at widely varying member images and evaluations of the group, to share both negative and positive feelings toward one another, to think about and decide inventively and readily how to deal with different members' preferences. The prevailing immediate mood was one of exhilaration and celebration. The group contrasted their daring and independence with the craven conservatism of the other groups who had stayed indoors.

After celebration came analysis and some historical reconstruction of the event. In the assessment of previous and subsequent events, this event became a peak experience within the group's subsequent time perspective. It had developed a sense of its own historic past and, in the same act, some sense of its potential future destiny—a destiny over which, within limits, members felt confident they might exercise collective and individual control. In other words, they had accumulated and constructed a conscious culture for themselves.

It was not the event alone which developed significant culture for the group. It was the event *plus* the group's "artistic" reconstruction of it, the "scientific" analysis of its generalizable meanings, and the "practical" translation of its significance into new, more livable policies for the control of ongoing adjustments and adaptations.

At this point, the reader may be feeling as some members do when they come in late to a T Group. They encounter a sense of history and of destiny in the group, but the events supporting this compelling common outlook seem too trivial to bear the weight of significance with which the group has endowed them. A deeper look reveals that the events were not so trivial after all.

The example used involves some of the deepest dilemmas of personal and social life, the dilemmas of self and society, of authority and freedom, of conservation and change. It involves the odyssey of human loneliness and of apartness partially overcome in an association which, while firm and security-giving, yet enhances and affirms rather than eclipses and derogates individual variation and difference. Although such dilemmas are part of the lot of all men, in the T Group they can be dramatized on a stage small enough so that they can be enacted as well as seen, worked through to some acceptable outcome, and the experience of their working out criticized and evaluated in terms of personally significant ideas.

In our own larger culture, which for many incorporates much vocational and personal loneliness in confronting the basic dilemmas of personal and organizational life, it is not surprising that the discovery and achievement of uncoerced community in facing and clarifying them should be of profound significance to the persons involved in such discovery and achievement. This community is the more significant because it is achieved not in opposition to the exercise of individual and collective intelligence, but primarily through the application of intelligence to the immediate problems of one's relationships with others. It is this sense of significant discovery and achievement that makes successful T Group experience a genuine alternative, in part, to a member's outside organizational life, rather than a willful escape or vacation from it; and it is in being seen, at least in part, as a practical alternative that some transfer of learnings from the training group to other social situations is made possible.

ONE IMPLICATION of the discussion of the accumulation and construction of a distinctive culture by the T Group is that it is achieved as members come to focus upon the control, appreciation, and understanding of the concrete realities of their immediate group experiences. Only as the group learns to focus upon its present experience can its own past and future attain clarity and significance and only thus can the outside experiences of the members be related meaningfully to experiences within the group.

Nevertheless, learning to face and to examine the here-and-now is a learning not easy to achieve. Members interpose a screen of assumptions, concepts, attitudes, and evaluations between themselves and what is actually taking place in themselves and between themselves and others. These patterns are drawn from members' outside experiences with other people, other groups and organizations. These are *transferred* to the T Group. Since it is set up differently, attempts to impose familiar forms upon what takes place there tend to compound rather than to clarify confusion. It is through factoring out the actualities of the here-and-now from the importations of the there-and-then that personal and collective patternings are opened up to conscious examination.

The phenomenon of status stripping has frequently been observed in the T Group. Outside statuses of members tend to be irrelevant. Members must establish anew their statuses, appropriate to the here-and-now social system of the T Group as it emerges. It is out of the shock of this stripping off of familiar statuses and the challenge of having to achieve new statuses that significant learning both about self and about social systems may emerge.

Actually, status stripping is only one aspect of a more general primitivization of member behavior that ordinarily occurs within the T Group. A whole range of familiar sophistications fails to work for members as they seek to negotiate a new and unfamiliar social environment. This phenomenon of primitivization of behavior extends not only to patterns of overt response and verbalization but to patterns of perception and evaluation as well. In many respects, members come to act in ways similar to ways in which adolescents act in our culture.[4] Questions concerning personal identity, vocational choice, sexual role, and world view, thought to be settled once for all during adolescence, are opened up for reexamination. Much of this reexamination goes on covertly but, in some measure, it comes to be acted out and verbalized publicly in the interactions of the T Group. As members turn to one another for help in redefining who they are and what they stand for, they are thrown back to the behavior evinced in the here-and-now of the T Group for dependable empirical evidence to validate their interpretations. And, confronted by various interpretations of "the same" behavioral events, they are driven further to distinguish idiosyncratic from common perceptions and evaluations of these events.

What is achieved at least by some members, as familiar sophistications are stripped away, is a kind of Socratic ignorance and humility before the complexities of human behavior. Of course, such "constructive" ignorance and humility are not achieved equally by all members. Nor do they extend to all areas of conduct and behavior for any member. But where members become secure enough to recognize limitations in their familiar sophistications about self and others, some processes of inquiry do take place and some willing use is made of other members in consensually validating or invalidating the results of personal observations and interpretations.

To be sure, a new sophistication develops in the group. This development was described in the previous section as the development and formulation of a group culture. The hope is that this new sophistication is based, not upon ignoring or explaining away the data of immediate experience when they clash with the "certainties" of previous indoctrinations, but rather upon respect for these data as potential levers in a "reality-oriented" extension, refinement, and revision of a cultural heritage. Taking account of the here-and-now, both when it fulfills and when it violates familiar and favored prophecies and predictions, becomes a part of the life-orientation, the "method" of the group.

It is this respect for the present, in its pains and frustrations as well as its fulfillments, which, seen as potentially an avenue toward the sober revision and improvement of the history and the destiny of the group, is among the learnings most beneficially transferable by members from the T Group in their other areas of social and organizational life. A sophistication which continually seeks learning from the here-and-now, which accepts "rebarbarization" of experience as a condition of significant personal and social growth, rather than one which attempts willfully to impose its familiar forms upon the facts, feelings, and potentialities of a novel and emerging present, is a sophistication become a tool of growth and change rather than an instrument either of dogmatic conservatism or of doctrinaire reform.

AN ADEQUATE language of interpretation has been said to partake of the linguistic requirements of "social science," "social policy," and of epic or dramatic "art." A part of the initial struggles of the T Group for security-giving patterns of organization centers in a struggle to define the "official" language of the group.[5] In a group where the trainer is seen as a social scientist, struggles over the proper relationship between the trainer and the group frequently involve related struggles over the place of social science jargon within the language to be employed habitually in the group. Those who attack the leadership, even when their training is in social science, may parody and satirize the *outré* language of the leadership of the group. Failures to "hear" the trainer's interpretations or comments frequently are attributed to his cruel and unusual vocabulary. Those who want more forceful leadership frequently copy the trainer's language. If he uses social science jargon, his words are not only used, but overused and misused, so far as their precise meanings are concerned. "Cohesion" or "role" or "power" function at least as much as weapons in the struggles for control of the group as they do as instruments for precise explaining of observations of behavior.

Members attempt to express questions in language systems which they can handle effectively and with authority. In a heterogeneous group, various vocational and academic jargons may struggle for supremacy as members jockey for statuses within the group. Attacks by some members on the unintelligibility or inadequacy of the special languages of other members are closely related to factional struggles within the group.

An assumption that underlies early factional struggles over language is that there should be *an* official language in the group. Just as the group often attempts to impose order on chaos of noncommunal struggle through precisely listed agenda, carefully codified procedures, or a proliferation of group officials, so does it often assume that the group should have an authoritative dictionary to control the "correct" usages of words. Sometimes attempts are made to develop a more or less elaborate glossary of key terms.

It is only as the group loses its need for the security of an official language that language begins to function imaginatively and flexibly as an instrument for establishing communications among members. Often this is seen first in a profusion of metaphorical expressions. Frequently, these come out as members try to express with some vividness how they felt during a certain event. A training group of industrialists in which I recently participated provides examples of what I mean. "I felt yesterday, when I was all alone, like a pygmy among giants. And all the giants had their faces turned away so I couldn't see which were friendly and which were angry with me"; and, "When Bill told me that he thought I disapproved of everything he stood for, when I thought I was supporting him, I felt suddenly like all of my clothing had been taken off. I guess I wasn't just supporting him, but actually trying to make him over in my image so I could feel more comfortable with him." Or as an observation of another's characteristic relations to the group: Jack looks to me like a little Indian peering out from behind trees at us as we work in an open space in a forest. He dashes in occasionally to touch one of us. Or I guess maybe he shoots an arrow at us occasionally—usually one with a soft point"; and "I feel like Ted sees himself as always presiding at our meetings, even when he is eagerly pressing the gavel into the hands of someone else—Murray usually. And I feel Murray doesn't exactly like being made king by somebody else."

This profusion of more or less apt metaphors is likely to

come during or following the "second" equilibrium period, which the group achieves following the breakup of its honeymoon ("first" equilibrium) period. Group members, with anxieties about "correct" and "official" language stilled, begin to "talk poetry" in efforts to achieve a more concentrated and concrete communication of feeling and perception than either the "morally" tinctured language of common sense or the designedly unambiguous and aseptic language of science can achieve. (This is not to say that there is no moral concern or concern for precision implicit in the disciplined use of poetic language.) As "experimental" exploitation of the "poetic" resources of language is achieved in some degree, both common preferences and valuations and a common appreciation of individual variations in preference and valuation are achieved by members. Without them, common action which is at the same time sensitive to the individualities of members cannot be accomplished.

The language of action must be "poetic" in the sense that it is inescapably a language of persuasion, mobilizing common attitudes, preferences, feelings, and motivations in relation to compelling images of "member" and of "group," or of group goal and of individual and group efforts to reach the goal. If the community of action is to be uncoerced and respectful of valid differences in individual orientation and valuation, each member—not one or a few—must use poetic language to get openly and tellingly before the others his "subjective" interest and stake in whatever is being considered and decided. This calls for mutual exploitation of the expressive and persuasive resources of language—not just its resources for unambiguous pointing and for logically consistent argument and demonstration. Feelings and attitudes cannot become "evidence" to a group until they are tellingly and convincingly expressed in the same processes of deliberation in which objective evidence is marshaled, and evaluated.

Yet, in a T Group, the goal is not action alone or primarily, but learning through action. Members are expected to function alternately as participants in full-bodied action and as observers and analysts of their joint and individual actions. And the reporting and joint analysis of observations call also for a common language. In the language of observation and analysis, where valid cognition of what is happening in the group is a requirement, the linguistic virtues of unambiguous reference, of clear and precise definition, of logical consistency, become necessary.

To the observer and analyst, the very poetic expressions which informed, influenced, and shaped group and member actions become data to be named and sorted. Let us suppose a group is analyzing a member's expressed feeling of being a pygmy in the presence of giants with averted faces. Here one talks about a member's inability to perceive the effect of other members toward his disagreement with them. Were cues of negative or positive feeling toward his disagreement given by other members? If so, why could not the disagreeing member see them or interpret them? If not, why did the other members hide their affective reactions? How far are personal and how far are group factors involved in "explaining" the event? These represent scientific approaches to the happening.

The event may be interpreted also by placing it in historical perspective. Has the member experienced similar difficulties in getting feedback from the T Group in the past? If so, under what conditions? Does this event show similarities with comparable events in the past life of the group? If not, how has the group or the member changed? How do we evaluate any changes that may have occurred?

The event may be assessed also for its "practical" sig-

nificance. Do we need more adequate ways of giving
feedback to an uncertain member? Should we have a
standard that a member may ask others how they are
reacting to him when he feels uncertain? This last type
of question pulls the group back again into a framework
of choice, decision, and action. In settling these questions,
the language of action again becomes appropriate.

It seems hardly necessary to state that in actual group
situations the language of action blurs and at times merges
into the language of observation. But the distinction between the two is still an important one to make and to
learn in a T Group, granted its professed goals.

"AND IN this staggering disproportion between man and
no-man . . . men build their cultures by huddling together,
nervously loquacious, at the edge of an abyss." Thus
vividly, Kenneth Burke characterized the precariousness
of the *human* regime within the world of *no-man*.[6]

In the regime of ordinary life, men are protected by
largely unquestioned routines and cultural patternings,
and by unquestioning acceptance of them, from looking
into the abyss of fundamental insecurity that stretches
beyond the man-maintained securities of social existence.
Individual men glimpse at times their basic dependence,
for order and meaningfulness in their personal lives, upon
the order provided by the institutions and ideological assumptions of their social group(s). They glimpse this dependence, and the prospect of individual loneliness and
un-sanity outside it, most readily in moments of radical
personal decision or when caught teetering and compelled
to choose between radically differing group demands and
loyalties. But this bleak vision for most men is difficult to
maintain for long and, typically, myth-making loquacity

quickly patches all frightening breaches in their personal-social systems of meaning and security.

In a T Group, members catch more than a glimpse of the personal insecurity that accompanies the absence of stable, common criteria for judging the rightness of actions and transactions, criteria of the sort that lend certainty and security to their judgments, evaluations, and responses in the everyday round of familiar associations. The most frightening insecurities come when the group-sanctioned ways of settling doubts imported and invoked by some members, encounter alternative group-sanctioned ways of other members, and neither is able to lend decisiveness to the choices of an unformed group.

It is as if the group were operating in that precontractual human state postulated by some political theorists which, taken literally as a datable historic (or prehistoric) condition of man, is mythical anthropology but, taken as an ever-threatening condition of human existence, embodies a profound truth.[7] Group members are thrust back upon their own resources to legislate and maintain a viable order of relationships. Men, as I have noted, typically take for granted the going patterns of their associational life. Some mythical "they" or "he" has fixed the orders of associational life as they are, and their legitimacy is acknowledged even in rebellion against them.

In the T Group, valiant efforts, like those of Kafka's "K" in *The Castle,* are made to detect the order which "he" or "they" really want for the group and tantalizingly are refusing to divulge. When these efforts fail, the group seeks to impose a rigid order which will shut out ambiguity. When these external and inappropriate social arrangements fail, as they must, members may try willfully to be good and kind to one another in what I have called a honeymoon period. But this effort must also fail, because it attempts to solve what is in part a social as well as an individual problem by individual restraints alone and because it rests on a denial of irrepressible psychological "facts" (of negative affect, differential feelings toward one another, or aggressive impulses, among others) and social "facts" (such as lack of viable patterns of social control, lack of mechanisms for consensually validating decisions and judgments). Group members finally come to accept, at least in part, the empirical reality of their plight. If they are to be saved from the threatening abyss of meaninglessness and ambiguity, they must save themselves through their own personal *and* collective "legislations." Commitment to an "experimental" quest for meaning, control, and communication, as it comes and is evaluated, is found to yield its own common security and authority, a security and authority based on affirmation rather than denial of member individuality, of personal and collective intelligence, and of the enduring paradoxes of social-personal life.

Why should contemporary "organization men" be brought to look into the abyss which lies beyond the conventional and parochial certainties of unquestioned group identifications and loyalties? Perhaps it is enough of an answer for the present to say that contemporary men cannot achieve a viable combination of "freedom" and "security," both of which they claim to prize, through rejection of group and organizational life in a spree of romantic individualism. But their affirmation of its practical necessity must not be a blind acceptance of the contemporary and traditional patterns in which their lives happen to be set historically. In affirming the inescapability of grappling with the demands of groups and organizations, contemporary men must at the same time learn how to alter, how to build and rebuild group and organizational patterns, even as they participate in them, with an eye to the values of community and of personal freedom and spontaneity. Such learning is facilitated by the kind of clear-eyed and socially supported look into the abyss which T Group experience provides.

THE T GROUP, I have said, finally finds or, better, constructs a basis of security and community in commonly acceptable ways of treating "experimentally" the concrete empirical "realities" of its here-and-now situation. These ways include approaches for eliciting honest evidence from all members relative to failures, disaffections, and conflicts, as well as to victories, euphorias, and resolutions, which occur in the course of group life. They include methods and mechanisms for analyzing and assessing the evidence in terms of its practical significance in the ordering and reordering of group activities and structures, in terms of its generalizable import as "knowledge" to be tested in various ways, and in terms of its meaning for imaginative and artistic construction and reconstruction of historic events and future destinies in the emerging culture of the group. They include the ways of managing, with increasing linguistic and behavioral skills, required shifts of membership between the postures and orientations appropriate to participant-actors and those appropriate to observer-analysts. These ways of group life do not eliminate pain and paradox, loneliness and suffering. But they do help members to sort the pain and paradox, the loneliness and suffering, which are self-imposed and organizationally imposed, from those which must be accepted as inherent—though not, therefore, incapable of future diminution—within the tragic human situation. The methodology developed for achieving consensual validations of perception and response should help members to distill from these latter limitations some measure of personal and collective clarity and wisdom.

The basic security of group members comes to be invested in this composite and complex methodology. The methodology is designed to support both individual and group growth in an inherently pluralistic community of constructive and reconstructive effort.

The nature of the "consensus" and "community," here described and normatively affirmed as "right," seems difficult for many contemporaries to envision and, so, to understand. The "positivist" mentality, draped in the robes of "scientific" sanctimoniousness, either denies rational meaning to the very notion of a community of ethical agreement or identifies it erroneously or perversely with a psychologically factual agreement attained by whatever means and resting on whatever grounds—spurious, fantastic, or perhaps by chance, correct. Arthur Murphy's statement seems to be particularly cogent at this point.

> To maintain the ethical agreement vital to such community it is indeed essential that its members think alike on fundamentals. That does not mean, however, that they must hold identical opinions on controversial issues, opinions maintained by indoctrination in all the various media of managed mass credulity. That is not to think alike, for so far it is not to think at all. It is, rather, the way in which men agree when they do not think, when their minds are the passive instruments of social forces they do not understand. To think alike, where doubt has arisen and a justification is called for, we must first of all think, and to think is to judge, to submit divergent claims and opinions to the test of examinable reasons and to decide, not arbitrarily, but fairly, on the merits of the case. An agreement thus maintained is an

> ethical agreement and the society that preserves
> and defends it a community. . . . The morally
> authoritative verdict of the community is the con-
> sensus maintained and validated in this process.[8]

Contemporary society is devoid of "community" in many of its parts. The T Group seeks to provide an experience in building and managing a "community," in the hope that through transfer of learning the normative drought of contemporary society can be reduced.

This involves, of course, an ideal, but hopefully not a sentimental, view of member maturity and of group maturity. It is not achieved equally by all members in the same training group or to the same degree by different groups. Nor are all areas of member experience opened equally to public examination. This is as it should be. Privacy is also a value within a well-organized community when not purchased at too high a price in terms of personal and social malaise. But some glimpse of such an ideal of social and personal organization and of its dependence upon the achievement, both at group and at member levels, of an adequate methodology for facing and dealing honestly and creatively with difference and conflict, comes to each member of a successful T Group.

A methodology adequate to the conditions and goals of training group life ordinarily makes its way against two sorts of methodological alternatives in the characters of its members. One kind of alternative is contradictory at some points to the rational-empirical-experimental methodology described above. One illustration is a thoroughgoing commitment to the method of authority in validating one's own critical judgments, valuations, and behaviors. Cognitively, this view denies the possibility of finding within the processes of personal and collective experience any norms for judging whether to believe this or that, whether to do this or that. Behaviorally, this view means a tenacious clinging to some authority outside the T Group as infallible, or a search within the group for an infallible authority-surrogate. The demands of a developing T Group upon a member with such a methodological commitment are excruciatingly difficult to meet.

The other sort of alternative is to take one part or aspect of the required methodology and to treat it as if it were the whole. An illustration would be a commitment to some strict version of "scientific method" as defining completely the necessary intellectual discipline of effective group membership. Consistent with this view, the stance of observer and analyst, not of participant, is the only proper stance for a member to take in the group. If this point of view were to be generalized to all members, the T Group would have no subject-participants to observe and analyze; or the group would be brought perforce to make of its observations and analyses *actions* for further analysis and observation. (This sometimes happens.) Again, this view tends to limit the function of observation and analysis to the formulation and checking of precise predictions about relations between isolable elements of group and member experience. The equally important "artistic" and "practical" (moral and political) functions of observation and interpretation, if I have been right in my argument, tend to be ignored and, thus, deprived of any conscious and critical cultivation in the group. The adaptation of the "scientistic" member to the full methodological demands of training group experience is, when healthy, not to forsake his commitment to "scientific method" but to learn to reconcile its legitimate demands with the equally exacting requirements of "historical-artistic" and of "practical" methods.

The clash of methodologies is never fully resolved. However, as some measure of genuine community is attained, these differences and conflicts among the members, along with others, may become accepted as sources of potential creativity, rather than proscribed as threats and blemishes to a soullessly efficient regime of social stability and order.

PERHAPS SOME comment on the attitudes and values which the trainer requires in giving help to others in learning for themselves will provide a useful conclusion to this essay. St. Thomas Aquinas, in his *De Magistro,* poses and discusses a question which all trainers should have pondered seriously before undertaking their roles. Can one be taught by another?

St. Thomas considers all of the then current arguments for and against the proposition that one can teach another and draws a qualified and conditionally affirmative conclusion. One can teach another only if he can enlist the other in thinking and learning for himself.

Whether or not the trainer reaches the conclusion which St. Thomas reached, he should have worked on the question seriously and should have attained the humility about helping someone else to learn for himself to which such serious consideration is certain to lead. This humility is needed by the trainer. Some people he probably cannot teach. Others he may be able to teach, but no two persons will learn in exactly the same way. Similarly, no two T Groups will develop in exactly the same way or present the same learning opportunities to their members.

What the trainer can predict are some of the major dilemmas and paradoxes of personal and social life which the group will encounter. What he cannot predict is the concrete form these problems will take in the life of a particular group or the distinctive shape they will take in the perceptions, feelings, and thinking of particular members. The trainer must be ready to let the group, and the individuals in it, find their own tortuous ways toward insight. He must be willing to let them try and fail as well as succeed. He cannot protect them from reality if his goal is to support them in facing the reality of self and others in all of its complexity and in handling such reality more creatively and rationally than before. What he can insist on is that realities be recognized, named, and analyzed, rather than ignored, denied, or oversimplified. But his version of reality is not reality, and he must be strong enough to have his version of reality challenged and changed if he is to be permitted to challenge the versions of others.

The main value that sustains him in his desperate resolve is that it is better for people to learn than to remain ignorant, that it is better for people (himself included) to change toward less distorted ways of perceiving and reflecting on themselves and their world than it is for them to remain chained to the comfort of false perceptions and crippled thinking processes. The faith that supports this value is a faith that he and others, through genuinely common efforts, can attain greater clarification in their insights and working assumptions than if they depend on their own unchecked perceptions alone. He must be ready to be used by others, and this frequently involves abuse, in order that they may discover how they are seeing and relating to themselves and other persons.

The trainer's ultimate reliance is on the institutionalizing of a methodology of participant-observation in a group as a self-correcting way for members to learn about themselves and about other people. His reward is increased insight into how this institutionalization can better be accomplished so that he and others can better teach and be taught by one another.

The Arts of
Democratic Citizenship

As IN the case of all other arts, the art of democracy draws its meaning from two sources. One source is a vision of perfection. In the fine arts, this vision is one of beauty and significant order. In democratic living, the vision is one of right human relationships, the vision of a social order built by free and equal men and women for the nurture and growth of free and equal men and women.

The other source of meaning in an art is derived from the materials to be shaped and built by the artist. The material never fits the form of beauty which the artist seeks to embody in it. The materials are never merely formless. They are in part already differently formed and so recalcitrant—resistant to the form the artist would realize in them.

It is in the process of reconciling his vision to the challenge of his refractory materials that the skills, the strategies, the arts and wiles of the artist are called for and are defined and refined. This is obviously true of the sculptor, the architect, the painter.

It is, though perhaps more subtly, equally true in the art of democracy. The materials to be shaped in the processes of democracy are people, individuals and struggling groups of people. They are sometimes formless, insofar as the vision of democratic perfection is concerned. But more often they are resistant and recalcitrant in part to the requirements of democratic living. Yet they are the materials which must somehow be formed to the demands of democracy, if there is to be democracy at all.

Moreover, every person is an artist in shaping and reshaping the network of human relationships in which he lives. And in this process of shaping his society each person is both artist and material. Each person must shape and reshape himself and his group to the vision of democratic living, even as he tries to shape and reshape other persons and other groups. Many of the failures of democratic artists occur when this simple but fundamental fact is forgotten. We too often seek to change others while holding ourselves apart from change.

Finally, it is not people in general or human nature in general, which the artists of democracy must seek to reshape toward their vision of perfection. It is actual, concrete people in this contemporary historical situation of ours which are our materials.

One may write historical romances about more or less idyllic agricultural and pastoral periods of history. But the arts of democratic action must be defined and learned within our own time and setting. They must be learned today and tomorrow in an atomic age, in an age of runaway cities and suburbs, in fragmented communities in which each group interest conflicts sharply at points with other group interests. And they must be learned in the presence of massive rejections of democratic ideas and ideals, at home and abroad.

It might be more pleasant to define and learn our arts of democracy in a more placid, less recalcitrant period of history. But we can't. We must behave democratically in our own historical situation. Our materials are people, ourselves and others, trying to live in and through this age. As artists we cannot neglect our materials if we are to produce any work of art, or to learn the skills which our artistry requires.

The arts of democracy, then, cannot be defined apart from some vision of democratic perfection, or apart from an analysis of people as they are in our own age. The arts of democracy are defined by the processes required to bring vision and reality nearer together than they now are. In discussing the arts of democracy intelligibly, we must be idealistic and realistic at one and the same time. At least, we must try to be so.

Let me now clarify both the meaning I give to the vision of democratic perfection, and the outlines of my diagnosis of our contemporary human situation, complicated as these statements must be. For there is currently consensus on neither. (And I would be derelict to my democratic vision if I did not prepare and open my views honestly to the rational criticism and attack of others.)

By democracy I mean a society or group of any size which operates on the principle of consent. Men prescribe rules and adopt goals for their common action on the basis of decisions reached through free study and deliberation. It is not enough that men should register their uninformed judgments on questions and issues. In the process of making up their minds they should have access to all facts and opinions and arguments relevant to an issue and problem. Men are legislators of authority at the same time they are subjects of the authority which they have collectively prescribed.

This vision rests upon the assumption that a policy or decision is most valid when it incorporates relevant experience and thinking from all men affected by the policy or decision—and not when it embodies the thinking of any few men, whether their right to rule is justified on the basis of wealth or learning or any other claim to prestige or excellence.

On any given issue the thinking of one humble or obscure man may be right, and all the sages and dignitaries may be in error. It is, therefore, necessary that all humble men be able and free to raise their voices and be heard in the process of public deliberation.

But minority voices will not be heard, however well articulated or informed, unless men are free to express "error" as well as "truth." When we don't know what the "truth" is in some controverted area, how can we in advance label "error" and silence it without drying up our very sources of new truth?

This means, further, that individual men and groups of men must be equal in their access to learning, equal in their opportunities for developing whatever unique talents they may have, equal in their rights to listen and be heard in the unending conversation through which men determine how to choose and to act as men—men who accept their humanity and strive to live neither as beasts nor as gods.

And what of the contemporary human situation? It is one in which these values are imperfectly embodied. It is not a democratic situation, but one instead which is filled with traditional institutions which reflect primarily authoritarian and aristocratic ideas of human relationships. And some of these institutions are powerful in the lives of people, especially in the lives of young people growing up.

Families, businesses, factories, unions, schools, military organizations, and churches reflect in varying degrees authoritarian ideas and ideals as well as democratic ones.

People growing up do not drink in democracy through every psychological pore. They learn authoritarian ideas and practices along with democratic ones. And the resulting conflict is reflected in the character of each of us.

Ours is also a situation in which it is increasingly difficult to build small democratic islands and let the rest of the world go by. People in Massachusetts are bound to people in Alabama, and less formally, but nevertheless actually, to people in Thailand and Tibet, in Israel and Iraq. We cannot be indifferent to what these people do, for our future as well as theirs is bound up with at least some of the things they decide to do today. And their future weal and woe are bound up in some of the decisions we are making today. Our collective problems are thus very large problems indeed. Moreover, they defy the comfortable provincialism and isolationism which mark much of our traditional mentality. Our provincialism resists the effective advance of democratic ideas and ideals.

Our traditional neighborhoods and communities have been fragmented and disrupted by the growth of industrial and urban ways of living. All of us tend to be more identified with some special interest or fragment of the geographic area in which we live than with the welfare of "the community as a whole."

In these conditions, common welfare tends to lose its meaning. It becomes a pious verbal mask which special interests put on to plead their case in the court of wayward and fickle public opinion. Actual common interest must be created out of the conflict of special interests as their proponents learn to integrate special outlooks and interests and invent new common ways of controlling their environment. But the voices of those who would create new common viewpoints and interests are frequently lost in the din of competing voices pleading for special interests and, what is more, masquerading as common interests.

Finally, knowledge is fragmented and unequally divided in our society today. Division of labor in our intellectual life has led to specialization of learning. Experts abound. The knowledge we need to make intelligent decisions is specialized in many people and in many places. We need to use the experts, frequently more than we do, but where are the men who help to frame the common view in which expert opinions and knowledges can be used in balanced ways? Without such men, experts, because we need them, can become the rulers of men rather than their servants—and dangerous rulers because their points of view are limited and unbalanced because of their very specializations.

These, then, are some of the refractory human materials in our situation which the artists of democracy must attempt to shape toward their ideal of democratic perfection.

To accomplish this task we shall need to master the following arts:

1. *The art of effective criticism as well as veneration of our traditions.*

Our traditions are the source of democratic ideals and attitudes and outlooks. True enough. But they are also the source of authoritarian and aristocratic ideals and attitudes and outlooks. How can we learn to criticize our traditions, which means criticizing ourselves as well as others—since our living traditions are within us—while still affirming the healthy and democratic parts of our traditions? This calls for art of a high order.

When we have learned to speak of our authentic democratic traditions in the same piece and paragraph and breath in which we also criticize our traditions of second-class citizenship for some, of arbitrary and irresponsible control of semipublic as well as public organizations, etc. —and when we learn to speak of both without defensiveness and oratory, we will have mastered the first art of democratic citizenship.

2. *The art of listening to opinions and attitudes and practices different from our own and answering these in the light of the full human meaning of what we hear.*

This is as hard as it is necessary to do in our fragmented communities and world. The other fellow's view must make sense to him. We must credit him with this if we are to respect him as a person. And this means usually respecting his group or groups as well as himself.

If his view makes sense to him, how does it? What needs, what aspirations, what traditions and what beliefs make his view sensible to him while it is so different from our own? Thus to entertain another's view, to take his role in our communication, is not to accept it as our own. It is rather to invite him for the time to see our world through our eyes as we are willing to struggle to see his world through his eyes. Only when this is accomplished can we together accurately identify our common ground as well as our differences and battle to good purpose to change each others' views.

Many well-intentioned attempts to change toward greater democracy fail because the spearheads of the change are unable to listen to their opposition and learn from them. To advance democracy, we must learn the art of listening sympathetically and understandingly to the opponents of democracy, even as we encourage and demand the same respect from them. When we can, without gullibility and without anxiety, state our opponents' views so that they agree, "Yes, that is what we are trying to say," and when we can help the opponents to state our views in the same spirit, then this second art of democratic citizenship will have been mastered.

3. *The art of dealing with conflict creatively and integratively.*

Many of us avoid conflict. Others of us join conflict and seek to prolong it because of its drama and excitement or for other unacknowledged reasons. But some have learned neither to avoid nor needlessly to precipitate and prolong conflict, but rather to welcome it as an opportunity for growth and learning all around.

Nothing new or significant gets formulated or accomplished without conflict. For conflict opens up the deficiencies of the status quo as well as the partiality of its reformers' views and makes it possible to invent new ways of thought and practice which avoid the difficulties and incorporate at least some of the goods of both parties to the conflict.

But this virtue of conflict will be realized only as men in conflict learn the complex art of creative bargaining, as Max Otto called it, or the art of integration of conflicting and partial interests and viewpoints, as Mary Follet called it. When we learn to welcome conflict which can be controlled toward new learning and growth for all, as Socrates did, perhaps we will have mastered this third art of democratic citizenship.

4. *The art of evaluating the virtues and limitations of the expert, of expert opinion and knowledge, and of using expertise rationally.*

When we are making policies or decisions, we know somehow that we may and should consult experts who know more about the questions under consideration than we do. And we frequently do one of two things in light of this knowledge.

We may deny the expert because he threatens our autonomy and our freedom to decide. On this view our decision remains less informed and more ignorant than it need be.

We may turn the responsibility for decision over to the expert and depend primarily upon his direction. This means we have denied the necessary part which our experience and our knowledge must play, as interwoven with expert opinion and knowledge.

But neither rebellion nor surrender is the answer. The expert because of his very specialization suffers from what Veblen called trained incapacity. The celebrated man in the street frequently knows better what the expert's knowledge should mean in a total practical situation than the expert himself can possibly know.

How can practical judgments be fused with the judgments of the specialist? This is a major problem of democratic deliberation at all levels of society and of government today. When we have learned to use expert knowledge—and I enter a special plea here for wider use of expertise in the social sciences, for the psychological, psychiatric, anthropological, sociological sciences of man—without self-defeating feelings of rebellion or of surrender, then we will have mastered this fourth art of democratic citizenship.

5. *The art of evaluating objectively the results in practice of decisions formed in the heat of controversy and conflict.*

Frequently, a policy we have fought for becomes our baby and we defend it against reason even when there is evidence that it is failing to meet, in practice, the objectives it was designed to serve. Its opponents similarly refuse to examine its virtues in practice. This delays the remaking of policies in the light of evidence and experience, a flexibility which democracies require and which is one of their fundamental boasts against the rigidities of dictatorships of any sort.

Can we learn to build plans (and funds) for reevaluation into all experimental legislation that we pass? No matter how enamored we may be with the beforehand wisdom of the plan, can we learn to collect and interpret evidence as to how well our plans work out? And can we include this in the original process of planning? When we can answer yes to these questions, we may have begun to master this fifth art of democratic citizenship.

There are probably many other arts which our view of democracy and the realities of our contemporary human situation require us to learn. But these five, I think, are among the fundamental ones. I believe we will be able to move more confidently toward fuller democracy when we learn the arts (1) of reverent criticism of our traditions, (2) of listening fully and of answering in the light of all that we hear, (3) of bargaining creatively within the heat of conflict, (4) of working with experts without either rebellion or surrender, and (5) of evaluating objectively our plans and policies as they work out.

NOTES

EDUCATION FOR TRAGEDY

[1] The following listing of names, brief and partial as it is, suggests the variety of thinkers—various in viewpoint as well as in field of specialization—who can today be called to support the thesis that our period of history is emphatically a period of cultural crisis— Charles Merriam, Karl Mannheim, Karl Marx, and the Marxians, Pitirim Sorokin, Arnold Toynbee, Emil Brunner, Jacques Maritain, Nicholas Berdyaev, T. S. Eliot, David Daiches, Walter Curt Behrendt, and George Bernard Shaw. Were my effort here to *explain* the current crisis rather than to suggest sources of documentation for its existence, the thinkers here named would compose a dissonant medley of contending and only partially communicating voices. The fact itself may be used as further documentation of the current crisis in culture.

[2] Kenneth Burke, *A Grammar of Motives* (New York, 1945).

[3] Eric Bentley, *The Playwright as Thinker* (New York, 1946), 190-91.

[4] Whitney J. Oates and Eugene O'Neill, Jr., eds., *The Complete Greek Drama* (New York, 1938), I, xxviii.

[5] Theodore Spencer, *Shakespeare and the Nature of Man* (2nd ed.; New York, 1949), 211.

[6] Reinhold Niebuhr, *The Nature and Destiny of Man* (New York, 1943), II, 110-12; Peter Drucker, *The End of Economic Man* (New York, 1939), 59-84.

[7] *Alcestis, Helen, The Bacchae, Andromache,* and *Medea.*

[8] Friedrich Nietzsche, *The Birth of Tragedy,* trans. William A. Haussmann, *Complete Works of Friedrich Nietzsche,* ed. Dr. Oscar Levy, I (Edinburgh, 1909), 69.

[9] Marjorie Grene, *Dreadful Freedom* (Chicago, 1948), 47.

[10] Jean Paul Sartre, *L'Etre et le néant,* quoted in Grene, *Dreadful Freedom,* 55-56 (italics mine).

[11] See, for example, Delmore Schwartz, *Vaudeville for a Princess* (New York, 1950), 4-6.

[12] Grene, *Dreadful Freedom,* 92.

[13] Robinson, Jeffers, *Medea* (New York, 1946), 107.

[14] Kenneth Fearing, *Collected Poems* (New York, 1940), 60-61.

[15] Kenneth D. Benne, "Toward a Grammar of Educational Motives," *Educational Forum,* XI (January, 1947), 239.

NOTES

EDUCATION IN THE QUEST FOR IDENTITY

[1] The notion of *mood*, as used here, was developed by the cross-disciplinary staff of the Pro-Seminar in Human Relations at Boston University in 1959 to order and analyze various contemporary and historical approaches and strategies with respect to the planning and direction of change in human affairs. The staff included Professors Kenneth D. Benne, Saul Bernstein, Theodore Brameld, Paul Deats, Don Kenefick, and Dr. Hesung Koh. A *mood* is an orienting set of attitudes toward man and his world, less crystallized and articulated than an ideology or philosophy of life. In fact, several ideologies may be developed out of a given mood, ideologies which differ in many details, yet reveal the "same" underlying mood. The staff identified four moods prominent in contemporary responses to social change—the liberal-optimistic, the therapeutic, the prophetic-revolutionary, and the neo-conservative.

[2] It may seem strange that I have omitted the neo-conservative mood as a source of challenges to educational liberalism. It is true that traditionally the major controversies in American discussions of education have swung around conflicts between liberal optimism and conservatism of one stripe or another. Liberal optimists are still enrolled for battle with conservatives, and their major rhetoric of attack and defense is shaped to the requirements of this battle. However, it is my opinion that the untenability of tradition-direction in our changing patterns and conditions of life and in the presence of the variety of traditions that characterize our pluralistic and fragmented society, national and international—deprives neo-conservatism of power to do more than fight rear-guard actions against educational or social innovation. A more ominous opponent of liberal-optimism is "totalism"—a life orientation to be discussed later.

[3] Erik H. Erikson, *Childhood and Society* (New York, 1950); Erik H. Erikson, *Young Man Luther: A Study in Psychoanalysis and History* (New York, 1958); Edgar Z. Friedenberg, "Society and the Therapeutic Function," *Adult Leadership*, V (September, 1956), 70-73, 94-95; Esther Milner, *The Failure of Success: the American Crisis in Values* (New York, 1959); David Riesman (in collaboration with Reuel Denney and Nathan Glazer), *The Lonely Crowd: a Study of the Changing American Character* (New Haven, Conn., 1950); and Allen Wheelis, *The Quest for Identity* (New York, 1958).

[4] In preparing this composite, I am much indebted to J. W. Getzel's brilliant review of Wheelis' and Lynd's books on the prob-

lem of identity—*American Sociological Review*, XXIII (December, 1958), 739-41. The quotation appears on page 739.

[5] Wheelis, *The Quest for Identity*.

[6] Riesman, *The Lonely Crowd*.

[7] Helen M. Lynd, *On Shame and the Search for Identity* (New York, 1958).

[8] See Karl Jaspers, *Man in the Modern Age*, trans. Eden and Cedar Paul (New York, 1933) and *The Future of Mankind* (Chicago, 1961); and Paul Tillich, *The Courage to Be* (New Haven, Conn., 1952).

[9] In *Growing Up Absurd* (New York, 1960), Paul Goodman presents a somewhat similar typology of youthful responses to a society that makes personal maturity difficult, if not impossible, to achieve.

[10] Robert Jay Lifton develops the psychological characteristics of "totalism" in his study of Red Chinese brainwashing, *Thought Reform and the Psychology of Totalism* (New York, 1961).

[11] Philip E. Jacob, *Changing Values in College: an Exploratory Study of the Impact of College Teaching* (New York, 1957).

[12] Stember's report of the minimal effect of education at all levels upon prejudices against minority groups gives some confirmation to this hunch. Charles Herbert Stember, *The Effect of Education on Prejudice Against Minority Groups* (New York, 1960).

[13] David Riesman, "The 'Jacob Report,'" *American Sociological Review*, XXIII (December, 1958), 738.

EDUCATION IN THE QUEST FOR COMMUNITY

[1] In this analysis of the eclipse of community, I have drawn heavily on my article, "Ideas and Communities," *Community Development*, No. 5, 1900, 90-100.

[2] David Daiches, *The Novel and the Modern World* (Chicago, 1939), 3-7.

[3] For a very able analysis of this fact and its educational implications, see William O. Stanley, *Education and Social Integration* (New York, 1953).

[4] Maurice R. Stein, *The Eclipse of Community* (Princeton, N.J., 1960), 282-84.

[5] This theme is suggested, though not so starkly stated, by Robert C. Wood in *Suburbia: Its People and Their Politics* (Boston, 1959).

[6] For a fuller treatment of this theme, see Warren Bennis, Kenneth D. Benne, and Robert Chin, *The Planning of Change* (New

York, 1961). This book deals extensively and intensively with methodologies for deepening the collaborative and scientific character and commitment of contemporary processes of change in persons and collectivities.

[7] See Kenneth D. Benne, *Group Dynamics and Human Relations Education* (New York, 1961). For an imaginative projection of a somewhat similar viewpoint in an image of the "ideal school," see also Herbert A. Thelen, *Education and the Human Quest* (New York, 1960).

[8] Martin Buber, *Between Man and Man*, trans. Ronald Gregor Smith (Boston, 1955), 31. See also Buber's earlier work, *I and Thou*, trans. Ronald Gregor Smith (Edinburgh, 1937).

[9] "The Interdisciplinary Frontier in the Study of Human Relations," partially reprinted in Bennis, Benne, and Chin, *The Planning of Change*, chap. I.

THE USES OF FRATERNITY

[1] See particularly David Riesman (in collaboration with Reuel Denney and Nathan Glazer), *The Lonely Crowd: A Study of the Changing American Character* (New Haven, Conn., 1950); also David Riesman, *Individualism Reconsidered* (Glencoe, Ill., 1954).

[2] William H. Whyte, *The Organization Man* (New York, 1956).

[3] Paul Goodman's comment on "progressive education" is eloquent on this point. "This radical proposal, aimed at solving the dilemmas of education in the modern circumstances of industrialism and democracy, was never given a chance. It succeeded in destroying the faculty psychology in the interests of educating the whole person, and in emphasizing group experiences, but failed to introduce learning-by-doing with real problems. The actual result of the gains has been to . . . foster adjustment to society as it is." *Growing Up Absurd* (New York, 1960), 225.

[4] "Creativity in Self-Actualizing People," H. H. Anderson, ed., *Creativity and Its Cultivation* (New York, 1959).

[5] See, for example, *Reaching the Fighting Gang* (New York, 1960).

[6] See Richard Bond and others, "The Neighborhood Peer Group," *The Group*, XVII (October, 1954); Ralph Kolodny, Samuel Waldfogel, and Virginia Burns, "Summer Camping in the Treatment of Ego-Defective Children," *Mental Hygiene*, XLIV (July, 1960).

[7] The ideal of a mature personality argued for in this essay is not really very different from David Riesman's "autonomous person," Paul Goodman's "independent" or Erich Fromm's "produc-

tive" personality. What the present discussion adds is the search for ways of deliberately creating the social (or group) conditions which make the development of such personalities most likely within the limitations and compulsions of an industrial society. This search has led me to reassess the potentialities of a means often used "naturally" to defeat the development of the kinds of personalities desired.

THE RE-EDUCATION OF PERSONS IN
THEIR HUMAN RELATIONSHIPS

[1] "Community animal" seems a better contemporary translation than the usual "political animal" for Aristotle's *zoon politikon*. For the Greek *polis*, or city state, fulfilled far more than political, in the sense of government, functions for the classic Greek. The *polis* was a basic organizational unit of social and cultural life—an organization of the entire range of human needs and interests and of ways of meeting these—political, economic, artistic, intellectual, and educational. Perhaps the last term signifies the basic meaning for the Greeks. For it is in education and reeducation that the continuity of human life and culture inheres. "Community" conveys this inclusive meaning better for contemporaries than "political," a term we have tended in modern times, however fortunately or unfortunately, to narrow and degrade.

[2] *Adventures of Ideas* (New York, 1933), 117.

[3] W. C. Behrendt, *Modern Building* (New York, 1937), 11-12, 15.

[4] *The Human Problems of an Industrial Civilization* (Boston, 1933); *The Social Problems of an Industrial Civilization* (Cambridge, Mass., 1945), *passim*.

[5] Kenneth T. Behnke, A Communication of Authority (New York, 1943), chap. V, *passim*.

[6] I realize that the question with which this section is concerned, if it is to be seen in the round, needs to be placed in religious, in psychological-psychiatric, and in historical perspectives, as well as in the four settings attempted all too inadequately here. Readers may wish to refer to the following three books as respectively "representative" of the several available treatments in these three neglected perspectives: Paul Tillich, *The Courage to Be* (New Haven, Conn., 1953); G. Brock Chisholm, *The Psychiatry of Enduring Peace and Progress*, reprinted from *Psychiatry*, IX (February, 1946); and H. Stuart Hughes, *An Essay for Our Times* (New York, 1950).

NOTES

FROM POLARIZATION TO PARADOX

[1] Out of a large and growing literature on laboratory methods of human relations training and the T Group, the best single reference is Leland P. Bradford, Jack Gibb, and Kenneth D. Benne, eds., *T Group Theory and Laboratory Method: An Innovation in Reeducation* (New York, 1961). In this book, I have published "A History of the T Group in the Laboratory Setting," which may be of interest to readers who wish to learn more of the origin and evolution of this educational innovation.

[2] Dr. Elvin Semrad is a Boston psychiatrist who has done pioneering work in group psychotherapy. I learned his ideas about "contract" in conversations with him.

[3] Kenneth D. Benne, *A Conception of Authority* (New York, 1943), *iii*.

[4] This observation of the "adolescent" quality of T Group behavior was worked out by Dr. Roy Whitman and me during our collaboration in a T Group in Bethel, Maine, in 1952. We hesitated to label the phenomenon "regression," in its usual psychiatric sense. The more neutral term, "primitivization" of perception, evaluation, and response, seems to me now a better label for it.

[5] So far as I know, only one careful report of language shifts in a T Group has been attempted. Herbert Thelen and Watson Dickerman, "Stereotypes and the Growth of Groups," *Educational Leadership*, VI (February, 1949), 309-16.

[6] Kenneth Burke, *Permanence and Change* (Los Altos, Calif., 1954), 272.

[7] On numerous occasions I have explored with Leland Bradford this way of describing the early condition of a T Group.

[8] "The Common Good," in *American Philosophers at Work*, ed. Sidney Hook (New York, 1956), 436.

ACKNOWLEDGMENTS

ALL OF THE ESSAYS in this volume have been published previously. I have reedited all of the pieces and, in a few cases, assigned a new title.

I acknowledge with thanks the permission granted by the following holders of copyright to republish my essays in their present form. "Education for Tragedy" appeared originally in the magazine *Educational Theory.* "Education in the Quest for Identity" and "Education in the Quest for Community" were first published by the College of Education, the Ohio State University, as the Bode Memorial Lectures for 1961. "The Uses of Fraternity" is reprinted from *Daedalus,* Vol. XC, No. 2, published by the American Academy of Arts and Sciences, Brookline, Massachusetts.

"Man and Moloch" first appeared in *The Journal of Social Issues,* published by the Society for the Psychological Study of Social Issues. "The Re-education of Persons in their Human Relationships" was previously printed in *Adult Education* and "The Arts of Democratic Citizenship" in *Adult Leadership.* Both these periodicals are published by the Adult Education Association of the U.S.A. The National Training Laboratories and John Wiley and Sons have given permission to reprint "From Polarization to Paradox," first published as the eighth chapter of a book, *T-Group Theory and Laboratory Method.*

W9-BVO-854

The World of Plymouth Plantation

THE WORLD OF
PLYMOUTH PLANTATION

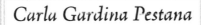

Carla Gardina Pestana

THE BELKNAP PRESS OF

HARVARD UNIVERSITY PRESS

CAMBRIDGE, MASSACHUSETTS

LONDON, ENGLAND

2020

Maps copyright © 2020 by Carla Gardina Pestana

Library of Congress Cataloging-in-Publication Data

Names: Pestana, Carla Gardina, author.
Title: The world of Plymouth Plantation / Carla Gardina Pestana.
Description: Cambridge, Massachusetts : The Belknap Press of Harvard
University Press, 2020. | Includes bibliographical references and index.
Identifiers: LCCN 2020003452 | ISBN 9780674238510 (cloth)
Subjects: LCSH: Pilgrims (New Plymouth Colony) | Massachusetts—
History—New Plymouth, 1620–1691. | Massachusetts—Social life and customs—
To 1775. | Massachusetts—Relations.
Classification: LCC F68 .P395 2020 | DDC 974.4/02—dc23
LC record available at https://lccn.loc.gov/2020003452

To my history teachers, beginning with Ruby Marquis at Ranchito Elementary and culminating in Gary Nash and Joyce Appleby at UCLA.

CONTENTS

AUTHOR'S NOTE   ix

Introduction   1

1. LOOKING AHEAD   13

Wives   15

Plantation   28

Guns   37

2. BRINGING ALONG   45

Transients   47

Refuge   59

Animals   68

3. MEETING AND EXCHANGING   75

Traders   77

God   86

Tobacco   95

CONTENTS

4. SETTLING IN   103

Escapees   105

A New England   114

Stockings   124

5. CREATING A COMMUNITY   133

Servants   135

Separatism   147

Furs   157

6. CONNECTING TO THE WIDER WORLD   165

Privateers   167

Kingship   175

Books   183

Conclusion   193

ABBREVIATIONS   205

NOTES   209

ACKNOWLEDGMENTS   221

ILLUSTRATION CREDITS   223

INDEX   225

AUTHOR'S NOTE

Quotations from original sources have been silently modernized. Names of people and places generally reflect usage in the original sources. Dates have been treated as if the new year began on 1 January instead of 25 March, the date the English considered the start of the new year in the 1600s.

The World of Plymouth Plantation

INTRODUCTION

Beyond Plymouth Plantation

Americans know their Plymouth Plantation history. Plymouth and its "Pilgrims" may be more familiar than the mystery of the "lost colony" of Roanoke or the legend of Pocahontas rescuing John Smith. Knowledge of Plymouth's past arises in part from the national holiday that commemorates the 1621 Plymouth harvest celebration widely known as the "first Thanksgiving." Popular images of the holiday celebrate intercultural harmony, with Indians and settlers sharing a meal. Americans also know of Squanto, the interpreter and "friend" to Plymouth and the star of numerous children's books. Most American history textbooks include a section on the founding of Plymouth Plantation and highlight the Mayflower Compact, an agreement signed on board the ship that carried the first settlers, one that purportedly established self-government among the men of the new settlement. American genealogists consider discovery of an ancestor who was on the *Mayflower* akin to winning the lottery. Tourists visiting Plymouth have, since the eighteenth century, gazed upon a rock designated many decades after the 1620 landing as the site where the first settlers stepped ashore. For the last seventy years, those tourists have ventured south of town to a living history museum, "Plimoth Plantation." There they visit a highly conscientious historical recreation of the village, complete with costumed actors portraying individuals present in 1627. Whether in school, in popular art, or elsewhere, Americans know their Plymouth.

Yet, how well do we really know Plymouth? These particular moments of Plymouth's history appear more like fragments of a still life than pieces of a historical narrative. As originally created, Plymouth's vignettes serve as part of the United States' origin story: the Mayflower Compact laid the foundation for American democracy; the religious piety and sacrifice of the settlers portended a later commitment to religious freedom. How did forty-one men signing a shipboard "civil combination" (as they called the agreement) lead to the American Revolution? How did their desire to practice their religion open the way to the First Amendment's prohibition on a religious establishment? Those who repeat the descriptions of these moments do so without tracing the unfolding history from 1620 to the revolutionary era, and Plymouth's own later history is little known. Each Plymouth image—Squanto, the Mayflower Compact—is as isolated as a tourist's snapshot, floating free. Today most of us see the plantation not as a real place in which people lived, worked, and died but only as a symbol of large, abstract concepts.

Fortunately, much more can be understood about Plymouth beyond this handful of well-known incidents. Those who participated in its first years described in their own words the world in which they lived. Two published narratives recounting events survive: *A Relation or Journall* (published in 1622) and *Good Newes from New-England* (1624). A number of different men contributed to writing *A Relation*, which strung together detailed descriptions of various events. Sent back by ship and printed in London, it appeared without any authors named; G. Mourt, who had not been in Plymouth, signed a preface written in London, and the little volume came to be known somewhat misleadingly as "Mourt's Relation." The twenty-seven-year-old Edward Winslow—who probably also contributed to *A Relation*—penned (and signed) *Good Newes*. At the end of the decade, William Bradford began writing a history that is today known as "Of Plimoth Plantation." When he first took up his pen, he described events only up until the time of the landing; later, he returned to the project, continuing his account to chronicle life in Plymouth through its first two decades. Although it remained unpublished for centuries, Bradford's history informed the writings of others because the original handwritten document circulated. Bradford's manuscript was especially important for his nephew Nathaniel Morton, who in his *New-England Memorial* (published in 1669) spread information gleaned from Bradford to a wider audience. A century and more later, readers of these books pulled out particular stories—of the signing of a governance agreement, of the meeting with Squanto (known more often in the original sources and therefore in later chapters here as Tisquantum), and of a multiday fall gathering celebrating a first successful harvest. Yet these famous tales represent a selection out of long and detailed narratives that tell many stories.

More than a century passed before the people of Plymouth began to promote their history as a significant founding moment. Interestingly, the rock—which is the only commemorative touchstone without any direct link to early writings—gained prominence first. In 1710, Plymouth residents trying to determine the landing site hit upon the rock with the assistance of an elderly inhabitant. Amid a rising interest in local history, Plymouth leaders in 1769 organized a Forefathers' Day. In addition to recreating the landing, the celebration included speeches, each of them extolling the importance of Plymouth. Over the decades that followed, these speeches—which were often published—contributed to the belief in Plymouth's significance. Invariably speakers extolling Plymouth after the Revolution linked its early history to the eventual creation of the United States. In these accounts, the Mayflower Compact held a key role; the agreement was depicted as establishing democratic principles of broad participation and community cooperation. Save for the improbably placed rock, all the well-known Plymouth scenes emerged directly from writings penned by participants, which were selected for their edifying lessons and repeated regularly.

Plymouth gained a place in our national mythology because eighteenth-century New Englanders—many of them descendants of the first colonists—sought to promote the region as the source of American values. Their efforts began even before the American Revolution, but expanded in the years after independence. Plymouth's advocates elevated it over other settlements in New England for a number of reasons: it was first, certainly; but Plymouth also escaped association with the worst of local history. Plymouth executed neither religious radicals (as the Massachusetts government did with four Quakers) nor witches (as the jurisdictions of both Massachusetts and Connecticut did, Massachusetts most infamously in Salem in 1692). Plymouth appealed because it could represent a heroic past in which valiant settlers faced and overcame their fears in a new land, and because it had no taint of religious intolerance. Those New England boosters who promoted Plymouth found in it a perfect foil for Virginia, with its story of "Princess" Pocahontas's rescue of John Smith. That southern colony had in fact been first among the thirteen that initially formed the United States, and Virginians were promoting their own early history in a bid to claim the status of most significant origin moment.

In the long run, Plymouth eclipsed Virginia. It entered early history textbooks as the representation of early colonization and of intercultural harmony, expressed in the stories of Squanto and of the first Thanksgiving. These advocates of the Plymouth story started the practice of referring to the "First Comers" as "Pilgrims," and coined the term "Pilgrim Fathers" as a way to distinguish them from other settlers. American awareness of Plymouth as a foundational moment had become firmly entrenched by 1863, when Abraham Lincoln declared the usually regional commemoration a national celebration of Union victories. That the New England holiday first went national at the height of the Civil War meant that Lincoln promoted a regional holiday dear to the hearts of many Union supporters at a time when the views of Southerners—who might have preferred a different story—carried no weight. Once the South returned fully to the Union, that region gradually adopted the celebration. Although today Southerners add their own flair to the classic New England meal (including macaroni and cheese as a side dish), they also eat the corn, cranberries, and molasses-flavored dishes that have long played starring roles in the iconic New England meal. Eventually named one of the first four official national holidays, Thanksgiving continues to symbolize family and gratitude for Americans with no connection to Plymouth and no broader understanding of its history.

Like the first Thanksgiving, which was based on a description in Winslow's *Good Newes* and never mentioned by Bradford, the story of Squanto also became part of the lore associated with Plymouth. Most fundamentally, his story argues that the inhabitants welcomed the new arrivals, a comforting idea given the later history of Native-White relations in the United States and the death, impoverishment, and displacement of Native people. Samuel Sewall, writing in 1697, sounded a standard note, treating Squanto as sent by God to aid the residents because he taught them how best to plant corn. Some authors also conveyed the story that a duplicitous English ship's captain had earlier kidnapped him from New England's shores and carried him to Europe to sell him as a slave. Despite this mistreatment, he went on to be "a warm friend to the English," according to Jedidiah Morse.[1] The tale of the kidnapping as well as the corn-planting instructions originated in the earliest writings.

The Mayflower Compact, perhaps today the least well known of the various images, was deeply admired at first. The chroniclers like Bradford and Winslow who signed the pact did not once mention the name of the ship in any writings, and as a result they certainly did not call the pact itself by the name we now use. Nathaniel Morton, nephew to Governor (and *Mayflower* passenger) William Bradford, recorded the name in his 1669 history. Over the years, *Mayflower* became shorthand for first arrivals, so that by the nineteenth century the name "Society of Mayflower Descendants" seemed a self-evident way to refer to those who could trace their family back to the "First Comers." By that time, the fashion for naming ships after mayflowers had faded, and no one confused this *Mayflower* for any other. If the ship's name seemed inconsequential in the moment, the pact itself received no formal name at the time either. When called upon to refer to it—as Bradford did in his manuscript "Of Plimoth Plantation"— participants simply described it. Bradford used the term "civil combination." In the nineteenth century, writers first linked the governance agreement with the ship. After the American Revolution, when the agreement became a key historical document for thinking about the founding of the United States—a foundational text for American democracy—it then gained the name by which it is now known. Editors gathering colonial-era documents that contributed toward the creation of the United States reprinted it in collections. Forefathers' Day lectures praised it. Artists painted its signing. George Bancroft, the New England resident who became the premier historian of the United States in the nineteenth century, referred to it as the "birth of popular constitutional liberty." Indeed, he asserted that "In the cabin of the *Mayflower*, humanity recovered its rights, and instituted government on the basis of 'equal laws' for 'the general good.'"[2] Bancroft bestowed high praise on the document, and his views convey the importance attached to the Mayflower Compact by his day.

Images of early Plymouth Plantation had formed a familiar constellation by the time Bancroft wrote. The nineteenth-century understanding of Plymouth took its place in the history of the new nation,

Plymouth and its "Pilgrims" became so much a part of the lore of the origins of the United States that its imagery could be used in marketing. This lithograph appeared on citrus crates in California to advertise Pilgrim Brand Oranges. The iconic image depicts the landing, with a boat ferrying a group of men and women who use a conveniently placed boulder to disembark. The snowy ground tells us it is winter, and the sober attire presents a common understanding of "pilgrim" dress. The distant ship is presumably the *Mayflower*.

as writers drew on the colonial past to explain why the United States had taken shape as a nation committed to religious freedom and democratic rights. These historians, as well as the men who gave the Forefathers' Day speeches or painted Plymouth scenes, drew upon the early published information describing the settlement's first years. Highlighting the first Thanksgiving, Squanto's friendship, and the initial governance agreement, they fashioned the series of images that continue to resonate with Americans.

In a strange historical turn, these authors shaped the idea of Plymouth without direct access to the single, most comprehensive account of the early decades. William Bradford's extended history of the endeavor, written in two periods (first in the 1630s and again in the 1640s), had disappeared by the time Plymouth began to gain prominence. Passed among different writers (beginning with Nathaniel Morton, who used it extensively), Bradford's handwritten manuscript traveled across the Atlantic during the American Revolution, coming to rest eventually in Fulham Palace's library, in the residence of the bishop of London. The history languished until it was identified and printed in the 1850s. It was not until 1897 that it was "repatriated" to the United States, where it has been held in Massachusetts ever since. Printed on numerous occasions, Bradford's original has become the main source for those writing about Plymouth. Today, popular accounts of the plantation usually adhere to Bradford's narrative arc, beginning the story of Plymouth with the Protestant Reformation, and then following the church founded in Scrooby, England, on its journey first to Holland, then on to southern New England. With the major plot points (as it were) of Mayflower Compact, Squanto, and celebratory meal all in place (absent the rock), Bradford's account added nothing new, but he did affirm most of those vignettes that had become so prominent in the Plymouth story. In the only exception, he made no mention of a harvest meal.

The vignettes that capture our collective imagination also limit our insight. As we debate how best to understand the encounter between Squanto and the English who moved onto his village site, or we gaze down at the rock caged in its seaside temple, we accept the idea that Plymouth arose out of the participants' wish to go it alone, to separate themselves from the wider world of European society, politics, economics, and religion. Plymouth Plantation, symbolizing "firstness" and New England's contribution to America, stands as an isolated early settlement. Its residents win our admiration for their fortitude and piety. Its very isolation adds to the heroism of the First Comers, but it gives the false impression that Plymouth was disconnected from the world that gave rise to it. Although a small and seemingly inconsequential settlement, Plymouth existed within a broader context. Its relative marginality did not prevent it from participating in the world beyond Cape Cod Bay. The vignettes detach the plantation, but in reality, Plymouth enjoyed, indeed utterly relied upon, links to the wider world. Considering Plymouth as a place connecting to other places shows us this familiar story in a strikingly different light.

The World of Plymouth Plantation reconnects our perceptions of Plymouth with the reality of the lives of its inhabitants. Reintegrating the plantation into its own time and place provides context for those who ventured to these shores as well as those they met upon arrival. This richer and deeper understanding not only makes sense of compacts and a meeting with a "friendly Indian." It permits us to appreciate the larger significance of the historic changes in which Plymouth planters as well as the indigenous people they encountered took part.

Debunking the myths of Plymouth by questioning the surrounding facts or the meaning of the various vignettes partakes of a long tradition. Many other writers have challenged the established images—a fact about which *Mayflower* descendant, attorney, and amateur historian Francis Russell Stoddard complained bitterly as early as 1952.[3] I confess to being deeply skeptical about the rock, since no one who has rowed a small wooden boat into shore would accept the idea that the crewmen navigated toward rather than away from rocks. I do take a certain perverse pleasure from the rather ludicrous fact that the tourist attraction Plymouth Rock is only a piece of the original boulder, which was hauled around town for display in a variety of

The boulder identified in the 1740s as the possible site of the landing has experienced
misadventures since that time. It was dragged around Plymouth to various display sites,
causing it to split. Various people chipped off bits as souvenirs. This chunk carries a
painted inscription from 1830 explaining its origins and significance.

locations and broken in the process. Given that it serves as a marker
for a landing site, the rock's journey around Plymouth itself seems
almost surreal. My only objection to the other vignettes (of meals,
compacts, and meetings) is that they ignore the wider history surrounding early New England. I would like to break the endless cycle
of writing about Plymouth, in which some repeat the traditional
vignettes while others debunk them.

Shaped by its larger context, Plymouth interests me as a small settlement far from any other English outpost, perched precariously on
the edge of the North American continent, a place eager to remain
linked to other places near and far. This book is organized around
the various ways this small settlement connected to the wider world.
Short chapters—each of which, in Plymouth tradition, opens with a

vignette—focus on a category of people, an idea, or a thing. Plymouth literally came into being as an English outpost because people moved across the Atlantic; despite our focus on that first ship, people continued to come (and leave) in the decades that followed. They brought with them ideas that shaped what they built and how they understood what they were doing, and they encountered new ideas once they arrived. Their lives were also shaped by the things they brought as well as by the people they met in North America. The chapters that follow cycle through a succession of triptychs, each considering a person, an idea, and an object. The ordering of these triptychs follows a roughly chronological logic. The first set have to do with anticipating what the settlers expected to find and to do; the second considers what they brought with them; the third centers on meetings and what they exchanged; the fourth evaluates what they established in settling at Plymouth; the fifth explores what they created; and the final triptych considers more far-flung connections. The categories overlap and intermingle, but overall each category encircles the previous one, expanding our vision and knowledge of this early settlement. This approach reflects my conviction that connections rather than isolation sit at the heart of the Plymouth story. Plymouth emerged out of and remained anchored to the world beyond its own shores as a result of the various people, ideas, and things that circulated into and through it. Capturing that history and that experience of connection is the goal of this book.

I

LOOKING AHEAD

WIVES

PLANTATION

GUNS

WIVES

IN MARCH 1621, after the English people had been in the area they knew as Plymouth for four months, they finally encountered the Wampanoag people who lived around Cape Cod Bay. First the two groups exchanged messages through various intermediaries, including Tisquantum (or Squanto), two other Native men (one of them Samoset, who had been the first resident to make contact), and Edward Winslow. Then, after arranging a hostage exchange to ensure the safety of the negotiators on both sides, the planters finally hosted the local leader, whom they called Massasoit, along with men who accompanied him.[1] Their party came to the half-constructed English village, where the colonists treated the occasion—the negotiation of a treaty of alliance—with all the pomp they could muster. They laid out a rug and cushions to welcome the king. The governor arrived to the sound of drums and trumpets, escorted by musketeers. After the ceremonies concluded, some of Massasoit's people desired to spend the night in the village. The Plymouth people declining, the men left the village to sleep nearby. As an anonymous chronicler explained, "the King and all his men lay all night in the woods, not about half an English mile from us, and all their wives and women with them." The narrative of the opening of diplomatic relations between the two groups included no mention of English women—although they were certainly present in the village where the meeting occurred—but it did note that Massasoit's nearby encampment housed not only the men involved in the negotiations but also wives and other women.[2]

English commentators thought it intriguing that women accompanied the negotiators. The English and the Wampanoags concurred that women did not partake in negotiations, but the latter saw no reason that a long-planned diplomatic journey ought to be undertaken by men alone. In contrast, Plymouth wives invariably failed to accompany men who went out to explore or visit other communities. Although the "First Comers" did not think of themselves as invading New England, they were at least aware that they might be received with hostility, making male-only expeditionary forces seem appropriate. The English observers assumed that the presence of women in Massasoit's company affirmed that he had come to negotiate an alliance rather than to attack. Similarly, the presence of European women on the first ship heralded to the region's Native peoples that this was no fishing or trading voyage. Upon first arriving, the *Mayflower* passengers cautiously ventured for a walk on shore after so long at sea. William Bradford remarked specifically that women were among these parties. With the area's residents surreptitiously watching (and occasionally sighted while doing so), the indigenous inhabitants soon knew that the ship's passengers included families and not just the men and boys that normally visited their shores.[3] The *Mayflower* women thus helped to set Plymouth on a peaceful path, signaling that this family-based community had intentions other than the merely military or commercial. Their small (and for a time declining) numbers made them seem unthreatening, an idea that the presence of women reinforced. Just as Massasoit's female companions demonstrated to the settlers that he meant them no harm, the women who arrived in 1620 helped to set the tone for initial encounters in New England.

Sixteen married women joined the first contingent to Plymouth. Every adult woman on board the first ship came as a wife in the company of her husband, with the possible exception of John Carver's maidservant (whose age is not known). In contrast, unaccompanied adult men were common: thirty-two of the voyagers were men without wives or children. Some of them were unmarried, such as the apprentice John Hooke or the servant John Howland. Others—including Samuel Fuller—left wives behind. Among the couples who journeyed together, all save five brought children with them. Two households included unrelated children: Desire Minter and Humility Cooper came with other families, one or both of their parents having died in Holland. Five husband-and-wife teams sailed without young children, although the adult son (Solomon Prower) of one of these women (Mary Martin) was also on board.

Other wives remained at home with the intention of joining their families later. Hester Cooke, for instance, stayed back while her husband and eldest son crossed in 1620. She and their other four children came on the *Anne* after a three-year separation. Degory Priest proved unable to send for his wife and children: he died in the first winter. After her remarriage, his widow arrived, also on the *Anne*, with the two daughters of her first marriage along with her new husband and their young son. A letter from William Hilton to his "loving cousin" survives, asking that his wife and children be sent to join him.[4] A number of men boarded with only a son. Thomas Rogers came with his eighteen-year-old son but left his wife and three younger children in Leiden. Uncertain about whether the journey and the first years would prove entirely safe, some families chose to undergo what they hoped would be a temporary separation. John Robinson, pastor of the church in Leiden, wrote in June 1621 that though he intended to join those of his former parishioners who had migrated to set up "the church of God, at Plymouth, in New England," he could not make the journey until all the remaining wives and children in Leiden had been transported to join their husbands and fathers.[5]

The presence of wives meant many things: home, permanence, peace; but, above all, wives meant babies. A pair of babies accompanied their parents on the voyage. Damaris Hopkins may have come as a toddler, with parents Stephen and Elizabeth as well as her older siblings. Samuel Eaton, son of Francis and Sarah, sailed as a "suckling child," meaning he was still young enough to be nursing. Two passengers undertook the crossing while pregnant. Elizabeth Hopkins—who joined the voyage in England, never having lived in Leiden—gave birth to a son. We can only imagine her experience, in labor on a damp, smelly, cramped wooden ship traversing the ocean. Another passenger, Susannah White, delivered a son after the ship had anchored off the coast but before she could disembark. The *Mayflower* at anchor might have been a preferable location for enduring childbirth, assuming the late autumn weather cooperated enough to allow some passengers and crew to grant her and her female attendants a bit of privacy by going onshore or at least on deck. When a second ship, the *Fortune*, arrived in November 1621, Martha Ford came ashore and went immediately into labor, delivering a son during her first night in New England.[6] Hopefully she found conditions in the primitive structures the *Mayflower* passengers had built in the first year a more welcome environment than shipboard would have been. Martha herself was probably recently widowed when baby John was born, and the infant did not long survive. Although no vital records (of births, marriages, and deaths) exist for the early years, genealogical research makes clear that—despite a high initial death rate of about half of the first arrivals—babies continued to be born in Plymouth to the couples who migrated or to pairs newly formed there.

William Bradford happily reported that after the first difficult winter, the death rate became negligible. Women, of course, continued to face the very real prospect of death in childbirth (which was apparently the fate of Isaac Allerton's first wife, Mary Norris Allerton, who died in the first winter); but otherwise life in New England proved remarkably healthful compared to Europe, as least for European settlers. Bradford's record of the descendants of the first migrants, made in about 1650, showed that births rapidly followed from a migration that included women. For instance, John Howland, John Carver's servant, "married the daughter of John Tillie, Elizabeth, and they are both now living, and have 10. children, now all living; and their eldest daughter hath 4. children. And their 2. daughter, 1. all living; and other of their children marriageable. So 15. are come of them."[7] By the time Bradford wrote, newer colonies had completely surpassed Plymouth in size and influence, and he eagerly asserted his little settlement's role in peopling the region with English residents. Later migration added to the population too, but that fact interested Bradford not at all. He wanted to prove the vast contribution made through the fertility of the first contingent of Plymouth wives. No one explicitly invoked the biblical command to "be fruitful and multiply," but Plymouth planters seemed to have taken it to heart nonetheless.

Although Bradford noted the booming birth rate that women made possible, the records—his or others—rarely noticed women by name. Well-behaved women, as Laurel Thatcher Ulrich once observed, seldom make history, and this omission was by design: they were not supposed to draw attention to themselves. Although Ulrich's phrase has been picked up in popular culture and used to urge women to make history by defying expectations for the well-behaved woman, Ulrich had no such intention. She instead described the cultural expectations for seventeenth-century English and New English women, expectations that brought women praise when they quietly went about their assigned tasks.[8] A well-lived life for a seventeenth-century English woman ideally passed with little notice. No woman wrote any surviving document penned in or about Plymouth in the first decades. In the records men produced, women mostly appear as wives and

...are come of them.

m[r] Brewster liued to very old age; about 80 years, he was when he dyed, hauing liued some 23. or 24. years here in my countrie. & though his wife dyed long before, yet she dyed aged. His sone Wras... dyed a yonge man vnmaried; his sone Loue, liued till this year 1650. and dyed & left 4 children, now liuing. His doughters which came ouer after him, are dead. But haue left sundry children aliue; his eldest sone is still liueing, and hath 9 or 10. children, one maried who hath a child, or 2.

Richard More, his brother dyed the first winter; but he is maried, and hath 4. or 5. children, all liuing.

m[r] Ed: Winslow, his wife dyed the first winter; and he maried with the midow of m[r] White, and hath 2. children liuing by her marigable. Besids sundry that are dead. one of his seruants dyed, as also the litle girls soone after the ships ariual. But his man Georg Sowle is still liuing, and hath 8. childre

William Bradford, his wife dyed soone after their ariuall; and he maried againe; and hath 4. children 3. whereof are maried. ... who dyed 9 of may 1650.

m[r] Allerton his wife dyed with the first, and his seruant John Hooke; his sone Bartle is maried in England But I know not how many children he hath. His doughter remember is maried at Salem, & hath 3. or 4. children liuing. And his doughter mary is maried here, & hath 4. children. Him selfe maried againe with y[e] doughter of m[r] Brewster & hath one sone liuing by here But she is long since dead. And he is maried againe, and hath left

Children by her; which are liuing and growne vp to years. But he dyed some 15. years agoe.

John Crakston dyed in the first mortality; and about some 5. or 6 y... after his sone dyed, hauing lost himselfe in y[e] wodes, his feet froze which put him into a feauor, of which he dyed.

Captain Standish his wife dyed the first sicknes; and he maried againe, and hath 4. sones liuing, and some are dead. ... who dyed 3. of octob. 1655.

m[r] martin, he and all his dyed in the first infection; not long after the ariual.

m[r] molines, and his wife, his sone, & his seruant dyed the first winter. only his doughter prisc... suruiued, and maried with Jo... Alden, who are both liuing, & haue 11. children. And their eldest daughter is maried & hath fiue children. See N. E. Memoriall p. 22.

m[r] White, and his 2. seruants dyed soone after ther Landing. His wife maried with m[r] Winslow (as is before noted) His 2. sons are maried, and resolu... hath 5. children; perigrine too... all liuing. So their Increase are

m[r] Hopkins, and his wife are now both dead; but they liued aboue 20. years in this place, and had one sone, and 4. doughters borne her. Ther sone became a seaman, & dyed at Barbadoes, one daughter dyed here. and 2. are maried, one of them hath 2. children, & one is ye... to mary. so their Increase, whic...

William Bradford calculated how many individuals were descended from the first group of migrants as of 1650 in an effort to demonstrate that Plymouth was an important source of New England's growing population. Listing couples and their descendants in "Of Plimoth Plantation," his record of necessity gave wives a prominent role in the population growth he extolled.

mothers. They earned mention as the mate of a man—sometimes only as his wife, with no name attached. Bradford listed Edward Fuller on board the first ship with his wife, known only as Mrs. Fuller. John Oldham, who arrived later, came accompanied by a wife, as did the aspiring minister John Lyford. The name of neither woman appeared in the Plymouth records, although we do know that Lyford's wife was called Sarah because of a record made at the time of her second marriage elsewhere. Women who garnered notice in the records often did so because of some trouble: they got pregnant before they were married, or—like the wife of John Weeks—they followed their husbands into religious error, in the case of the Weeks, to "become very Atheists."[9] Similarly, the court cited Samuel Gorton's wife for joining him in leaving the colony in the company of a widow who was wanted for questioning; their aid allowed Widow Aldrich to flee. Whether pregnant out of marriage or led astray by an erring husband, even much of women's occasional notoriety involved men.

Some of these women experienced hardship because of the men to whom they were attached. Certainly, such was the case with Sarah Lyford. She feared God would punish her family for her husband's many sins. Sarah, buffeted from one location to another until Lyford's death allowed her to rest, remarried and remained in Hingham, Massachusetts.[10] John Oldham's wife was allowed to stay for one more winter in Plymouth when he was banished.[11] The wife of Ralph Smith moved with him from England to Salem, from Salem to Nantasket, where they lived among "some straggling people," until finally landing in Plymouth. The church there called him as its minister and the couple settled while Smith preached. Bradford never named Mrs. Smith, who wandered about with her husband before Plymouth first gave them a place to stay—referred to as "house room" in the records—and then employed him; nor do we know if she shared the religious scruples that made her husband unwilling to remain in either England or Salem.[12] Other men similarly subjected their families to serial displacement, trying to find a suitable home. Roger Williams dragged his wife Mary from England to Boston to Plymouth to Salem before striking out for the area that would become Providence, Rhode Island. To add insult to injury, at least to hear his critics tell it, he later became so unwilling to enter into religious communion with anyone who might be tainted that for a time he refused to pray even with his own wife and children.[13]

In a most interesting turn of events, one woman headed an isolated household outside of any colonial boundaries to the north of Plymouth. Between Plymouth's founding and the advent of Massachusetts, the area became dotted with tiny enclaves in which single households tried to make their way alone. Many of the men who established these outposts, known later as "Old Planters," came to New England with the intention of participating in one trade or fishing endeavor or another. When a collective enterprise fell through, most participants departed, but a few men independently chose to stay. In a few rare cases wives accompanied or joined them, enduring these trying conditions along with their husbands. When one such man, David Thompson, died on the island in Boston Bay that bears his name, he left behind a wife, child, and servants. It would be another two years before Boston was settled. Meanwhile his widow managed this small and isolated household.[14]

Most wives, however, conformed to the ideal that proper women avoided the gaze of history: they were either absent from the record or they can be only vaguely glimpsed in passing references. Two years into Plymouth's history, clergyman John Robinson wrote to Bradford from Leiden, and among other news conveyed the greetings of his unnamed wife. The next day, writing to Plymouth church elder William Brewster, he mentioned that the arrival of her two daughters must have comforted Brewster's nameless wife, who was then ill.[15] When Edward Winslow wrote to John Winthrop he noted that his letter would be carried "by my wives sonne." The letter carrier may have been Peregrine, then seventeen, or his older brother Resolved, twenty-two, as his wife had at that time two living children from her first marriage.[16] Wives, the essential companions to Plymouth men, remained in the background when all went well.

Wives were indeed essential. When a wife died, a man rapidly remarried for practical reasons among others: no seventeenth-century household ran without the skills a woman provided. In the absence of a servant with similar skills, a household without a wife barely functioned. Yet William Bradford waited almost three years from the drowning death of his first wife, Dorothy, shortly after their arrival at Cape Cod before taking as his second wife the widow Alice Southworth, who came on board the *Anne* in 1623. Bradford presumably figured out another way to manage his household, relying on his neighbors or servants for the women's work Dorothy no longer performed. Other second marriages occurred more rapidly: Edward Winslow lived a widower for just two months between the death of Elizabeth in March 1621 and his marriage to Susannah (mother of Peregrine) in May. Rarely did an adult woman remain long unmarried.

With a dearth of women, unmarried men eagerly sought out women who could become their wives. When Mary Moorecock was bound to serve Richard Sparrow and his wife Pandora for nine years, her contract had an escape clause in the event she wanted to marry; her master and mistress would not prevent her from doing so, but her new husband would have to pay them for the remainder of her time at a rate set by two impartial men brought in to determine a fair fee.[17] In this case, Pandora had to be named in the record—which was otherwise unusual—because another escape clause gave Mary immediate release from service if both Sparrows should die. In other words, her contract would not be sold to a new master if the couple with whom she was to live could no longer house her.

Many new settlements experienced a dearth of women. This imbalance made it hard for men to live within a traditional family structure, much less to start families of their own. Even in Plymouth, acquiring a wife was not a foregone conclusion. The search for a wife in fact prompted one of the only examples of levity in the official records of early Plymouth. In 1632, the government of Massachusetts wrote to express concern that servants and others with obligations in the more northern colony would leave their responsibilities to make a new life in Plymouth. In responding, the governor and assistants of Plymouth addressed each case the Bay colony had raised. Of John Pickworth, they noted he "came but as a sojourner to work for a few weeks, in which time he got a wife, and so is long since returned double, and hath no cause to complain," unless, of course, "he hath got a bad wife."[18] Jokes about the quality of wives aside, that Pickworth came to Plymouth and found one suggests the demographic success of that colony, with at least some unattached but marriageable women after only a dozen years in existence.

Native society placed a similarly high premium on women. The economic calculus differed, but only in detail. Native women grew corn, the region's main crop, a fact that prompted Winslow to comment that runaway wives would always be sheltered wherever they went because those who received them would benefit from the wealth their labor brought. While he may not have grasped the dynamic of indigenous marriage practices, he did appreciate the essential economic role of women. Winslow also remarked on what he understood of Native marital customs. He observed that Native political leaders sought wives who were equal to them in nobility, although these men also had relations with concubines and lesser women, who obeyed the principal wife.[19] William Morrell, a clergyman, also described a practice of taking multiple wives, explaining that the attractions included getting more children and "A second profit which by many wives They have, is Corn, the staff of all their lives."[20] Children and corn represented the contribution of Native wives, at least as Morrell understood it.

Morrell's and Winslow's interest in understanding marital practices was shared on the other side of the cultural divide as well. Captain Christopher Levett recounted a conversation he claimed to have
had with some Native men on the subject of wives. Supposedly they
asked him why he did not beat his wife, who wanted him to come
home; her desire indicated to them (at least according to his account)
that Mistress Levett did not know her proper place. He reportedly
replied that beating wives "was not the English fashion, and besides,
she was a good wife and I had children by her, and I loved her well."[21]
He did not note whether this answer satisfied his companions. Certainly, his understanding that Native men lorded it over their wives,
beating them if they did not obey, represented his own interpretation of Native culture. In reality, indigenous women often exercised
considerable power, including the right to divorce at will. Nonetheless he may have had a version of this conversation, however dimly
he understood the status of Native wives and the extent of their
authority.

In another attempt at cross-cultural communication, some early
Plymouth men reported an exchange with Massasoit in which they
described to him their king, James. Learning that after the death of
his queen, Anne of Denmark, in 1619, James had not remarried, Massasoit's response was "marveling that he would live without a wife."[22]
Assuming Winslow's description of Wampanoag elite marital practices is correct, Massasoit would have had multiple wives. Not only
did wives bring wealth, for a major leader (like Powhatan, whom the
English encountered in Virginia) multiple marriages cemented alliances across numerous subordinate communities. Whether Native
or English, the men living in the Plymouth region in the first half of
the seventeenth century agreed on the necessity of a wife.

English men in North America occasionally entered into relationships with Native women, and Plymouth offers a few known examples. When discussing allegations against Thomas Morton, who led

a nearby trading outpost, Plymouth leaders cited sexual abuse of Native women to prove that Morton was immoral and profligate. If their claims about the outpost can be taken at face value, he and his men were guilty of "abusing the Indian women most filthily, as it is notorious."[23] So many of the allegations against Morton were exaggerated that it is difficult to determine whether this claim was accurate. William Baker, who began as a servant in Plymouth but eventually worked as a trader with Native communities, was alleged to have had sexual relations with numerous Indian women. Community leaders saw his relationships as wrong because they occurred outside of marriage. Unlike John Rolfe in Virginia, no early settler in Plymouth proposed to marry an indigenous woman, as far as the surviving records suggest. As a general rule, Native wives in New England's first years had Native husbands while English men took English wives. Whether planters migrated as families or formed them in Plymouth, the Plymouth experience was rooted in the family life that wives made possible.

Plymouth Plantation was conceived as a family affair. Unlike Virginia, originally a military and trading outpost, Plymouth included men, women, and their children from the first. In contrast to the previous ships that had visited the shores of southern New England, the *Mayflower* came not merely to fish, trade, or explore but to stay. Women's presence among the passengers signaled a different intent to Native observers. The presence of women promised families and households. If the military danger posed by this group appeared lessened by the women among them, women also contained an implicit threat. Women and the children they bore would inexorably expand the English presence. A rising population, augmented by later arrivals heartened by Plymouth's seeming ability to live peacefully with their Native neighbors, endangered indigenous lifeways. The rapid demographic growth (after the first sickly winter) of the first Plymouth families—so gleefully touted by Bradford—eventually created pressures on Native lands and resources. Wives made New England more English, both in the settlement's initial population and also, over time, in the population explosion that followed. Commemorations of Plymouth since the eighteenth century have exalted the "Forefathers," but it was in fact the women, as wives and mothers, who made the plantation a lasting presence in southern New England.

PLANTATION

PLYMOUTH PLANTERS, when first exploring the area around their village, bemoaned the fact that the recent epidemics had left fertile agricultural land without "men to dress and manure the same."[1] (In this case, by "dress" they meant prepare for planting.) Promoters of English colonization thought that comparatively empty lands in America cried out for the introduction of the idle men of England: "the Country wants only industrious men to employ, for it would grieve your hearts (if as I) you had seen so many miles together of goodly rivers, uninhabited," while at the same time you "consider those parts of the world where in you live, to be ever greatly burdened with abundance of people."[2] Besides supporting the self-serving assumption that land was freely available for the taking, these observations also anticipated the transfer of English land-use practices to the shores of America. The first migrants to New England understood their project in terms of such a transfer: they wanted to transplant their familiar agricultural practices and social organization. In their terms, they envisioned a "plantation" rather than simply a trading outpost or military installation. While those other models depended on male participants stationed in a location only temporarily, the vision for Plymouth included families that would remain permanently. A plantation from the outset, Plymouth was established with that goal in mind.

The new arrivals embraced the idea that theirs was a plantation. The first published account describing their undertaking frequently referred to the project in precisely those terms. Not only was the work published under the title *A Relation or Journall of the English Plantation setled at Plimoth*, but the authors and editors sprinkled the term liberally throughout the text as well. Participants in the project were "planters," not "settlers," as we often refer to them today. A few years later, Edward Winslow penned another account in the interest of relating, as the subtitle of *Good Newes* put it, *Things very remarkable at the Plantation of Plimoth in New-England*.[3] When, after a decade, leader William Bradford composed his account of the gestation of their project, he famously titled his record "Of Plimoth Plantation." After Plymouth was founded, John Smith—a man most commonly associated with Virginia—published his *Advertisements for the Unexperienced Planters of New England*, referring to Plymouth as a plantation and to those who might venture to the region as planters. In 1669, Bradford's nephew, Nathaniel Morton, described the "Transplantation of themselves and Families."[4] "Plantation" remained the most common term participants used, a word that described their fundamental goal: the transplantation of English families to a new place. Plantation meant permanence, sustenance, and familiar practices.

To modern ears, "plantation" has a different meaning. We envision a plantation as a large-scale agricultural concern in which European masters lived in luxury while enslaved Africans toiled their lives away in bondage. This definition has led some activists to question the continued use of the term in such names as that of the state of Rhode Island: "the state of Rhode Island and Providence Plantations." That term does not imply, as its critics suspect, the existence of slave plantations. Prior to the advent of American slave plantations, and for many decades after they were launched, "plantation" carried a broader meaning, that of permanently transplanted groups of Europeans living in families. Edward Winslow, writing general advice for anyone wanting to set up a plantation, listed three dangers: expectation of quick profit, ambitious leaders who make "slaves of all that are under them," and unqualified men. In Winslow's warning, the men in danger of enslavement were English men who signed on to help settle a plantation but found themselves bound to an unrelenting taskmaster.[5] In his understanding, plantations were perfectly possible and indeed preferable without slaves. They were made up of English people who went as "Tillers of the Earth."[6] Plymouth Plantation and later Rhode Island and Providence Plantations bore the name "plantation" to indicate that they housed English families. Whether or not they held slaves (and initially neither place did), both New England jurisdictions carried the name. The first publication about the effort to establish Massachusetts Bay Colony similarly discussed it as a "New-England plantation."[7] Modern critics can fault them as examples of settler colonialism, intent on taking the land of others for their own purposes, but not, at least initially, for profiting from the mass enslavement of their fellow human beings. The distinction, as far as the term "plantation" is concerned, is one that we have lost but which they fully understood.

Plymouth people were in fact conscious of the problem of taking the land of others for their project. The site where they located their town had been a Native village prior to devastating epidemics (from disease brought by visiting Europeans). The new arrivals learned this history not only through their observations of the land itself but also in conversation with area residents, including Tisquantum, who resided in that village at the time of his 1614 kidnapping. They came to think of the fact that they entered unoccupied land as an important aspect of their experience. It meant their movement into the area (although watched from afar) did not involve direct confrontations over land. Plymouth residents told a visitor in 1624, "Here is not one living now, nor not one living which belonged to this plantation before we came, so that the ground on which we are planted belongs to nobody."[8] Some English observers saw the hand of God in the widespread death that paved the way for them to move into the Wampanoag village site. John Smith remarked in 1622, after hearing reports of the Plymouth settlers, "God had laid this Country open for us, and slain the most part of the inhabitants by cruel wars and a mortal disease."[9] For Nathaniel Morton, it was axiomatic that God swept away the original inhabitants in order to make way for the Plymouth people.[10] Whatever God's intention, moving into land that belonged to nobody was surely an easier proposition than taking the land that someone else actively used and would doubtless defend.

When the English author expressed grief over untended tillable land, he imagined bringing that land under English cultivation practices. Seemingly available lands caused many visitors to think of all the idle men of England who might be employed upon the land. Such observations, published out of Plymouth almost immediately, helped in fact to prompt the schemes to set up other such plantations throughout the region. Although Massachusetts Bay was officially called a "colony" in line with terminology used in its charter, it was understood in precisely the same terms of transplantation. In that regard, Plymouth not only led the way but sent the signal back to England that here was land available for the taking, wanting only "men to dress and manure the same."

The goal of transplantation assumed the transfer of English approaches to land use. The idea that "the Country wants only industrious men" announced English expectations. While it was true that the initial expeditions into the countryside found places that had once been populated and were currently abandoned, the agricultural laborers who no longer lived to plant and harvest were not Native men, as these observers supposed, but rather women. Native women took charge of planting, manuring, harvesting, and grinding the staple crop

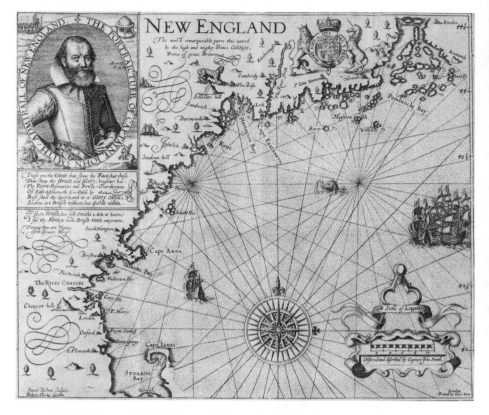

Published four years before Plymouth Plantation's founding, this map named locations in New England after places or royalty in England. Many of the names never came to be applied beyond Smith's early map, but Plymouth was an exception. John Smith's place named for the English port city appeared in the general vicinity of the future village of that name. Clearly Smith, like those who later came to Plymouth Plantation, envisioned transplanting English people to this place bearing (new) English names.

that sustained their communities. Men performed all these tasks in England, and the Plymouth people thought such labor an exclusively male province. They brought their cultural assumptions not only about proper agricultural practices but also about gendered labor.

Even as they pursued their goal of transplanting English agricultural practices to the New World—no mean feat since many of them had lived in an urban environment before migrating—their perceptions of Native practices were skewed by their own cultural expectations. Observing Native women doing agricultural work, they decided that the women were being degraded and likened their lot to that of slaves. William Wood, when he wrote an early description of New England, included an entire chapter on the roles of women in Native society. Addressing this chapter directly to English women, Wood expected his female readers to be especially interested in the lives of their counterparts in America. He explicitly instructed them on the lesson he wanted them to take from his description: they should be grateful for their easier lives.[11] English men writing about Native people invariably remarked on the difficulty of the work the women among them performed: Edward Winslow, William Morrell, Francis Higginson, and the unnamed authors of *A Relation or Journall* all noted that Native women suffered the abuse of performing agricultural labor.

The men, in contrast, spent their days engaged in recreational activities, or so declared William Morrell. Like all these authors, he came from a culture in which hunting was reserved for the elite and enjoyed as a recreational activity, so he perceived Native hunting in a similar light. If he had paused to consider the implications of the fact that indigenous people kept no livestock, he might have realized that any meat in the Native diet came of necessity from hunting. Yet so entrenched were expectations of European agricultural practices, with men behind the plow and meat provided by the slaughter of farm animals, neither Morrell nor anyone else pondered the obvious differences. Instead, even when they noted the centrality of women's agricultural labor—Winslow for one realized that "where are most women, there is greatest plenty"[12]—they still discounted the complementary and equally important contribution of Native men.

Even as they misunderstood how Native practices differed from their own, the men who wrote about early Plymouth seemed at times to overlook how the effort to transplant English ways affected the women who participated. At times, they appeared to dismiss the work performed by the women in their own communities. Women in Plymouth labored intensively: no clothing was sewn, no food was processed or prepared, no kitchen garden was tended, and no children were cared for without the physical labor of Plymouth's women. Households could not function without the contribution of adult women, who were trained as girls in the skills needed to feed, clothe, and otherwise care for their families. Remarkably, given the narrative about Native gendered agricultural labor, Plymouth women did sometimes work in the fields. This necessity arose particularly during the plantation's first years, when food was scarce and laborers few.

A moment in the first year in Plymouth, later remembered and mentioned by William Bradford when he sat down to describe important early events, brought home the occasional invisibility of women's work. When the first arrivals set up their small settlement, they tried to create household units that would work well given the gendered nature of work roles and skills. Each household had to be headed by an adult male who was responsible for all members—wife, children, servants, and any other residents within the household. Although the Plymouth leaders identified twenty-four distinct families, they decided initially to build only nineteen structures. Thinking to save on the (male) effort of building dwellings, they instead silently added to the expectations placed on women. They directed "all single men that had no wives to join with some Family, as they thought fit, that so we might build fewer houses, which was done, and we reduced them to 19."[13]

This policy, besides reducing the number of structures needed, also hinted at (without fully acknowledging) the essential nature of women's work. Men alone could not easily live without women's labor. William Bradford later suggested that this strategy—saddling the community's women with the care and feeding of unrelated men—prompted resentment. Labor that women willingly performed for the benefit of their own families they saw as "a kind of slavery" when it fed and clothed men other than their husbands or his dependents.[14] Such resentment might have been particularly acute in this situation, in which the community's men simply expected the women to cook and clean for anyone placed in their household. In England, it would not have been unknown for households to take in unmarried men, but they usually entered as servants; and the sort of large households that employed male servants also retained the services of female servants who joined in the cooking and cleaning, tasks that in Plymouth under this arrangement fell to these hardworking and exhausted wives. A departure from English practice, the placement of unattached men had been organized without regard for the women's expectations or indeed for usual household arrangements. That the men in their community did not see them as slaves—even if the women themselves might say they were being treated as such—arose out of their own expectations about the work appropriate to women. It was less an assessment of the work's demanding nature than it was an unthinking assumption about who did what sort of work in a properly organized English plantation.

Both men and women in Plymouth understood their project as one of plantation. For them, plantation meant transplanting the society they knew as well as the household work regimens that made it possible. Plantation proposed making the outpost in New England into a place where they could live, work, and raise children. They looked at unoccupied land and pictured English farms, with fields and livestock. They balked when the pressures of the first year forced a departure from usual household practices. Their own ideas about how a society was organized were so deeply engrained that they interpreted Native society within the terms of their own familiar ways and judged it lacking. Despite an early period of adjustment—in which women complained that they were treated as slaves—they gradually succeeded in their project of transplantation.

The plantation of New England involved many facets, including the migration of English families and the recreation of English ways. Their goals and understanding of land use led the English arrivals to read American lands with English eyes. The idea of plantation contained a constellation of other ideas: expectations for how best to use the land, hopes for what such bounty would mean for their countrymen and women, and blindness to other ways of living on the land. Plantation, a goal dear to the settlers (or rather planters), shaped their project in Plymouth and beyond.

GUNS

IN DECEMBER 1620, their ship sat at anchor off of Cape Cod. On
5 December, Francis Billington was playing with a gun—"a fowling
piece"—and gunpowder in the tiny ship's cabin where his family
resided. The teenager started a fire, which blazed "within four feet of
the bed between the Decks, and many flints and Iron things about
the Cabin, and many people about the fire, and yet By Gods mercy
no harm done." In relating this brief tale, the unnamed writer mentioned God's mercy twice. Fires aboard wooden sailing vessels had
potentially devastating consequences, and Francis's play might
have destroyed the entire ship. The writer clearly imagined the nearby
bedding catching easily, as well as an explosion, caused by the gunpowder, picking up the "many flints and Iron things" to hurl them like
shrapnel, killing those nearby. With or without an explosion, once the
wooden ship caught fire, the passengers and crew would have had
little recourse but to flee. The boy, this author declared, was foolish.
At some time—whether then or on an earlier occasion—Francis "in
his Fathers absence had got Gun-powder, and had shot off a piece or
two, and made squibs," a sort of firecracker. Once again playing with
gunpowder and fire, he might have killed most of the people—both
passengers and crew—who had journeyed on the *Mayflower*.[1] Only
ten passengers and a few sailors were then ashore—men exploring in
search of a settlement site. Had the ship blown up, everyone else might
have died. Certainly, all their supplies would have been destroyed. At

the time of this incident, no one in England knew where the *May-flower* had touched land; so those on shore would have been stranded, hoping someone would happen upon them. Theirs might have been a second lost colony.

This near disaster might have ended Plymouth Plantation before a settlement site had even been selected. If, as Americans are taught, Plymouth was a founding moment in U.S. history, Francis's foolishness launched a long history of accidents and near-accidents prompted by children playing with guns. This story also shows that guns came to North American shores with the first English people. Settlers brought both fowling pieces and more substantial muskets, intending to use them for hunting and for fighting. The settlers felt the fear of death or destruction from fire and powder continually, and it was only a few months later that numerous ill people resting in a newly built house barely escaped being "blown up with powder" after a thatch roof caught fire. The "house was as full of beds as they could lie one by another, and their Muskets charged, but blessed be to God there was no harm done."[2] As always, observers noted God's role in protecting them.

In Plymouth, guns took on many meanings: they divided Native and English technologies of both warfare and hunting (although not for long); they had ceremonial purposes; and they became a source of contention among various parties. The first arguments for gun control would be articulated in Plymouth, too, as William Bradford and others tried in vain to keep guns out of Native hands. While the hapless Francis Billington escaped becoming the first young person to kill inadvertently with a gun in New England, his father's relationship to firearms resulted in far worse: he would be the first convicted murderer in New Plymouth (as the plantation was sometimes called). A decade after his son almost destroyed the *Mayflower*, John Billington shot and killed John Newcomen "about a former quarrel." Tried by a jury, Billington died by hanging.[3]

The people of Plymouth considered guns necessary tools for their undertaking. When Edward Winslow compiled a list of items to bring to a new plantation, he included firearms, either a musket or fowling piece, along with much powder and shot. He also noted that a heavy gun would work, since most of the shooting was done from "Stands," a stationary position (as when shooting at a flock of birds).[4] Incidental mentions make clear that the settlers realized the need even before Winslow wrote. A few days before young Billington found his father's piece and gunpowder, a whale came to float for a long while near the ship. A couple of men prepared to shoot at it "to see whether she would stir or no." The first man encountered trouble: "his Musket flew in pieces, both stock and barrel." This mishap saved the whale, who "gave a snuff" and swam away. For the writer, the fate of the man holding the malfunctioning weapon was more important; he declared "thanks be to God, neither he nor any man else was hurt with it, though many were there about."[5] The early records make numerous references to fowling, as the Plymouth men were best prepared to take birds of all the varied wildlife that the environment periodically offered. When the settlers finally made contact with the local residents, two men went out to parlay with a group they saw at a distance. Between them, Stephen Hopkins and Miles Standish carried only one gun, which they laid down as a sign of peaceful intent.[6] Guns, although considered necessary, were not all that numerous, as various mentions of pairs of men with just one between them made apparent.[7]

Plymouth men also used guns for ceremonial purposes. When Standish and Master Williamson went out to meet Massasoit and accompany the Wampanoag leader to the site of the treaty negotiations, they greeted him "with half a dozen Musketeers," who then escorted the "king" to the rendezvous point.[8] When Conbatant, another Native leader, questioned Winslow about the practice of saluting dignitaries with shots fired or setting armed men to escort them, he explained that such treatment was considered an "honorable and respective [meaning respectful] entertainment." Unimpressed, Conbatant declared his dislike of the practice.[9] Not only Native leaders were honored thus. According to a 1627 visitor, the governor and the preacher (who at this time would have been William Brewster, the ruling elder who led services in the absence of a minister) routinely processed to Sabbath meeting with an honor guard—"each with his musket or firelock." On the governor's "left hand, the captain with his side-arms and cloak on, and with a small cane in his hand; and so they march in good order." Once in the meeting place, "each sets his arms down near him." The Dutch visitor who penned this description approvingly observed, "Thus they are constantly on guard day and night."[10] The practice kept the community leaders safe, but it was also, as Winslow noted, "respective," or conveying respect.

In other cases, as Conbatant suspected, guns could be used to humiliate. After John Oldham returned from banishment to taunt the Plymouth authorities, Bradford reported, "They committed him" to prison until "he was tamer, and then appointed a guard of musketeers which he was to pass through, and everyone was ordered to give him a thump on the breech with the butt of his musket, and then he was conveyed to the waterside where a boat was ready to carry him away."[11] This ritual—forcing a man to run the gauntlet while being struck with the butt of many muskets—was intended to cause pain as well as humiliation.

Guns also symbolized European warfare in the interchange with Native America. When the settlement received a snakeskin wrapped around arrows, Tisquantum explained that it was a threatening gesture. The settlers responded by wrapping powder and shot in a skin and sending it back. In this exchange, arrows symbolized indigenous military might, while powder and shot did the same for the English.[12]

Plymouth men believed their guns would keep them safe from the Natives, intimidating them at least and also checking any inclination toward violence. Initially the new arrivals and the local residents kept one another at arm's length, observing and assessing. At one point, feeling threatened by a contingent of Native men who made noise nearby, Plymouth men "shouted all together two several times, and shot off a couple of muskets and so returned: this we did that they might see we were not afraid of them nor discouraged."[13] While it could be doubted that the settlers accomplished much with this show of bravado, it does seem that Native people were hesitant at first around their guns. When Quaddequina came to visit along with a "troup" of men, "he was very fearful of our pieces, and made signs of dislike, that they should be carried away, whereupon Commandment was given, they should be laid away."[14] On another occasion, Tisquantum urged the men to discharge their guns to impress a group of Native peoples. Later, when Native men traveling with English men expressed fear of meeting their enemies the Narragansetts, the English "bid them not to fear; for though they were twenty, we two alone would care for them."[15] This scenario, in which Native people looked to better-armed European allies for protection from traditional enemies, suited the English sense that access to firearms ought to give them a decided advantage.

Yet the settlers very soon lost any advantage arising from their exclusive access to guns. With the newly arrived Europeans showing off their guns, Native peoples wanted to acquire them. The Plymouth authorities forbade trade in guns to indigenous residents, a policy that soon earned the backing of King James. The king issued a proclamation in 1622 against trading any "warlike weapons." The royal proclamation enumerated the metal weaponry that distinguished Native from European tools of war, including swords and pikes as well as guns, along with the accoutrements necessary to firearms, including shot, match, and powder.[16]

This fanciful image depicts a group of armed English men guided by a Native man, which was created to illustrate a Henry Wadsworth Longfellow poem about Miles Standish. Every man in the party carries a gun, including Hobomok, whom Longfellow calls "a friend of the white man." The image vastly overstates the availability of guns.

The efforts of authorities near and far made little difference, as many Europeans (whether fishermen or traders) offered guns for sale. Sometime Plymouth resident Phineas Pratt later described the small and ill-fated settlement at Wessagussett, in which the starving men received offers of corn from the Natives if only they would trade away their firearms.[17] Bradford wrote, both in his manuscript history and in various letters, a series of blistering attacks on this trade. He attributed the expansion of gun-wielding Indians to "the baseness of sundry unworthy persons, both English, Dutch and French."[18] Most aggravating were the English men who set up nearby settlements and began trading guns. With a rising competition for furs along the New England coast, indigenous hunters soon learned not to settle for the "trifles" that they had originally accepted and began demanding guns instead. Thomas Morton, a trader, reputedly taught Native hunters to use the firearms, which they then employed in bringing in more pelts to his outpost at Mount Wollaston.[19]

It would not be long before Native people near Plymouth obtained firearms. In 1621, when the Plymouth people negotiated terms of a treaty with Massasoit, one clause had each side leaving their weapons aside when they visited the other. The wording made clear the sharp division between the long-time residents and the new arrivals on this score: "That when their men came to us, they should leave their Bows and Arrows behind them, as we should do our Pieces when we came to them."[20] Yet, within a decade, the plan to keep firearms exclusively in English hands had entirely failed, and this neat division between Native men with "Bows and Arrows" and English men with "Pieces" had broken down.

Nothing better captured the failure of the Plymouth scheme to keep guns away from indigenous men than the story told of the assassination attempt on Edward Winslow. In 1641, John Winthrop recorded the tale in his journal. According to Winthrop, the Indians at Kennebec in Maine, learning of a general conspiracy planned against the English, decided to set it in motion by killing Winslow. Knowing he "did use to walk within the palisades" of the trading fort that Plymouth maintained there, a Native man "prepared his piece to shoot him, but as he was about it, Mr. Winslow not seeing him nor suspecting anything, but thinking he had walked enough, went suddenly into the house, and so God preserved him."[21] This story—whether true or not—revealed much. It indicated the importance of Winslow, a leading man in Plymouth but also a well-known figure throughout the region. He frequently negotiated with Native communities in New England or traveled back and forth across the Atlantic on business. The incident also made apparent the fact that a Native would-be assassin not only carried a firearm but was well practiced enough to target a man on a distant rampart. Only some twenty years before, Plymouth men, among them Winslow himself, had reassured their Native traveling companions that they had no need to fear their enemies because the guns that English men alone wielded would protect them.

Not only the early English arrivals but also later observers have placed great emphasis on the role of firearms technology in giving Europeans an advantage in the encounter with indigenous Americans. Yet firearms never granted vast benefit. The technology was cumbersome to use and did not routinely give those who had guns a clear edge over those skilled with other weapons. Guns, and especially the powder they required, carried their own dangers, as young Billington amply demonstrated aboard the *Mayflower*. In addition, firearms were, then as now, not easily kept out of the hands of those who wanted them. Whether for teenagers playing with them or indigenous would-be assassins aiming them at English leaders, guns were accessible. If the English gained any superiority from bringing this technology to Native shores, that advantage proved somewhat illusory.

2

BRINGING ALONG

TRANSIENTS

REFUGE

ANIMALS

TRANSIENTS

IN THE WANING DAYS of the first winter, two well-traveled men met. Before their first encounter on the American shore, both had been in England and on the European continent. Neither was a stranger to transatlantic crossings. Both had considerable linguistic skills that somewhat eased their movements among peoples who spoke different languages. The two men gave evidence of the increasing interconnectedness of people living on either side of the Atlantic, as wooden vessels carried people to distant lands. The older of the two encountered the younger standing on his Native ground, having been born nearby decades before. The other man had journeyed many miles from his native place, Droitwich, Worcestershire, in the Midlands of England. While the local man would be dead little more than a year after their meeting, the transplant would live another thirty-four years, re-crossing the Atlantic repeatedly. He would die on a ship, traveling between two West Indian islands, in 1655. Despite their very different personal histories, both Tisquantum and Edward Winslow exemplified the increased mobility that shaped their world.

Although we tend to think of Plymouth as a place created by the movement of European peoples, their migration to the shores of Cape Cod Bay made up only part of that story. Long before anyone contemplated the *Mayflower* voyage, the area that would become New Plymouth witnessed routine as well as extraordinary instances of

Native mobility. The coastal region where the settlers would alight had been the site of a Native village, where the Patuxet people spent summer months every year. In the winter they dispersed inland to hunt, returning to the coastal site in the warmer months to plant and to gather the bounty of the sea. Tisquantum had been a member of that community when an English ship's captain named Thomas Hunt kidnapped him—along with numerous other Native men—in order to sell them into slavery in southern Europe. Alone among that group of captives, Tisquantum made his way home. His travels took him first to Spain, where the nefarious Hunt's efforts to sell him were thwarted when local friars recognized Tisquantum as a Native of the Americas. Spanish law treated such people as vassals of the king of Spain (and therefore not eligible for enslavement). Removed from Hunt's grasp, he was taken in by the friars, who aimed to convert him to Roman Catholicism. Eventually he traveled on to England, where he was able to join several voyages west. After a journey to Newfoundland, he finally undertook a voyage that brought him near to his destination. At Patuxet he discovered that a major epidemic had wiped out his village in his absence, and the surviving people had dispersed into other Native communities. Learning of the arrival of the Plymouth planters while in the area the English called Maine, Tisquantum came south, where he met Winslow and other men who had survived their first winter on the shore of Cape Cod Bay. Coerced into his first transatlantic crossing—an experience he shared with other kidnapped indigenous peoples from the far north down to Brazil—Tisquantum came to use English sailing ships to his own ends, voyaging back to North America despite arduous circumstances.

Edward Winslow, when he encountered Tisquantum, was the less well traveled of the two men. Before his recent voyage to New England, Winslow had lived in his native England and in the Dutch city of Leiden. As a child, he had moved to the nearby city of

Edward Winslow returned to England from Plymouth for the final time almost a decade before his death, and while living there he sat for this 1651 portrait by an unknown artist. Winslow was one of many people who moved in and out of Plymouth during its first decades

Worchester to attend school, and from there to the fast-growing metropolis of London to serve an apprenticeship to a printer. Although these experiences were not unusual for a youth of his background, his next move, across the English Channel to Holland at the age of twenty-two, brought him into more exclusive company. Still, the path from England to the Protestant Netherlands was well worn, and Winslow found an enclave of English speakers already in Leiden, drawn by commercial opportunities, family ties, and the availability of religious options beyond that offered by the English church. There he joined John Robinson's English congregation. Three years later, with other church members, he journeyed to North America. Over the course of Winslow's lifetime, the Anglo-Atlantic colonies would absorb tens of thousands of migrants, but at the time when he stepped onto the *Mayflower*, a transatlantic crossing remained unusual. Besides fishermen who visited seasonally, the only English residents on the western shores of the Atlantic at that time resided in Virginia, a struggling colony not yet a decade and a half old. Others lived in the middle of the ocean on the small island chain of Bermuda. English people were still not often resident in the Americas in 1621, although more circulated all the time. After their meeting, these two highly peripatetic men—one American and the other European—would be joined by rising numbers of transients who moved in and out of the Plymouth area.

The English people who came in the winter of 1620–21 set foot on Native land with a long history of human habitation that included seasonal migrations. They soon learned that the cleared site where they located their own cluster of houses had been a Native village. Previous European transients—traders and fishing crews, not to mention kidnappers—had brought disease microbes into the area that had drastically reduced the resident population. This steep population loss left the immediate area largely uninhabited, opening the way for the quiet occupation undertaken months before the meeting between Tisquantum and Winslow. Once Plymouth was established, the village site became a Native destination again. Tisquantum himself would play a key role as interpreter and mediator over the year to come. From 1621, various local people came to see the new settlement or to trade. After Plymouth men and local leader Ousamequin (referred to in English records by his title, Massasoit) entered into a treaty, interactions between the two groups became commonplace. The first Native to visit had been a man named Samoset; he had been sent to open relations with the new arrivals. Tisquantum's superior grasp of English meant that his presence fostered greater interaction. The English learned about the patterns of movement that supported indigenous people's sustenance. Massasoit's people informed them that they would return in the summer months to avail themselves of local seafood and planting opportunities.

The regular coming and going of the Native inhabitants was, from 1620, overlaid with increasing European movement. The best-known arrivals are those who came intending to make a commitment to Plymouth and who did indeed become settlers. Others came and left, either because they never intended to reside permanently or because, like Winslow, they changed their plans. Many came only for the short term: seamen plying the Atlantic or coastal waters, settlers who were intent on making their way to other destinations, and visitors who came specifically to look at Plymouth itself. The transient population of Plymouth reflected larger trends as populations within England journeyed to an increasing number of Atlantic settlements. Temporary sojourners joined migrants, creating a more fluid environment than our focus on those who came on the *Mayflower* would suggest. Transients created connection, but they also brought change.

While moving back to England occurred—involving perhaps 10 percent of the colonial population—some people also made repeated crossings, journeying back and forth to see to private business and in some cases to the plantation's concerns as well.[1] Winslow himself crossed the Atlantic on multiple occasions before remaining in England, never returning to Plymouth after his 1646 journey to the metropole. Other Plymouth men—Isaac Allerton and Miles Standish among them—made the transatlantic circuit, Allerton repeatedly. Steven Hopkins had already been across the Atlantic once when he arrived on the *Mayflower*: his previous voyage, in 1609 to Virginia, had been interrupted by shipwreck on Bermuda. That incident inspired the subsequent colonization of that mid-Atlantic island chain, as well as Shakespeare's play *The Tempest*. Hopkins continued on to Virginia eventually, returning to England to be present in London so that he could set out for Plymouth in 1620. Such transatlantic peregrinations, while not the norm, were on the rise. The mobility of a growing number of people contributed to an English presence in the wider Atlantic and also to its integration. Plymouth, along with other outposts, took part in that circulation of peoples.

Among the settlers, others besides Winslow joined the community only to leave later. William Bradford (who wrote "Of Plimoth Plantation" and served more than once as the plantation's governor), when reviewing the demographic contribution made by the first settlers, reported on deaths, departures, and descendants. Bradford's interest was in showing that Plymouth migrants founded New England by expanding its English population through their fertility. With this aim, he produced a demographic study focused on numbers, different than the sort of genealogical study so dear to the hearts of *Mayflower* descendants: he cared less about individuals and more about documenting an overall upward trend in population. His compilation showed some people leaving and many more who died. Edward Winslow's own brother Gilbert departed after many years in Plymouth. Desire Minter came as part of the Carver household but subsequently returned "to her friends" in England, where she "proved not very well, and dyed." Another girl, Humility Cooper, came over in the household of her cousin Edward Tilley, but when he and his wife both died, she returned. One of Stephen Hopkins's servants lived in Plymouth only until his contract expired, at which time he went to Virginia. Among the servants who came with the Carver family, a boy named Latham "after more then 20 years stay in the country, went into England, and from thence to the Bahamy Ilands [the Bahamas] in the West Indies, and ther with some others, was starved."[2] The first English settlement in the Bahamas proved a deadly place, and Latham, after surviving the first winter in Plymouth, had the misfortune to meet his end there. While Winslow was doubtless the most promi-nent member of the early Plymouth community to depart perma-nently from the settlement, he was far from the only one.

The departures that Bradford described appear to have been vol-untary, but other settlers were forcibly removed. One case of a forced departure involved a former (and aspiring) clergyman, John Lyford. He brought a large household, with wife, children, and servants, with the intention of making his home in Plymouth. Lyford quickly began feuding with the plantation's leaders over religious and political prac-tices, and eventually they ordered him banished. Going first north to Cape Ann, Lyford finally migrated to Virginia, where he died in 1634. John Oldham, one of his allies in the fight with Bradford, Brew-ster, and the others, also received a sentence of banishment. Oldham returned shortly thereafter, verbally abused the local leaders, and was ritually driven from the town, forced to walk a gauntlet of musketeers. He remained in the region and eventually made his peace with the Plymouth authorities. He never returned to Plymouth, however, but resided in neighboring Massachusetts after it was established in 1629. He died along the Connecticut River in a 1636 altercation that helped to prompt a war between Connecticut and Massachusetts on one hand and the Pequot people on the other. Although he does not seem to have been formally banished, Samuel Gorton—whom author John Josselyn characterized as "a pestilent seducer, and blasphemous Atheist, the Author of the Sects of Gortonians"—was at least made to feel unwelcome, in part because of his religious views. Like Roger Williams, who temporarily ministered to the church at Plymouth, Gorton left the plantation after living there only briefly in the 1630s.[3] In 1637, the Plymouth court banished a man guilty of "lewd behavior and unclean carriage," after first branding and whipping him. The term "unclean" covered a whole range of sexual transgressions, from masturbation to fornication. Two years later, John Dunford, "for his slanders, clamors, lewd & evil carriage," had to get out of Plymouth in three months. Carriage, in these instances, meant behavior. The court further ordered with regard to Dunford that if he returned, the constables would whip him from town to town until he reached the border. Not always with the same violence meted out to Dunford, Plymouth nonetheless forced out various would-be settlers.

Besides those who came to stay but eventually departed, some transients merely visited Plymouth without intending to take up residence. Some of these wayfarers can be identified, although others no doubt passed through without making an impression on the historical record. In 1621, Robert Cushman, although a former member of the Leiden church who had at one time planned to migrate, visited only briefly when the settlement was just a year old. While there, he preached a sermon, subsequently published as *A Sermon Preached at Plimmoth in New-England December 9. 1621*. He also later arranged for the publication of a multiauthor account of the first months, the important *A Relation or Journall*. A Plymouth advocate, Cushman never lived there, although his son Thomas stayed in Plymouth permanently after his father left.

Others passed through without the firm connections that drew Cushman. In 1622, John Pory stopped on his return journey after spending three years in Virginia. At Plymouth, he assessed the little settlement's progress and prospects. The same year, a group of men who were sent out to start a new outpost at the behest of former Plymouth investor Thomas Weston resided in Plymouth before setting up their new undertaking. Bradford complained that they came without provisions and ate up those of the inhabitants.[4] Another visitor, more elusive than Cushman, was John Hampden, "a gentleman of London." Edward Winslow explicitly described him as visiting in 1623, noting that he came to learn about the area. To that end, Hampden accompanied Winslow on what must have been a fascinating journey up the coast to the ailing Native leader and Plymouth ally Massasoit. Along the way, they met other English men, some of them residing at a small and ill-fated trading post established by sometime Plymouth investor Thomas Weston; one of the workers employed by Weston, a man named Phineas Pratt, remembered meeting Hampden years later.[5] Some historians have speculated that this man might have been the English parliamentary leader later active in the early struggles of the English civil wars. The famous John Hampden did have interests in New England, so conceivably he visited either on a fact-finding mission or with a purpose more akin to the first tourist. Other short-term visitors joined Hampden in brief sojourns.

As Plymouth and New England more generally became integrated into the burgeoning trade networks of the Atlantic world, traders came to Plymouth to pursue their business interests. Isaack de Rasieres, merchant for the Dutch West India Company at New Netherland along the Hudson River, came to Plymouth in 1627 hoping to establish a relationship with Plymouth. Bradford, while intrigued by the prospect of nearby trading partners, feared offending English authorities by seeming to support Dutch claims.[6] Emmanuel Altham, one of the investors in Plymouth, visited for the first time in 1623 (one of only a couple of investors to do so). He came as the captain of the *Little James.* The investors sent out this forty-four-ton pinnace to fish and trade. Altham and the *Little James* plied local waters for a year before returning to England. Altham ventured back the following year as a passenger and remained for some months before returning again to England. Local traders, such as Isaac Allerton, who pursued Plymouth's business and his own, joined these more transient traders pursuing economic opportunities offered by the establishment of the plantation.

The most peripatetic men of all were those who served as ship's captains and crew members. They came to know well the Atlantic crossing and the waters around the various English settlements. The seamen who sailed the sea lanes made it possible for these circulating people to move in and out of Plymouth. Not only did they transport temporary sojourners and settlers, they themselves added to the transient population during their time in port. The famous *Mayflower* passengers spent the first deadly winter in the company of the crew members of the ship. Anchoring on November 11, the *Mayflower* did not sail away until the following April. Crew members sickened just as passengers did, and illness further postponed their departure. The captain remained an extra month waiting for enough men to recover to make the return voyage. During that time, they shared the fate of the passengers, participated in their expeditions ashore to find a settlement site, and helped set up the guns on their small fortification once it was built. Two seamen—William Trevore and a man named in the records only as Ely—stayed for the entire first year, as required by the contracts they signed, and at the end of that time both returned to England.[7] Plymouth also produced a few mariners of its own. Oceanus Hopkins, born as his parents Stephen and Elizabeth crossed the Atlantic on board the *Mayflower*, took up the occupation appropriate to his name as an adult and became a seaman. He died while in Barbados sometime before 1650. Richard Gardner, listed as a *Mayflower* passenger, soon pursued the life of a sailor, dying either in England or at sea, according to Bradford.

Some captains—and no doubt crew members as well—became regular visitors. Such was the case with William Peirce, who supported Plymouth in a feud with John Lyford and carried passengers and goods for the plantation on numerous occasions. In fact, when the settlement's backers in England challenged Winslow about the treatment of Lyford, Peirce supported the Plymouth leader. The ship's captain eventually settled in New England—but in Massachusetts rather than Plymouth—while he continued to ply the seas as a trader. He carried Plymouth furs in 1632 but never reached his English destination because his ship, the *Lyon*, wrecked near Virginia. Although Peirce survived, twelve people died, and the cargo was lost. Like Winslow, Peirce himself would die in the Caribbean. In the summer of

1641, he carried settlers from New England to join an English colony, Providence Island (off the coast of modern-day Nicaragua). To his great misfortune, he arrived just as the Spanish had retaken the colony and died when the Spanish shot at his ship from the island's fort. He was much lamented afterward.[8] An early supporter of Plymouth, Peirce helped to knit that settlement into the wider Atlantic. He moved people and things for the plantation.

Both Winslow and Tisquantum are firmly associated with Plymouth Plantation in the popular imagination. Even though their mobility shaped their life histories, we remember them in their Plymouth context: Winslow arriving on the *Mayflower*, Tisquantum greeting him and other planters in their own language. Yet Tisquantum's coerced journey to Europe has long been known, for it was recounted and decried in the early sources. Indeed, the language skills he acquired through travel facilitated the role he famously filled in Plymouth's first year. Winslow's later life story is less well known, possibly because he abandoned Plymouth for other places and projects. His role in revolutionary England and his willingness to support Oliver Cromwell's attempt to conquer Spanish America fits poorly into our narrative of early Plymouth. A major figure in its early history, he arrived with the first settlers, served as the colony's governor thrice and its representative to the Natives in the region more often, wrote one early account of Plymouth, and contributed his writing to others. Yet he ultimately did not settle permanently, although he did leave lands and family members there. Winslow at his death was on a mission to expand militant Protestantism and English rule in the Caribbean. That fact connected his Plymouth story to wider currents and concerns.

Transients each had their own personal histories, ones which carried them into and out of Plymouth. Collectively, they added to the fluidity of the population and to the plantation's connections beyond its borders. If Plymouth's story only matters in relation to the founding of the United States, then the people who left or who visited only briefly seem to have little significance. Yet these visitors shaped Plymouth too, not the least by connecting it more firmly to places beyond its boundaries. There would be no Plymouth and no United States without the mobility of many who sometimes stayed but sometimes moved on. Peregrine White, born on the *Mayflower* while anchored off New England, stayed in the place where he was born despite his name, but many others underwent peregrinations, creating a world that was dynamic and changeable.

REFUGE

BEFORE ONE OF THE London presses issued a little book collecting various accounts of Plymouth Plantation's first year, Robert Cushman penned a brief statement laying out "Reasons & Considerations touching the lawfulness of removing out of England into the parts of America." Cushman had yet to cross the Atlantic, but he would soon journey to New England. Despite his belief in the "lawfulness" of leaving England to live in America, he would linger only a month, returning on the ship that carried him out. He had, however, been involved in the plantation from its inception. A member of the Leiden church, he helped to make the arrangements for the passengers who sailed in 1620. He had deeply pondered the undertaking, which he was prepared to defend. His "Reasons & Considerations" imagined the people who went to New England as analogous to the Jews of ancient times, wandering but finally ending in their appointed place. Except that, sadly for the Plymouth people, the promised land was not to be: for "now we are all in all places strangers and Pilgrims, travelers and sojourners, most properly, having no dwelling but in this earthen Tabernacle; our dwelling is but a wandering, and our abiding but as a fleeting, and in a word our home is nowhere, but in the heavens."[1] Cushman's long-winded sentence constituted the first time that anyone involved in the settlement used the term "pilgrim" to refer to those who lived in the plantation. He understood pilgrimage to be, for this community, a lifelong journey rather than a temporary activity that would land them in their appointed place. Never resting, they lived without a real home until they died and went to heaven.

Cushman's reference drew on an Old Testament passage, Hebrews 11:13: "All these died in faith, and received not the promises, but saw them afar off, and believed them, and received them thankfully, and confessed that they were strangers and pilgrims on the earth." In this vein, Cushman imagined the Plymouth people as wanderers. Their displacement was of little consequence, however, because they did not care about any earthly home, but only about heaven. Although John Bunyan's great work *Pilgrim's Progress* had not yet been written, Cushman's use of the term was similar to Bunyan's: pilgrimage constituted a journey through life toward a heavenly reward.[2] He chose not to follow Samuel Purchas, another contemporary, who used the term in a different sense. A compiler and editor of travel writing, Purchas cast his stay-at-home self as a pilgrim who metaphorically journeyed around as he related the histories and attributes of distant locations.[3] For Cushman (as for Bunyan), it did not matter where pilgrims lived, as long as they were faithful. Besides the spiritual journey through life, Cushman also emphasized the literal experience of displacement. For him, the sojourners in New England's Plymouth were refugees, foreigners displaced from their homes and forced to live as strangers elsewhere. Their journey was not a purposeful mission but just one in a series of displacements.

Cushman's concept of a refugee wandering resonated with one of his fellow Leiden church members, a man who did find a home in America. In 1630, William Bradford sat down to compose a history of the founding of Plymouth Plantation, a decade after he landed on New England's shores. His narrative—which would become the first book of his manuscript "Of Plimoth Plantation"—carried the story forward only to the moment when the settlers prepared to move on shore from the shelter of the ship. He began his tale in the previous century, with the welcomed but incomplete reformation of the English church. This starting point has become standard for histories of Plymouth, which faithfully follow Bradford. In this telling, a religious awakening among a few Christians in sixteenth-century England led them to form a church outside of the established religious structure and later to move to Holland where they could pursue their vision free of harassment. Bradford's story briefly considered the group's interval in the Netherlands, then described the decision to migrate again, this time to a location in North America. As some of the church's members parted from the rest of their community and journeyed to Delft Haven to sail to England as the first step of their voyage, Bradford paused his narration to ruminate on their status. "So they left that goodly and pleasant country which had been their resting place near twelve years; but they knew they were pilgrims, and looked not much on those things, but lift up their eyes to the heavens, their dearest country, and quieted their spirits."[4]

Again, like Cushman, Bradford saw "strangers and pilgrims" wandering, without a home but aware that what really mattered was their faith and prospects for life after death. Both men imagined departures, whether from England or, later, from Leiden, as exile. For them, the people who set off to cross the Atlantic in the fall of 1620 sought a refuge. Bradford described them as having "suffered this hazardous & voluntary banishment into this remote wilderness" in order to protect their church.[5]

Although Bradford only uses the term "pilgrim" once (and his example joined Cushman's as the only two such references in the original sources), the first book of his manuscript history, taken as a whole, did present his community as refugees repeatedly in flight. The departure from Leiden, the occasion that prompted his reference to the passage from Hebrews, proceeded in an orderly fashion. The church held a day to pray for the success of the voyage in Leiden; the migrants then journeyed south to Delft Haven, the port where they were to

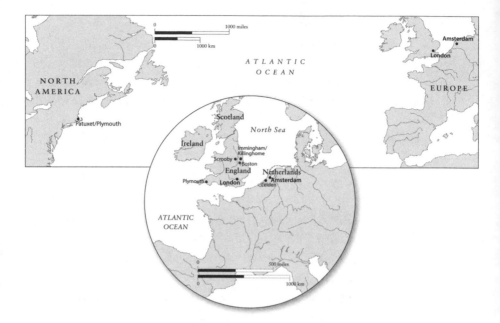

The founders of Plymouth Plantation were English people, some of whom had lived for the previous decade or more in the Dutch city of Leiden. From the areas of Immingham and Killinghome, not far from the town of Scrooby where their church had been founded, they made two attempts to depart for Holland, which Bradford narrated so dramatically.

meet their ship for travel back to England; and there they said a tearful goodbye to friends who had escorted them to the port.

In contrast, the earlier departure from England had been harrowing. The church members who decided to migrate to the Netherlands did so illegally, attempting to sneak out of the country without being detected. The decision was difficult, since it took them "into a country they knew not but by hearsay, where they must learn a new language and get their livings they knew not how, it being a dear [expensive] place and subject to the miseries of war, it was by many thought an adventure almost desperate; a case intolerable and a misery worse than death."[6] Despite these worries, they agreed to go.

Their first attempt to leave England ended in catastrophe, as the ship's captain they hired betrayed them. Meeting him in secret, they boarded his ship not at a dock in a regular harbor but in an out-of-the-way spot. Rowed out in small boats to board, they were at his mercy when he ordered his men to search through their belongings and take anything of value. The mistreatment they received shocked Bradford—and was intended to shock his readers—as he recounted the crewmen "searching to their shirts for money, yea even the women further than became modesty." After this abuse, the captain carried them not to the Netherlands but to a nearby English port, that of Boston, where he turned them over to the authorities. Having broken the law by trying to sneak out of the country, they could not call upon the authorities to punish the duplicitous captain for theft. Rather, the local magistrates committed them to prison to await the word of the Privy Council, a body of noble lords who advised the king. After a month of hearing nothing, most were released, but seven were held to appear at the next session of the court of assizes. Bradford's account of betrayal, theft, and incarceration calls to mind the human traffickers of today who abuse the refugees they are paid to aid.

The next attempt went only marginally better. This time they arranged to sail with an honest Dutch ship's captain. Again meeting the ship in secret, the men who had arrived on foot boarded first. Before the sailors could row the women, children, and supplies out to the ship, the crew saw approaching "a great company, both horse and foot,"—by which he meant men mounted and on foot—"with bills [a staff with a hooked blade on the end] and guns and other weapons, for the country was raised to take them." With this force advancing, the captain swore an oath, "and having the wind fair, weighed his anchor, hoised sails, and away." This turn of events left some men, along with all the women, children, and belongings, to the mercy of the approaching force, while the majority of the men departed, panicked that their loved ones would be harmed. To make matters worse, the ship "endured a fearful storm at sea." The passage, which normally took a week, lasted two weeks or more, a week of which "they neither saw sun, moon nor stars." Indeed, they were driven far to the north, almost to the coast of Norway. Bradford believed that only the prayers of the faithful saved them.

His description of the sailing was so vivid, readers might assume he had been in the contingent that boarded early and endured the storm, but he was similarly eloquent about the fate of those who stayed behind. He described the plight of the "poor women in this distress," with their "weeping and crying on every side, some for their husbands, that were carried away in the ship . . . , others not knowing what should become of them and their little ones; others again melted in tears, seeing their poor little ones hanging about them, crying for fear, and quaking with cold." The authorities faced a problem of how to handle this group once it was apprehended. Bradford noted,

> they were hurried from one place to another and from one justice to another, till in the end they knew not what to do with them; for to imprison so many women and innocent children for no other cause (many of them) but that they must go with their husbands, seemed to be unreasonable and all would cry out of them; and to send them home again was as difficult; for they alleged, as the truth was, they had no homes to go to, for they had either sold, or otherwise disposed of their houses and livings.

Again, the parallels to modern-day refugees are obvious. Luckily for those who remained, in the end they did make it to the Netherlands, although as Bradford observed, "in the meantime they (poor souls) endured misery enough."

This dramatic and prolonged effort to get to Holland, so vividly told by Bradford, concluded with his theme of displacement. He underscored "their wanderings and travels both at land and sea" before they were finally reunited with their loved ones. Although he does not, in this passage, use the term "pilgrim," the meaning here, that they were forced to wander and seek refuge, made a similar point to that which he offered as he ruminated about their departure from Holland years later. They had to leave their homes and roam, enduring misery. Bradford advised that they think of heaven as "their dearest country" and not ponder excessively on their worldly sufferings.[7]

Although Cushman (who in the end was not a Plymouth resident, dying in London in 1625) and Bradford were the only ones to use the term "pilgrim," other participants in the plantation's first years left hints that they considered themselves wanderers. Most tellingly, the two children who were born on the *Mayflower* were given names that accorded with the circumstances of the journey. Oceanus Hopkins, child of Stephen and Elizabeth Hopkins, bore his unusual name because of his birth during the crossing. While the Hopkins family joined the America-bound travelers in England, the other parents, William and Susannah White, were part of the Leiden contingent; William, in fact, was brother-in-law to the Leiden church's pastor, his sister Bridget having married John Robinson. The Whites gave their baby an equally unusual name, Peregrine.[8] The bird that bears the name, the peregrine falcon, migrates over great distances, and its name translates to "wandering falcon." Although Peregrine's parents and older siblings had wandered far—William and Susannah were born in England, migrated to Leiden, then left for America—Peregrine himself stayed close to home, living in the vicinity of his birthplace until his death in the next century in the nearby town of Marshfield. Like Cushman in 1622 and Bradford in 1630 looking back at the departure from Leiden a decade before, the elder Whites thought of themselves as displaced wanderers. For them, arrival in America meant refuge, a respite from their experience of repeated displacement.

Today we think of Pilgrims as synonymous with settlers in Plymouth Plantation, but that terminology in its modern form does not mean today what it meant in the 1600s. Modern Americans may not pause over the idea of a Pilgrim when they picture the first arrivals, in supposedly drab attire with buckles on their shoes. Pilgrims, for many, simply denote those English people who arrived first in New England. This branding campaign proved so successful that all modern accounts of Plymouth use the term as if it were a label used by that group at the time. If you could visit Plymouth Plantation in its first decade—rather than the living history museum that depicts life in 1627—no one would know why you were referring to them as "the Pilgrims." In contrast, if you went to neighboring Massachusetts in the next decade and addressed the people you met as Puritans, they would know what the term meant, although they would assume you meant to insult them. "Puritan" was a critical term—a taunt—but it was at least in wide circulation, unlike the "pilgrim" moniker.

The association between Pilgrim and Plymouth came about many decades after Cushman and Bradford passed from the scene. It only came to refer to Plymouth planters in the late eighteenth century. The people who promoted the name (as opposed to mentioning it in passing as Cushman and Bradford did) imagined a more purposeful pilgrimage than what in fact took place. After the American Revolution, New England clergymen and historians promoted the idea of Plymouth as a defining moment in U.S. history (and advocated for it over the earlier but less—to them at least—satisfying tale of early Virginia). With the term, they suggested that those who journeyed to New England arrived with a purpose: that they meant to create the new nation that arose a century and a half later. In making this connection, they drew on a different version of the idea of pilgrim: one associated with pilgrimage as a purposeful religious journey. As used in medieval Europe, a pilgrim went on a religious mission to visit a holy place. Medieval Christianity revered holy sites where people could find comfort, healing, or forgiveness. This association is ironic, in that Catholic pilgrimage and even the concept of a holy site—indeed, all things Catholic—were anathema to Cushman and his associates. To view the early Plymouth people as pilgrims pursuing a goal—analogous to a pilgrimage to Mecca—misses the core idea of aimless but ultimately insignificant wandering found in Hebrews and picked up by Cushman and Bradford. If our image of a Plymouth Pilgrim includes any sense of purpose, it connotes a mission to found America or at least to establish the religious liberty that would become a founding principle of the United States. For that reason, nineteenth-century Americans began to visit Plymouth Rock as a sort of patriotic holy site. But in the 1620s, the people who founded Plymouth thought not of the United States—how could they?—but of themselves as refugees wandering in a strange land. They sought refuge, a temporary stopping place, and many of them found that in southern New England.

ANIMALS

IN 1623, chickens traveled from Plymouth village to the winter encampment of the Wampanoag leader known to the English as Massasoit. Carried by an unknown runner—an unnamed Native
man—the chickens were intended for a broth to help the seriously
ill leader. The fowl's journey had been prompted when Edward Winslow sent a messenger to the settlement to request that some birds
be hastily delivered. The healing qualities of chicken broth would, he
hoped, provide a cure. Doing what he could, Winslow attempted to
prepare a number of foods used in England to nurture the sick. Sub-
stituting local plants when English medicinal plants were unavailable,
he also dispatched one of Massasoit's men to Plymouth for chickens.
By the time the messenger returned with the birds, however, Massasoit had mended enough that instead of drinking a broth he asked
Winslow to give him the chickens. He hoped to breed them in his
own community.[1] Winslow did not speculate as to whether Massasoit
saw the domesticated fowl simply as a potential addition to Wampanoag diets or expected to use them as status objects, to demonstrate
his ability to acquire the exotic European birds.

Since the Wampanoags kept no farm animals, such creatures
invoked European dietary and agricultural practices. The desire for
English fowl readily explained why the chicken crossed the Atlantic:
they made the transatlantic voyage in the settlement's very first years.
Along with dogs, they were the first animals brought to Plymouth.[2]

Whether Massasoit's birds made the sea voyage or had been bred subsequently in Plymouth, their presence made a striking addition to a Native village that previously kept no animals for food.

While a chicken in a Wampanoag village would serve as an exotic addition, poultry and other farm animals formed a routine part of English farm life and of the English diet. English people regularly ate meat—if they could afford it—and that meat was acquired almost exclusively through the slaughter of animals raised for the purpose. Except for wealthy elites whose deer parks yielded venison or for the poor who trapped small game in common lands or as poachers on estates owned by others, meat seldom entered the English diet through hunting. Wild fowl were more readily available, although hunting them was reserved for those with sufficient wealth to own a gun. Many of the guns brought to Plymouth were in fact intended for taking birds, the oft-mentioned "fowling piece." Although Winslow's description of the first Thanksgiving made no mention of wild turkeys specifically, that bird was presumably consumed in New Plymouth; in its wild form it would have been scrawnier than the modern farm-raised bird, the latter having been bred for its outsized breast. The men who came to Plymouth, although they brought guns to take fowl, were not adept hunters of larger game. Given their lack of skill in hunting and their familiarity with farm-raised meat, they wanted English poultry and livestock as part of their diets. Chickens came first—small and easily transported, they also had the benefit of laying eggs that sustained hungry people. Winslow appreciated their healthful qualities. Dairy cattle—which could also continually provide milk—were harder to bring and more difficult to maintain in an early settlement without fences or barns. As Winslow intimated, access to English foods was familiar and comforting.

Those who thought about making the region habitable placed great emphasis on the need for imported animals. Before any English people had settled there, John Smith promised in his description of

GOOD
NEVVES
FROM NEW-ENGLAND:

O R

A true Relation of things very remarkable at the Plantation of *Plimoth*
in N B VV - E N G L A N D.

Shewing the wondrous providence and good-
nes of G o D, in their preſervation and continuance,
*being delivered from many apparant
deaths and dangers.*

Together with a Relation of ſuch religious and
civill Lawes and Cuſtomes, as are in practiſe amongſt
the *Indians,* adjoyning to them at this day. As alſo
*what Commodities are there to be rayſed for the
maintenance of that and other Plantations in the ſaid Country.*

Written by *E. W.* who hath borne a part in the
fore-named troubles, and there liued ſince
their firſt Arrivall.

L O N D O N
Printed by *I. D.* for *William Bladen* and *Iohn Bellamie,* and
are to be ſold at their Shops, at the *Bible* in *Pauls-*Church-
yard, and at the three Golden Lyons in Corn-hill,
neere the *Royall Exchange.* 1 6 2 4.

Edward Winslow wrote *Good Newes from New England* describing events in the first years
in Plymouth Plantation. An essential source for understanding this early history, *Good
Newes* contains the story of Massasoit's chicken, among many others.

the land that cattle would thrive, allowing settlers to recreate that aspect of their lives and diets.[3] The first residents, in their earliest
writings, declared that if they had "Kine [plural term for cows],
Horses, and Sheep, I make no question, but men might live as contented here as in any part of the world."[4] When minister Francis Higginson described what New England needed, he listed "Horses,
Kine and Sheep to make use of this fruitful Land."[5] His account also
printed "A Letter from New-England, by Master Graves, Engineer
now there resident" who attested to the fruitful nature of the country.
Graves mentioned in particular the prospects for raising cattle as well
as growing barley and vines. Had he been right on all three counts,
New England would not have needed to import wine, as England did;
but the other items (barley and cattle) aimed precisely at reproducing
what England provided itself. Animals—whether European or
American—meant food, but English creatures meant familiarity, a
recreation of the foodways of their home. In a land without cattle or
familiar breads—where Natives hunted wild game and ate corn—the
English adapted somewhat but longed to ignore local foods and sit
down to familiar English fare. Looking back, Nathaniel Morton noted
how the difficult conditions dismayed the first arrivals. While some
had apparently realized "they could not expect it should be better,"
even they were shocked to find they had not only no bread but also
no cattle. This situation made them less well-off than the biblical
Jacob, who in his lowest moment at least enjoyed meat.[6]

Within the first half decade, a great variety of domesticated animals traveled to New England to fulfill this wish for familiar flesh. A
year after Winslow and Hampden journeyed to Massasoit's bedside,
the first livestock (larger farm animals) arrived. The English investors
wrote to announce that they were finally able to send cattle.[7] Both Nathaniel Morton and John Josselyn thought the arrival of three heifers
and a bull worthy of note when they wrote about early New England.[8]
Writing in 1631, John Smith enumerated the human population and

noted the presence of livestock. He reported "In this Plantation there is about an hundred and fourscore [or 180] persons, some Cattell, but many Swine and Poultry."[9] Sheep arrived in numbers more slowly. After a few decades, a Plymouth poet felt the need to urge people to bring in more sheep in order to reduce the population's dependence on imported clothing.[10] Animals for food came first, and sheep for wool, although important, were a lower priority.

Some livestock were more readily introduced than others. As William Morrell reported after his visit to New England, "Hogs and Goats are easy, present, and abundant profit, living and feeding on the lands, almost without any care of cost."[11] Goats had the benefit of being relatively small and transportable; they could be penned on-board ship or staked in a farmyard once in New England. While clearly in residence, goats garnered little notice from authors and from the courts. Pigs were especially hardy and thus became the imported animal of choice, since they could be let loose to fend for themselves until slaughter time. As a result, pigs rose in importance in the diets of English Americans. Transporting the larger animals proved more difficult. For instance, the *Handmaid* on its 1630 voyage had a rough crossing, during which it lost ten out of the twenty-eight cows that it carried.[12] Higginson thought settlers should bring cows and goats. He did not mention pigs except in the form of bacon, but in fact pigs would proliferate in colonial New England.[13] Large draft animals also crossed the ocean. They could haul wood out of the forests, to be burned in fireplaces or used in construction. Besides those brought for meat, such livestock eased burdens otherwise borne by people and sped the process of building.

Pigs, which adapted best to the new environment, introduced problems of their own. Building pens for animals was time-consuming work, and pig owners were tempted to avoid the effort by leaving swine free to forage on their own. The practice of turning them out into the woods became so common by midcentury that it could be used metaphorically to refer to the neglect a young person experienced if they were left without proper spiritual guidance. In addition to providing rhetorical fodder, pigs created conflict by indiscriminately damaging neighbors' garden plots. Plymouth court ordered owners to pay for any damage caused by semi-feral animals and further declared that great swine in particular be driven out of town.[14] In addition to conflicts among planters over damages caused by free-ranging animals, the pigs' destructive tendencies caused numerous legal conflicts between European and Native residents. Those great swine driven out of town to spare English gardens instead attacked Native plots. Indignant Indians sometimes killed foraging pigs and thereby infuriated their neglectful owners.[15]

It took some time, but New England eventually became a center of livestock production. Plymouth farmers initially used the imported animals to meet pressing local needs. Once the deluge of settlers began pouring into the newly founded Massachusetts Bay Colony, a local export market opened. Plymouth men sold animals to the new arrivals, helping them fend off hunger but also allowing them to start their own herds. The authorities wanted the few sheep in the plantation as of 1633 retained rather than sold away, ordering that no sheep be sold out of Plymouth's jurisdiction.[16] When migration to Massachusetts dropped drastically at the end of that decade, Plymouth's leaders worried that the loss of income from the local livestock economy would hamper their ability to pay off the plantation's lingering debt.[17] After midcentury, they, along with other New Englanders, sold locally raised animals to Caribbean island colonies to work in the sugar mills. By that time the presence of cattle and other English farm animals was sufficiently entrenched that one visitor noted that where the animals churned up the ground, new plants had begun to take root. Environmental degradation followed the introduction of numerous new species and of novel herding and farming practices. Before the descendants of livestock from Europe could sail south to the West Indies, however, animal husbandry was made to flourish—just as John Smith promised that it would—in New England.

3

MEETING AND
EXCHANGING

TRADERS

GOD

TOBACCO

TRADERS

THOMAS WESTON SAW POTENTIAL for profit in southern New England and pursued various means to achieve it. He connected London investors to prospective migrants in Leiden, contributing to the founding of Plymouth but failing to benefit himself in the process. Deciding to establish his own trading venture near the new plantation, he dispatched sixty men in 1622 to set up an outpost north of Plymouth. Many of those men resided for the summer in Plymouth before moving twenty-five miles up the coast, to the site of what is today Weymouth, Massachusetts. Weston's scheme fared poorly, as indeed all his undertakings seemed to do. After living off of Plymouth for some months, his men failed to apply themselves in Wessagussett (as his outpost was dubbed). Like the early arrivals in Virginia, his crew neglected basic tasks necessary to survival. Later Plymouth author Nathaniel Morton attributed their failure to the fact that theirs was "an unruly company, that had no good government over them."[1] Soon desperate and hungry, the men either stole food from nearby Native communities or traded their possessions (including clothes and guns) for food. Having fomented their neighbors' animus, the starving Weston men feared an imminent attack and turned to Plymouth for help. A company under Miles Standish journeyed north and there assailed Wessagussett's long-suffering neighbors, an unjustified assault that prompted Leiden pastor John Robinson to chide his former parishioners.[2] With any chance of trade squandered, the men soon abandoned the site. Weston's hopes for profit were dashed, rendering him nearly destitute.

Traders in early Plymouth have often been presented as problematic outsiders, like these Wessagussett men. The Weston men certainly caused numerous difficulties: depleting Plymouth stores during the early, lean years and sparking conflict with the local peoples (not to mention failing to set up the trading post Weston desired). His outpost was one of a number of lesser efforts that brought a scattering of mostly men to the area in the 1620s. These endeavors aimed to trade, and they were staffed largely by hired men or servants. Such outposts had little in common with Plymouth. Most of the men involved went as employees. Weston's men seemed ill-prepared for the enormity of their undertaking and the work that would be needed to make it succeed. Plymouth's complaints about the purported laziness of the Wessagussett men echoed similar criticisms aimed at the first English in Virginia, another group initially made up only of men and seeking immediate profit.[3] These complaints suggested that the men involved were of a different sort, in this case not the hard-working planters of Plymouth but a dissolute band of lazy freeloaders. Although at least one of Weston's men, Phineas Pratt, later lived in Plymouth—there marrying, raising a family, and pursuing a career as a joiner (or skilled carpenter)—most of the men disappeared from New England with the collapse of the endeavor, sealing their status as interlopers.[4] Nathaniel Morton, noting that they departed without repaying any of the aid Plymouth had given them, further remarked that it was a providence of God that such strong and capable men (he used the contemporary equivalent, "lusty") failed when Plymouth, burdened with women and children, succeeded. Morton's implication was clear: God smiled on Plymouth but not on such men who neither pulled their weight nor paid their way.[5] Traders in and around Plymouth are generally treated in exactly that light: as outsiders with a potential to create trouble.

The men associated with another trading attempt—that at Mount Wollaston—proved the point even more decisively. Captain Richard Wollaston established an outpost in 1624 or 1625, in what is now Quincy, Massachusetts. He staffed it with three or four gentlemen and a great number of servants. It too disappointed, and Wollaston decided to make a try in Virginia instead. Before he had a chance to move all his laborers south, Thomas Morton, one of the elite men involved, enticed many of them to join him in his own endeavor. His "Merry Mount" became a site of debauchery—according to the outraged William Bradford at least—and he irked all his nearby countrymen, not just those in Plymouth but also those living scattered in households that had sprung up in the vicinity of the future Boston. His critics cited gun sales to Native peoples as one reason to drive Morton away, but the whole tenor of his undertaking offended, assuming the stories of excessive drinking and sexually abusing Native women were accurate. English men with property feared servants out of control—the infamous problem of "masterless men"—and Morton, an elite man who encouraged rather than controlled these men, earned their particular ire. The trajectory from Mount Wollaston to Merry Mount confirmed in Plymouth leaders' minds that trading outposts and the men who staffed them were potential sources of grave difficulties.

The Wessagussett and Mount Wollaston undertakings were launched on different terms than Plymouth, in that they focused on trade over plantation. In this respect, they bore more similarity to trading forts (often called factories because they employed merchant factors) in the Indian Ocean or other remote locations. To use their own language, whereas the Plymouth endeavor was a plantation since it intended to transplant people permanently, these neighboring projects used employees with only a short-term commitment to pursue profits through trade. Their residence in the area was incidental, a means to another end, instead of being the point of the undertaking.

English men initially came to Virginia intending to trade rather than settle, and the investment company overseeing that effort moved only gradually toward colonization as residents began to produce and ship tobacco that required additional workers to make profits. Most trading outposts around the globe relied on an area's original inhabitants to generate trade goods, leaving those in the factory simply to purchase and ship the items. They did not intend to take territory and institute their own land-use practices—as the Plymouth people did—and in many locations they would have been unable to do so had they wished to displace the inhabitants. Instead they aimed to extract things of value, working with the residents to acquire them. The best-known trading forts in the Atlantic world were those that marketed slaves on the coast of Africa, but that trading factory model also applied where the trade was in spices, silks, or other valuable items. New Netherland was initially organized around this model, with furs being the object in that case. The staffing of these outposts differed from the population of Plymouth, reflecting their different purpose.

Plymouth's difficulty with traders arose not solely in regard to annoying nearby settlements, but also in relations with one of its own. Isaac Allerton's business dealings eventually drove a wedge between him and his fellow Plymouth leaders, a fact that has been cited to suggest that Plymouth was uncomfortable with trade in general. Allerton came to Leiden in 1608, where he joined the church and married a fellow member. One of the better-off English men in Robinson's church, he worked on the arrangements for the move and journeyed to New England on the first ship. When the settlers in 1621 decided their governor needed an assistant, they chose Allerton. In the same year, having been widowed, he married Fear, daughter of William Brewster, the church elder. Like Edward Winslow, he negotiated with local Native leaders and traveled back to England repeatedly on plantation business. He played a key role in replacing the large investment group that initially backed the migrants with a smaller partnership between a handful of London investors and a number of Plymouth men (including himself), designated as "Undertakers."[6] This term referred to the fact that they undertook to pay off the debt incurred in planting Plymouth, just as the investors who had risked (or adventured) their money were "Adventurers." In subsequent years, he continued to oversee plantation business affairs.

Eventually his dealings led to a falling out with his fellow Plymouth Undertakers. Allerton may have been guilty of defrauding his friends or his failing may have been sloppy bookkeeping that made it difficult to separate his private affairs from his work for Plymouth. He certainly made commitments on behalf of Plymouth that his compatriots did not accept. Charles McLean Andrews long ago suggested that Allerton was at least "unbusinesslike and careless."[7] While Bradford and others came to suspect him of cheating, their own poor bookkeeping practices foiled their efforts to prove these suspicions. The culprit on their side was Edward Winslow's newly arrived younger brother Josiah, who proved a disastrous choice as their clerk but never earned their personal ire as Allerton did. In fact, the younger Winslow became a longtime resident and leading magistrate.[8] Allerton eventually left Plymouth, living in other parts of New England. He died insolvent in New Haven Colony in 1659, his commercial efforts having failed to bring him the financial success he sought even as it drove a wedge between him and the Plymouth community.

Adding Plymouth's differences with their agent Allerton to their disgust with the Weston trading post and their outright hostility to the Thomas Morton endeavor, it seems possible that Plymouth leaders generally opposed commercial exchange. This idea ties into an older view that New England sought religion while other places—the primary example being Virginia—sought profit. This idea has long permeated college textbooks and popular

understandings of regional differences in early America. Supposedly, Plymouth—and indeed all of New England—sought to separate from the wider world and avoid commercial interactions. In
this view, a trader like Allerton could not long reside in Plymouth,
since he rejected shared attitudes that bound the community.

This way of understanding Plymouth's relationship to trade and
traders is simplistic and, at root, incorrect. Plymouth eagerly engaged
in trading activities. From the moment of their arrival, the first
planters wanted to trade with local peoples. They appointed Allerton
and others to act as agents because of their engagement in commerce.
Trade served as means to two ends. Like any European residents in
the Americas at this time, they wanted the ability to buy items from
Europe—everything from clothing to books, guns to kettles—and
for that, they needed money. At the same time, the plantation carried a heavy burden of debt to the investors who financed their voyages and sent supplies, and trade permitted them to discharge those
obligations. Farming New England's rocky soil could not generate the
kind of income the plantation required, for no northern crop could
hope to compete with the success of tobacco in Virginia. Nor was
Plymouth well placed or its residents sufficiently skilled to exploit the
region's fisheries to the extent that would have been required. Hence,
the Plymouth people turned to trade, and especially to the fur trade,
to produce the needed income. Plymouth objected to outposts such
as Weston's not because they were hostile toward trade or unwilling
to deal with outsiders, but rather because these enclaves competed
for the very trade they themselves wanted to capture. Plymouth Plantation was indeed made up largely of planters, as its name implied,
but the residents—most especially Plymouth's leaders—pursued
local trade to benefit the plantation.

Strategies for trade in Plymouth shifted over time. Initially, the first
arrivals attended to the fact that the Native people they met sported
beaver pelts, and they discussed trade with Massasoit as part of treaty

negotiations. As the limitations of the Plymouth location became apparent—and as rival trading entities started to box Plymouth in—the plantation claimed distant sites that were better able to tap into Native networks. They set up satellite locations where trade could be regularly conducted away from Plymouth itself, including on the other side of Cape Cod (at what is today Bourne, Massachusetts), on Cape Ann (where they obtained a patent for a tract in 1624), on the Connecticut River, and on the Kennebec River.[9] Through these various efforts, Bradford felt certain that they had sent hides sufficient to cover their debt by the mid-1630s, although it was not until 1641 that all parties agreed that the debt had been fully discharged. At first trade was conducted by whomever went out to treat with the local Native communities, but soon men were designated to staff outposts and manage transactions. Once responsibility for the debt fell to the eight men known as Undertakers, either one of them oversaw outposts or they assigned other men to do so. The Undertakers—of whom Allerton was one—did not object to trade. They simply wanted to harness its benefits.

If Plymouth was primarily a plantation (in 1620 terms), intent on transplanting English life in all its detail to a new location, then its satellite trading posts were akin to the trading factories that dotted the Atlantic and indeed the globe. These trading forts aimed merely to extract profit, using traders in residence to manage transactions with local populations. Using a combination of models, Plymouth both planted a settlement and extracted local resources for profit. Plymouth leaders objected to the activities of traders only when they threatened Plymouth's success, either by siphoning off trade through rival factories or by mismanaging their own trading interests with ill-conceived deals or shoddily kept books. Far from objecting to trade and traders in principle, they eagerly embraced them. Trade would lead to economic viability for the plantation and an end to the crushing debt that threatened Plymouth's future. For planters themselves, trade drought, & no raine for many weeks togeather, so as all was burnte vp, hay, at 5. a load; and now all raine, so as much sommer corne, & later hay is spoyled. Thus y lord sends iudgments, after iudgments, and yet we cannot see, nor humble our selues; and therfore may iustly fear heauier iudgments; vnless we speedyly repente, & returne vnto him, which y lord giue vs grace to doe if it be his blessed will. Thus desiring you to remember vs in your prayers, & euer rest

Sep: 14 · 1636.

your louing friend
James Sherley

This was all y answer they had from m̃ Sherley, by which m̃ Winslow saw his hops failed him. So they now resolued to send no more beauer in y way which they had done, till they came to some issue or other aboute these things: But now came ouer letters from m̃ Andrews, & m̃ Beachamp, full of complaints, that they marueled y nothing was sent ouer, by which any of their moneys should be payed in; for it did appear by y accounte sente in Añº 1631. that they were each of them out, aboute a leuen hun=dered pounds a peece, and all this while had not receiued one penie to=wards y same. But now m̃ Sherley sought to draw more money from them, and was offended becaus they deneyed him. And blamed them hear very much that all was sent to m̃ Sherley, & nothing to them. They marueled much at this, for they conceiued, that much of their monies had been payd in; y yearly each of them had receiued a proportionalle quantity out of y larg returnes sent home. For they had sente home since y accounte was receiued in Añº 1631. (in which all, & more then all their debts, with y years supply) was charged vpon them) these sumes following.

Nou: 18. Añº 1631.   By m̃ peirce — — — 0400ᵗ waight of beauer, & oters 20

July 13. Añº 1632. by m̃ Griffin — — — — 1348ᵗ beauer & oters — 147

Añº 1633 · by m̃ Graues — — — — 3366ᵗ beuer & oters — 346

Añº 1634 · by m̃ Andrews — — — = 3738ᵗ beauer & oters — 234

Añº 1635 · by m̃ Babb — — — — — 1150ᵗ beauer & oters — 200

June 24 fiñ: 1636 · by m̃ Wilkinson — — — 1809ᵗ beauer & oters — 010

y̅ s̅idem   by m̃ Langrume — — — 0719ᵗ beauer & oters — 199

{ 12150 }   · 1156 ·

All these sumes were safly reciued, & well sould, as appears by letters. the coat beauer vsualy at 20. 21. pound, and some at 24. the skin at 15. & sometimes 16. & doe not remember any vnder 14. yt may be y last year might be something lower, so also ther were some small furrs that are not reconed in this accounte, & some black beauer at higer rates, to make vp y defects provided an opportunity to acquire necessities and, eventually, luxury items.

Plymouth's location in New England limited its ability to succeed in trade. Its hinterland was not especially fertile; its harbor not particularly useful; its access to fish or to furs paled in comparison to that of other locations. For a short period, Plymouth operated the only sustained English trading venture in the area, but it was quickly displaced by others. It then made do with satellite outposts that kept it active in commerce until its debt was cleared. After that, Plymouth lapsed into backwater status, pushed to the margins by the advent of new colonies, especially the populous and well-located Massachusetts Bay. Its marginality as a trading center did not arise out of hostility toward trade or lack of interest among its residents. Rather, location tamped down Plymouth's ability to become a foremost site of merchant activity: Rhode Island, Boston, and Salem all soon surpassed it in this sphere. Some Plymouth residents interested in pursuing a trading career, such as Allerton, moved to other locations. Many others remained to participate in regional economies, such as selling livestock to newly arrived settlers in Massachusetts. Later, Plymouth would join in the livestock trade beyond the region, especially in the West Indian islands. Never did anyone actively oppose these sorts of economic activities. Never was it the case that Plymouth planters, out of hostility to outsiders or fears that religion and commerce were incompatible, opposed trade and traders for their own sakes. Long before Boston became a leading center of Atlantic commerce, the first English arrivals in New England embraced trade (if not every trader) and tried to find profit in it.

GOD

DESPITE THE DIFFICULTIES of language and cultural differences, the new arrivals and the original people of southern New England engaged in theological discussions. The English, as Protestant Christians, explained their belief in one God, an all-powerful and distant deity who could alter the course of human affairs, and who did so to test and to punish. They also, somewhat contradictorily, mentioned a second figure: Satan or the Devil, who tempted Christians to sin. God and Satan represented the limits of the new residents' cast of spiritual characters. Unlike other European Christians, they ignored the possible intervention of others, holding no faith in aid offered by Mary, the earthly mother of Jesus Christ, or a host of saints, deceased Christians of deep faith whom Roman Catholics revered. Bringing these ideas to Native New England, the planters tried to understand how the residents' view related to the reality of the unseen. Edward Winslow decided that Natives had a vague idea of God, a distant creator figure whom they called Kiehtan, as well as an alarming intimacy with Satan, or Hobbamoqui, who concerned himself with their day-to-day affairs. After these exchanges, Winslow remained satisfied that he knew the truth both about the existence of God and Satan, and about how Native peoples mistook the situation with their only partial understanding. For their part, the original residents must have wondered whether the God Winslow spoke of was the same as Kiehtan—and if so why he bothered with daily needs. Native people found even stranger the idea that Hobbamoqui, who cured and otherwise cared for them, represented evil. In such incomplete exchanges, Native and English beliefs circulated in New England.[1]

For the planters, God affected their lives constantly. Seventeenth-century English people believed in divine providence, the idea that God shaped daily events, and they often cited what we might see as fortuitous happenings as part of divine design. Epidemics wiped out many of the region's inhabitants prior to the arrival of the *Mayflower,* a fact which numerous Europeans cited as reflecting God's care in clearing the land for their arrival.[2] According to *A Relation or Journall,* many aspects of their experience represented divine providence at work. God directed their course to "one of the most pleasant, most healthfull, and most fruitfull parts of the world." Finding (and taking) buried corn soon after their arrival offered another concrete example of God's care. When a musket blew apart without inflicting injury, or a teenager started a fire that did not spread, or armed Natives ran away rather than attacking, or sick people in a burning house full of gunpowder got out in time, all these averted disasters gave credence to the view that God watched over them.[3]

God concerned himself with all manner of events, according to the settlers. Edward Winslow gave God credit for the increase in the number of residents, which prepared them to withstand the "savages." Under the new conditions, should the region's residents decide to overcome Plymouth, doing so "will be more hard and difficult, in regard our number of men is increased, our towne better fortified, and our store better victualed."[4] Solidifying a new business partnership with London investors, William Bradford observed, "doubtless this was a great mercy of God unto us."[5] Reporting on an alleged assassination plot against Winslow, John Winthrop concurred that "God preserved him."[6] With God caring for them so assiduously, the settlers could confidently enter a potentially hazardous trade relationship, noting that God's providence had heretofore been good to them, and they had no reason "(save our sins)" to expect it to change.[7] For the Plymouth people, God busied himself with their epidemics, sailing voyages, firearms, population increase, assassination attempts, and even trade. Anything that concerned them might draw the attention of the deity as well.

They knew that their sins could change the outcome because God also meted out punishment. That idea lay behind the comment that their sins might cause trade to falter. Bradford, for one, thought anyone hostile to Plymouth itself risked God's anger. In his view, the Lord so firmly supported the settlement that its enemies needed to beware. His "Of Plimoth Plantation" frequently explained that God would judge anyone who opposed the undertaking. He described retribution against a seaman who abused the passengers on the way from England; against John Pierce, who tried to profit from their work through specious claims; and against John Lyford, who was guilty of sexual assault and denigrating the church. His kinsman, Nathaniel Morton, amplified Bradford's theme, expanding on that aspect of God's protection when he wrote his own account.

The men of early Plymouth were far from alone in expecting God to punish sins, which represented a common way to think about how God interacted with the world. A visiting ship's captain, Christopher Levett, cited God's potential anger as a reason to keep his wife. He described one particularly sinful and lazy migrant as justly dying, having done nothing to earn God's protection and much to deserve his wrath. When settlers arrived at Salem, the first party to launch the colony of Massachusetts Bay, they were soon consulting with Plymouth leaders about how to assuage God's anger as indicated in a high death rate among the migrants.[8] People in both Salem and Plymouth agreed that they ought to accept God's judgment and not become impatient with "such afflictions" that God visited upon them.[9]

Living in this world of reward and punishment, settlers tried to please God and avoid his ire. They struggled to figure out what God wanted and to comply with his wishes. In this project, they relied heavily on the scriptures, which they viewed as God's word. A very early assessment by a participant in the plantation judged that "Our company are for the most part very religious honest people; the word of God is sincerely taught us every Sabbath." As a result, he offered his opinion that nothing was lacking, at least nothing "a contented mind can here want."[10] Everyone agreed that a successful settlement had to observe the proper religious forms, even if they might disagree about what those forms entailed. As their London financial backers advised, their best course was to "walk close to God, being fervent and frequent in prayer, instruction, and doctrine, both openly and privately."[11] Bradford wrote A Dialogue in which he depicted young men eagerly seeking the guidance of their elders, while the elders routinely cited God's word as the ultimate source of authority. This fanciful account exactly reflected Bradford's ideal. Although gratified to learn that their community enjoyed a reputation as godly, Samuel Fuller warned that they had better live up to that reputation, "that it may be more than a name, or else it will do us no good."[12] Plymouth would succeed only if its inhabitants did right. Otherwise God would make sure they failed.

Given this high level of engagement with their God, these English people thought it their duty to alter the beliefs of the region's original residents. When writing to an English audience, Plymouth authors frequently noted the goal of converting the Indians, declaring it one of their purposes. Such was the case with the dedication to Edward Winslow's Good Newes, which noted the fact that "the Church of God being seated in sincerity" in the area held out hope for converting the "heathen."[13] Those investors who continued to back Plymouth over the years supported "their ends and intents," which they summarized as "the glory of our Lord Jesus Christ in the propaga-tion of His gospel and hope of gaining those poor savages to the knowledge of God."[14] References to the need to convert the Natives were as common as they were unfulfilled, not only in Plymouth but throughout the English settlements around the Atlantic.

This oft-repeated theme produced no serious or sustained effort at conversion in the first years. In general, theological discussions in-volved comparing beliefs rather than trying to persuade anyone to change those views. Exchanges with residents were limited by lan-guage mastery, since only a few Native people knew English initially and others on both sides only slowly picked up the new language. No English person on the *Mayflower* arrived able to speak an American language. Only in a few rare cases did English migrants arrive with indigenous language knowledge. Thomas Harriot, who did so, proved the difficulties involved: he arrived in Roanoke already conversant in a local dialect because he had lived in the household of Sir Walter Raleigh with two Native men for years. They taught him their lan-guage prior to sailing home with the settlers. In Roanoke, Harriot conversed with the inhabitants about their beliefs, leaving an impor-tant account of what he heard.[15] No one arriving in Plymouth was similarly prepared.

Even when language posed no barrier, the first arrivals made little effort. The local man with the greatest facility with English in 1620, Tisquantum, became an interpreter and adviser to the Plymouth com-munity. He spent most of his time with the settlers in the eighteen months before his death in 1622. Yet Bradford seemed almost sur-prised to note that as his death approached, Tisquantum described himself as "desiring the governor to pray for him that he might go to the Englishmen's God in Heaven."[16] Although he had been frequently in Plymouth in the company of Bradford, Winslow, and others, no reference survives to indicate that anyone conversed with him about his beliefs or tried to get him to embrace their own. When the English

This page from the 1619 Book of Common Prayer depicts Adam and Eve in the Garden of Eden surrounded by their family tree. While seemingly no one brought this book—which contained the liturgy of the Church of England—to Plymouth, its imagery nonetheless conveys the complex Christian theology which all English people did bring. The nature of the early communications between Native and English was incapable of conveying the wealth of complex ideas on either side.

made statements to Native people about their God, they tended to be straightforward references to what their God wanted of them. Captain Levett explained that his refusal to beat his wife arose out of his desire to please God, and some Plymouth men told a Native man that they could not accept a gift of possibly stolen tobacco for fear of being punished by God. Neither conversation involved directly urging their listeners to change their own behavior in these exchanges. They simply noted the way in which their understandings of sin and punishment guided their own actions.[17]

While direct missionary effort did not occur, some settlers did engage in exchanges that seemed to pit the two religious views against each other. When both the Natives and the settlers worried over a drought, Winslow was pleased to report that the Christians got results when the Native spiritual leader could not. After they held a community day of humiliation (including fasting and prayer), rains came and saved both Native and English crops. Winslow interpreted this as "showing the difference between their conjuration, and our invocation on the name of God."[18] Treating the two belief systems as dueling efforts to gain supernatural support, they asserted that their own faith better protected its followers. Such observations served as a sort of indirect effort to persuade, since a spiritual authority that could protect its followers was attractive to Natives and English Christians alike. If Christianity proved more effective, the Natives might eventually be convinced to adopt it. In the meantime, the timely rain after fervent prayer certainly reassured Winslow that his own religion was superior.

Mostly English Christians did not move beyond tentative efforts to understand Native belief. Some of them fell back on the idea that Natives had no religion, a view both Thomas Morton and one of the anonymous Plymouth men who contributed to *A Relation or Journall* (1621) expressed. Yet Morton—who resided in a nearby trading outpost and so encountered many of the same people as did the first

Plymouth residents—went on to describe aspects of the local belief system that seemed to contradict his general assessment. He clearly knew they adhered to what we today would recognize as a religion, but because it was not the same as his own, he was unwilling to label it as such. The author contributing to *A Relation or Journall* noted with surprise that despite a lack of awareness of God, the Natives were "very trusty" (that is, trustworthy). He believed that only fear of God's punishment made Christians good and wondered why someone lacking "knowledge of God" could behave well.[19]

What especially struck English observers was the fact that Native peoples looked to multiple sources of spiritual power, whereas Protestant Christians limited themselves to revering only God. English authors translated Native belief into a variation on (or misunderstanding of) the Christian cosmology. The Americans living in New England, rather than recognizing the single deity, acknowledged two, according to many English authors. The Church of England clergyman William Morrell declared that the locals worshipped two gods, an idea that not only Winslow but also Captain Levett and the Salem minister Francis Higginson repeated. Levett and Higginson both offered names for these figures that differed from what Winslow heard: they learned about Squanto (or Squantam) and Tanto (or Tantum).[20] Levett assumed that those spiritual leaders who dealt with Tanto, whom he equated with Satan, were witches. Making this equation, he placed the supernatural being and the religious system it represented in a recognizable context. When the English posited Native belief in two Gods, they revealed the depth of their misunderstanding and their own inability to reach across the cultural divide to comprehend a different belief system.

Just as the Natives wondered how to think about the Christian God within their own accustomed framework, the English could only understand Native belief through their own. Hence, they described Native belief in terms of heaven and hell, God and the Devil, and witches. God to the English meant guidance, punishment, and reward, with the ultimate reward being eternal salvation. Although they could hardly conceive of life outside this framework, confronting Native beliefs gave them a glimpse of a different view. On the Native side, more flexibility reigned. To their way of thinking, the insistence on a singular entity was unnecessarily limiting, and their initial impulse was to incorporate this seemingly new being into their own complex and populous spiritual world. If the English God proved powerful and effective, he would be worth knowing, but they were a long way from thinking that they needed to reject aid from all other beings as a result of learning about God.

Both Native peoples and English settlers changed as a result of exchanging their religious views. God was an English concept, not a Native one. Still, both groups held broadly analogous beliefs about how forces beyond human control shaped their lives. Over the centuries after 1620, Native peoples gradually came to terms with the English God, accepting the idea and making it their own. Plymouth conversations offered an early, tentative introduction on both sides to vastly different understandings. When English people wondered how Native goodness came about in the absence of the threat of divine punishment, their ideas about God were being challenged, just as were those ideas of the Natives who wondered how God fit into the world they knew.

TOBACCO

DURING THEIR FIRST YEAR in New England, the people of Plymouth allied with the Wampanoag leader Massasoit Ousamequin. The negotiations brought a Native encampment near to the newly constructed village and gave an opportunity for much interaction between the two. On the day after the negotiations, Massasoit sent to the village asking that some of the English come to visit him. Two men—Captain Miles Standish and Isaac Allerton—accepted the invitation. The anonymous author who described these events hinted that their willingness gave evidence of their bravery: they "went venturously." In the presence of "King" Massasoit, they received a welcome "after their manner," as well as a gift of "three or four ground Nuts, and some Tobacco." After the two men returned to Plymouth, the governor sent a gift of English peas, "which pleased them well."[1]

The exchange of Indian tobacco (and groundnuts) for English peas might seem to capture the respective spirits of English and Native cultures, each side bestowing items familiar to the giver and exotic to the recipient. Yet the tobacco that Standish and Allerton received was not an unfamiliar gift for the two men newly arrived in New England. Both knew the plant and quite likely had smoked it before landing on the American shores where it originated. Although an anonymous author who described the encounter made clear that on both sides the meeting brought wonders, tobacco did not fall into that category. The English author thought he needed to describe in detail the

Native complexion (like that of "our English gypsies") and attire. He also explained that the Wampanoag were equally interested in such novelties as a trumpet.[2] Yet tobacco proved one aspect of Native culture that the author felt no need to describe. As an English man—and quite possible one who had lived in Leiden for a time— he knew this American plant, and he seems to have expected his readers to know it too. Tobacco, a plant central to Native cultural practice, had also—over the previous decades—become firmly embedded in Western European culture.

An American plant, tobacco grew as far north as New England and as far south as the Caribbean islands and South America. In many locations, Native peoples used it for ceremonial purposes. When Massasoit shared tobacco, his action was of course sociable, but it also had a ritual component related to cementing an alliance. In that meeting, the English observers noted that Massasoit carried tobacco in a pouch on his person; they also observed that his people awaited his permission to partake. Hence, in this moment at least, no Native person casually smoked—or in the English term of the day, "drank"—tobacco; they waited until their leader invited them to do so.[3] As they described: "In his Attire little or nothing differing from the rest of his followers, only in a great Chain of white bone Beads about his neck, and at it behind his neck, hangs a little bag of Tobacco, which he drank and gave us to drink."[4] On other occasions, Native men offered tobacco as a way to make amends. When a party of English men journeying through the country encountered a former guide who had abandoned them earlier, the erstwhile guide tried to mend their relationship by sharing tobacco. They declined—believing the tobacco to have been stolen—but his gesture hinted at the symbolic use of the plant in sealing friendship.[5] On other occasions, Native peoples marked moments of reconciliation by sharing tobacco.[6]

Native peoples also used the plant for personal needs, possibly even for its appetite-suppressing qualities. The early accounts of

Plymouth—especially the *Relation or Journall* that recounted the events of the first year—mentioned tobacco frequently. Besides remarking on tobacco's symbolic purposes, the various narratives included in the *Relation* refer to tobacco use at other times. On a later, less formal visit to Massasoit, a group of Plymouth men sat with him smoking tobacco and discussing England. It was on this occasion that Massasoit learned that the widowed King James had not remarried, a revelation that caused the Native leader to marvel.[7] The English undertook that particular journey during a time of want, when the local population had no food reserves. Massasoit himself apologized for having little to give them, and the Native men with whom they traveled ate little, tightened their belts, and smoked tobacco.[8] For their part, the English found it excruciating to hike through the woods without food and tried to hurry home where their own stores could sustain them.

Tobacco, an integral part of Native cultural practice, also had a place in English experience by 1620 as well. English awareness of this American plant dated to the previous century when travelers encountered it and brought it to England. Sir Walter Raleigh—who encountered the plant on a voyage to the Americas—offers a famous case in point, but other seamen no doubt gained access to tobacco in their journeys as well. Its use was sufficiently widespread by 1604 that the new king, James I, authored a pamphlet against the "loathsome" custom, *A Counterblaste to Tobacco*. His efforts had no discernable effect on rising use. In fact, during the decade that followed, the Virginia Company hit on tobacco as an export crop, and by 1620 Virginia planters shipped a great deal of the plant to be consumed in England. By that time, tobacco had become a standard vice, to the point that Captain Levett, explaining why one prospective settler's efforts came to naught, declared that the man, "a base lazy fellow," had run through his funds in London before embarking by spending on wine, women, and tobacco.[9] At the same time, mariners and traders

This image, "The Landing of the Fathers at Plymouth, Dec. 22: 1620," communicates the challenges faced by the first arrivals. Its inscription refers to "the desert land." Far from a desert land—whether we understand that to mean empty or unproductive—New England included people (although no one that dressed as the figure depicted here) and the crops, like tobacco, that they grew.

from other European countries were similarly introducing the tobacco leaf to consumers. Leiden residents were familiar with it, as the local university was known for its tobacco-obsessed students.[10] Whether in England or in Leiden, many Plymouth residents would have been familiar with the plant before they arrived in America.

Tobacco was an established Atlantic commodity by the time Plymouth was founded. That people native to the Americas were its original users, that it had been introduced to Europe, and that it had become a desirable consumer good for many Western Europeans made it the first commodity from the Americas to be widely consumed elsewhere. In that regard, it anticipated other American goods like chocolate, which had long since been served as a beverage in Spain but which had yet to become a widely enjoyed drink in Europe more

generally. Unlike sugar or coffee, which would also become important crops grown in America for export to Europe, tobacco had in
common with chocolate the fact that it came originally from the
Americas: both were American plants that became transatlantic commodities. While it is likely that someone on the *Mayflower* brought
tobacco with them for their own use, the new arrivals in Plymouth
soon found themselves consuming the locally grown plant, first with
Indian hosts who shared and then by acquiring, and eventually
growing, the leaf for their own use. In an interesting contrast to other
commodities, the familiar plant no longer circulated as far as it once
had in order to fit into Plymouth consumption habits. The settlers
had come to tobacco, having already experienced it coming to them.

As with many innovations, the far-sighted Edward Winslow perceived that tobacco might become a New England export crop. In his
Good Newes from New England, he departed from his narrative of
events to include a chapter on the area's prospects. In it, he mentioned
that New England might in fact be an island, with the Hudson River
dividing it from the mainland. He then went on to describe the local
climate and the ubiquity of Native corn—"Indian Maize or Ginny-
Wheat"—as a staple of the residents' diet. He extolled the prospects
for a trade in furs and ended noting that tobacco might also offer a
modest hope of yielding profit.[11] The quality of New England tobacco
made it unlikely to compete with that grown in Virginia, and Winslow's
demur no doubt arose from that awareness. A later Plymouth law—
only briefly on the books before it was repealed—illegalized the import
of "foreign" tobacco, probably a reference to that grown farther south
in either Virginia or the English Caribbean colonies. Presumably
the law intended to keep local consumption confined to locally grown
product.

By that time, New England tobacco had become an object of local
consumption. While records of who consumed it, when, and how are
few, when Plymouth decided to regulate its consumption, the court

records revealed some answers both to how the leaf was used and how magistrates wanted to see it used. A law passed in 1638 focused on where it was smoked. The court objected that people were "taking Tobacco in a very uncivil manner openly in the Towne streets." They also expressed alarm that men smoked as they "pass upon the highways" as well as while at work "in the woods and fields." The problems that arose were described as twofold: the men neglected their labors with frequent smoke breaks; they also brought "great reproach" on the government. Why the latter was the case, the record did not state. In any event, the government imposed a fine on anyone found taking it in the outbuildings, highways, and fields, anywhere "he doth not dyne or eat his meat." As a concession to the inveterate smoker who needed a pipe of tobacco during his workday, the court agreed that a man working a mile or more away from home could enjoy the weed without punishment.[12] Clearly by this time, Plymouth residents consumed a great deal of tobacco. Soon the grand jury presented three men for ignoring the rule, but did not explain where the trio had imbibed or indeed whether they had been together at the time that they did so.[13] Jurors were not immune to the allure of tobacco either, and the courts eventually declared it illegal to smoke while sitting on a jury.[14]

Tobacco in Plymouth proved far more than an Atlantic commodity. In Native culture in New England as elsewhere, tobacco had ceremonial purposes but was also used medicinally and socially. Plymouth migrants entered a Native world in which tobacco had an established place. Local uses—the details of its place in Native New England—may have been unfamiliar but tobacco most assuredly was not. The European arrivals were familiar with this American commodity that was readily available in London and Leiden. In Plymouth, colonists quickly incorporated the plant into their regular routines, presumably growing it for personal use. No notable export market ever developed, nor is there any indication that New England tobacco was sufficiently prized to warrant sending it as a gift to any English correspondent.

Tobacco meant many things in Plymouth: used in ritual and medicine in Native communities, it became an object of consumption and contention among the English.

Even as tobacco became part of the European experience on both sides of the Atlantic, it continued to carry associations with America. Emmanuel Altham, Plymouth investor and occasional resident, gifted his brother with a tobacco pipe (or perhaps two) acquired in New England. In 1625, he wrote that he had entrusted to Edward Winslow, "an Indian tobacco pipe, being the first and rarest that ever I saw. I desire you keep it for my sake, it being a great king's pipe in this country." He also felt the need to apologize for the pipe's odor, noting "the pipe cannot be transformed to a better smell, for it doth stink exceedingly of Indian tobacco."[15] While not offering a ringing endorsement of either the local product or, for that matter, his gift, Altham still thought his brother should give Winslow some wine for his trouble. Altham's gift traded on the exoticism of an Indian king's tobacco pipe, a novelty item that his brother might be pleased to show off (in spite of its nasty odor). His brother might well have been a smoker already, as many English men had come to partake over the previous decades. In any event, the pipe referenced the connection to America that his brother's Plymouth business ventures and occasional visits created. Tobacco, both increasingly familiar and still decidedly American, bridged the Atlantic.

Tobacco would of course have a long history. It remains an important crop in some regions in North America, and it is increasingly derided for its addictive qualities and its deadly side effects. To this day, inveterate smokers like to partake after a meal, and those who give up tobacco often complain that they miss its appetite-suppressing qualities. Long before it became a multimillion-dollar industry and the subject of studies and lawsuits, tobacco had an important role in the English Atlantic. Tobacco reveals the transatlantic circulation of things as well as any item can.

4

SETTLING IN

ESCAPEES

A NEW ENGLAND

STOCKINGS

ESCAPEES

In 1624, the Reverend John Lyford arrived in Plymouth aboard the *Charity*. Traveling with a household that included his wife, children, and servants, Lyford arrived hoping that Plymouth offered an opportunity to escape his past. An educated man and an ordained minister, he expected the church to call him to serve. Having previously guided a Protestant church in Ireland, Lyford had the requisite experience to fill the post. At the very least, he sought employment as a teacher for the infant colony, and the Plymouth investors promised him, before he sailed, a salary for that work. Lyford came to join the small and rudimentary community, despite his educational attainments and lack of ties to the Leiden church, because he had seriously damaged his prospects at home. He fled Ireland and ultimately went to Plymouth to avoid the consequences of having raped a member of his congregation. Asked by a parishioner to examine the spiritual fitness of his prospective bride, Lyford took the opportunity of a private interview with the young woman to assault her. He then reported back to her intended husband that she was a fit companion. When the rape was revealed, Lyford lost his post. Returning first to England, he moved on to Plymouth ahead of the rumors about what he had done. Lyford was the first person known to have traveled to Plymouth to evade a sordid past, though the strategy would come in to play throughout English America.

Had Lyford made himself inconspicuous, he might have left the Irish incident behind. Instead, he quickly became embroiled in controversies with the Plymouth church and the town's leaders. After joining Plymouth's congregation, he quietly moved to gather other new arrivals into a rival church without the permission (or even at first the knowledge) of his fellow church members. He also tried to write, surreptitiously, to the investors to accuse the main body of settlers of various abuses. While his accusations were being mediated in London, Lyford's history of sexual assault came to light. His wife, Sarah, confided in her friends at Plymouth, among them a church deacon. She claimed that he lied to her before their marriage, denying that he had fathered a "bastard." Later, after their marriage rendered her powerless to object, he brought the little one into their home for her to raise. She also described how he repeatedly assaulted the serving maids, even "meddling with them" as these young women slept at the foot of the couple's bed.

When Lyford and his family were forced to leave Plymouth, Sarah expressed her great fear that God would punish the family for her husband's many sins. In particular she worried that she would fall into the hands of the Indians, "to be defiled by them as he had defiled other women."[1] With this fearful fantasy, Mistress Lyford revealed a great deal about herself. She feared Native peoples—despite the lack of any evidence that indigenous men were inclined to rape English women; she believed that God punished sin with suffering; and she felt that her husband's sin, for which she had already suffered, might be punished with torment meted out to his family members. Her comment exposed her fear and misunderstanding of the people among whom the Plymouth planters lived; her providentialism—the idea that God punished sin in this life with misfortune; and her society's patriarchal household organization, in which a man's dependents were thoroughly identified with him. While Mistress Lyford's fears proved unfounded—since the Natives never defiled her or any other woman in Plymouth—"her grief and sorrow of mind" at being shackled to this hypocritical rapist came through with stark clarity. Although Lyford proved unable to reform his ways or fully to escape the consequences of his crimes, his wife did eventually gain her freedom through his death in 1634. At that time, she returned to New England, married a local man, and lived in apparent peace. She lapsed into the obscurity appropriate to the well-behaved seventeenth-century woman.

Lyford's case was the most dramatic but not the only example of transatlantic travel being used to escape the consequences of misbehavior. Thomas Weston—an early supporter of Plymouth who had tried unsuccessfully to launch a rival trading outpost—visited the plantation in 1623. His recent attempt to establish a neighboring outpost at Wessagussett had collapsed, and his finances were in disarray. He traveled under an assumed name, fleeing his creditors in England. Despite complaining of the unexpected expenses they had incurred aiding Weston's people at Wessagussett, the Plymouth leaders assisted his next attempt to trade along the New England coast. He never repaid them. Subsequently, he ran afoul of Sir Ferdinando Gorges, a member of the Council for New England, and left for Virginia.[2]

Bradford worried about the influence of those who chose to migrate to escape shame at home, but who would necessarily follow their dissolute courses" after their arrival.[3] In this case he seemed not to be thinking of Weston, who had racked up additional unpaid debts in Plymouth after fleeing creditors in England. Rather, he feared immorality, such as that involving Sir Christopher Gardiner. Gardiner came to New England in 1630, apparently aiming to leave two wives behind and possibly to enjoy a new liaison with a third woman. His ostensible reason for the journey was to work as the silent agent of Sir Ferdinando Gorges of the Council for New England, which had the king's permission to colonize the region. Behind his role as

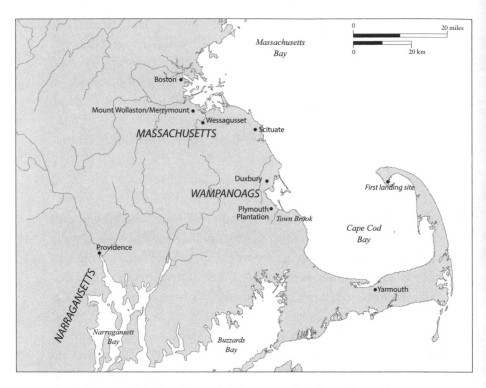

Plymouth was established on the site of a Wampanoag village (Patuxet), amid the Wampanoag people. The Narragansetts to the west and Massachusetts to the north also interacted with the newly arrived English. Eventually the English established other enclaves of rival traders (Wessagusset and Mount Wollaston / Merrymount) or of towns (Scituate, Duxbury, Yarmouth) that grew out of Plymouth.

Gorges's agent—and his possible intention of spying on Plymouth and the colonists who were just then setting up Massachusetts Bay Colony—Gardiner also reputedly hoped to get away with bigamy. Bradford and others were suspicious about his companion, "a comely young woman whom he called his cousin; but it was suspected that she, after the Italian manner, was his concubine."[4] John Winthrop, governor of Massachusetts, received a complaint from Gardiner's abandoned wives and moved to have him arrested. Once back in England, Gardiner did his best to create problems for New Englanders, working with another foe of Plymouth and Massachusetts, Thomas Morton. He seems to have escaped punishment in England for his bigamy (and the accusation that he stole from one of his wives), and his "cousin" went on to marry another and live in Maine.

Gardiner was not alone in hoping that crossing the Atlantic Ocean might permit him to hide illegal activities like multiple marriages and theft. Another man, a Mr. Fells, came to the region aboard the *Sparrowhawk* in 1627, with a maidservant who was also suspected to be his "concubine." When she proved to be pregnant, he attempted unsuccessfully to run away with her to avoid detection by the authorities and the punishment for unwed pregnancy. Upon his return, "they packed him away and those that belonged unto him by the first opportunity."[5] Bradford, ever anxious to protect the reputation of Plymouth, wanted nothing to do with the Gardiners and Fells.

The Plymouth authorities worried in one case that residents who had been accepted into the colony may have used transatlantic travel to flee responsibilities in England. As with Lyford, Gardiner, and Fells, this case involved sex. A married couple in Plymouth—Luce and Thomas Boardman—were found to have indulged in premarital sex while still in England, prior to their marriage and their migration. In the words of the court, they had been "living incontinently." For this crime, committed far from Plymouth, the magistrate ordered Thomas whipped "severely" while Luce was to be censured with some as yet undetermined penalty once she gave birth to the child she was then carrying.[6] Although a punishable offense, as the Boardmans learned, sex before marriage was not an unusual occurrence. The Plymouth court recorded numerous instances of couples caught and punished. These indiscretions came to light most often when a baby's birth occurred too soon after the wedding date. Routinely, the midwife who attended the birth would be asked if the early baby seemed to have been premature. If not, the couple was presumed guilty and punished with whipping or time in the stocks. The first case of an early birth uncovered in the new town of Duxbury earned the errant couple, Francis West and his new wife Margery, an order to sit in the stocks. The magistrates further ordered Francis to build the stocks for the town first, as part of his punishment.[7] Throughout New England and indeed colonial America more generally, marriages that started in this way, and couples who indulged in this transgression, faced no long-term consequences. The community accepted the Wests and other couples like them without pause, treating them— once they endured their punishment—just as they did others whose babies were born the requisite time after marriage.

The Boardmans faced possible censure because Thomas and Luce had left their first baby in London when they migrated to Plymouth. Someone, possibly one of the Boardmans, must have revealed the existence of the child. In a small community, the information circulated, and the magistrates learned that the pair had not only indulged in premarital sex but had left behind the resulting child. The authorities wanted assurances that the child "(so unlawfully begotten)" had not been abandoned but was receiving proper care. Besides punishing the couple—which involved the court handing down a sentence for a transgression committed before they resided in the colony and under its jurisdiction—the court ordered that Thomas post a bond for £80 until he was able to document their son's well-being. The court sought to learn whether the infraction stretched to child abandonment as well as the more routine sex before marriage.[8] What precisely had the couple sought to escape by migrating to Plymouth: just the stigma of Luce bearing a child out of wedlock or also the cost of the care of their first child?

These twin concerns—the commitment to punishing the sex itself and the need to see that any resulting child received the proper care—meant that the authorities deemed sex not followed by marriage a more serious problem. When two people who were not married and had no intention of marrying nevertheless produced a child, they introduced to the community a baby who had no male household head to assume financial responsibility for it. The magistrates' desire to learn whether Thomas Boardman had indeed arranged care for the baby left in London motivated their insistence that he post a bond until he could prove he had done so. Within Plymouth itself, when extramarital sex produced a child, the court forced the father to pay for the child's upbringing. When Stephen Hopkins's serving maid Dorothy Temple proved to be pregnant and the father was revealed to be the recently executed murderer Arthur Peach, the court faced a more difficult question: with Peach dead, who would pay for the baby's upkeep? The court decided that Hopkins, as Temple's master, had failed in his duty when a woman under his authority entered into an unlawful sexual relationship. Hopkins was outraged and at first refused to pay. The court held him in contempt, and he eventually raised the money by selling Temple's indenture to another master. In the case of the child of Temple and Peach, the court demonstrated a typical concern that the costs of a fatherless child be covered by a responsible party. Their concerns were predominantly financial, although the concern to ascertain whether Boardman had escaped his responsibility by abandoning his son suggested that they were also intent on having parents behave conscientiously.

Adultery brought out a different set of concerns. In the case of a married woman having sex with a man other than her husband, the resulting baby would be born into a marriage—which was generally considered ideal—but the couple's illicit union passed the financial responsibility unfairly on to the unrelated husband. In such a case, circumventing the financial problem appeared less significant than the need to punish the sinning pair and protect the cuckolded husband from being saddled with the expense of another man's child. Outrage over the act of adultery—an act explicitly forbidden in the sixth commandment—also dictated a harsher punishment. Initially the Plymouth court agreed that adultery would be punished by death, but that extreme penalty was never carried out. The colony faced few cases of adultery. In one instance that would seem particularly ripe for a harsh response, Mary Mendame, the wife of Robert, allegedly enticed the Native man Tinsin into having sex with her. The court did not order either partner executed. Still, her punishment did stand as one of the more unusual in the record book. The court ordered her whipped at the cart's tail—meaning she would be tied to the back of a cart that processed down the street as a constable followed behind laying on the whip—and it consigned her to wear a badge on her sleeve for as long as she lived in Plymouth. If she was caught without the badge, she was to be branded with a hot iron in the face. Tinsin, in contrast, was only whipped and made to stand "with a halter about his neck at the post." The magistrates gave him a lesser punishment because they believed that the sex resulted from "the allurement & enticement of the said Mary."[9] The badge—despite its association with New England history through *The Scarlet Letter* of Nathaniel Hawthorne's later imagining—was an uncommon and rather odd form of punishment. It certainly had no earlier precedent in Plymouth. Notably, the court record revealed no particular concern for the fact that the sex occurred between an Indian man and an English woman: the issue was her status as a woman married to another. Adultery, not cross-cultural sexual encounter, earned the ire of the court.

Given the dedication of its leaders when it came to ferreting out transgressions, Plymouth seems an unlikely place to go for those trying to hide from the consequences of their actions. Regardless of the vigilance of the authorities, New England did offer the advantage of a remote location. Distance removed people from the places where they and their crimes were well known. John Smith, writing to re-cruit prospective settlers to move to New England, assured his readers that "My purpose is not to persuade children from their parents; men from their wives; nor servants from their masters: only such as with free consent may be spared."[10] He anticipated the worry about escapees, although he envisioned those fleeing responsibilities rather than crimes. Weston, evading debt, fit Smith's pattern more than others. Lyford tried to leave behind the ignominy of rape, and Gardiner abandoned two wives and allegedly absconded with stolen jewelry. Even the Boardman couple attempted to slip into Plymouth without revealing that they had a son born before marriage. As many others in Plymouth could tell them, the magistrates were alert to the need to find and punish sins of a sexual nature, whether they violated marriage vows—as in the case of Mary and Tinsin; left a child behind—as did the Boardmans; or simply resulted in a birth too soon after the wedding. In the end, we may never know how many sexual transgressions went undetected and therefore unpunished in Plymouth.

Escape to Plymouth offered a refuge of a different sort for those who skirted the law or challenged social conventions. Escape could mean a blank slate, with a new start and a chance to live by society's rules, or it might mean simply avoiding punishment or debtors' prison with no aim of reform. Whether escapees came to make a fresh start in a law-abiding way or to continue their objectionable activities, crossing the Atlantic did not always protect them from their pasts.

A NEW ENGLAND

IN SEPTEMBER 1638, the government of New Plymouth impaneled a jury of twelve to try four men for robbery and murder. The jurors concluded that the accused had robbed a man they met in the highway. Assaulting him, they took his possessions—three coats of woolen cloth and wampum, beads made from a shell with various uses in Native communities, valued as a means of exchange among Europeans—and left him for dead. The victim managed to travel home before dying, there relating his tale to various people, including Roger Williams, a former Plymouth resident and founder of Rhode Island. One of his four assailants, Daniel Crosse, escaped before the trial. The court sentenced the others to death. In accordance with both English and Plymouth law, they were executed by hanging. William Bradford—who that year served as an assistant to Governor Thomas Prence—bemoaned the fact that this incident marked the second trial for murder since the founding of Plymouth eighteen years before.[1] The court case, however much it dismayed Bradford, demonstrated that Plymouth had indeed imported the forms of governance and justice of his native England. Trial by jury and treatment of murder as a capital offense both supported the assertion that Plymouth instituted governance "after the English form," as a Dutch visitor described it. The case nonetheless prompted some grumbling. No one objected on principle to death for murderers, a well-established and uncontroversial punishment. Rather "Some have thought it great severity, to Hang three English for one Indian."[2] The victim, Penowan-yanquis, was a Narragansett man.

The trial for the killing of Penowanyanquis showed observers that Plymouth would conduct business as an English outpost. The forms of justice—the trial and the sentence—reflected standard English practice. Before the trial, Plymouth and its larger neighbor, Massachusetts Bay, debated which colony held responsibility to punish the crime. Aware that the murder might spark retribution from the Narragansett, a powerful neighboring community, colonial leaders agreed that the transgression had to be addressed forcefully. Yet authorities in Massachusetts pushed the case to Plymouth, claiming that the crime's location—at Misquamsqueece (present day Seekonk, Massachu-setts)—put it within the smaller jurisdiction. Bradford later observed that subsequently the larger colony would reverse this geographical claim, asserting a right to the area based on its own land grant.[3] Even these debates over boundaries and jurisdiction reflected European ways of organizing society. Punishing Penowanyanquis's killers both protected settlers from retaliatory attack and demonstrated the legiti-macy of English practices. What made some planters grumble—one dead Indian for three dead English—aimed to prove the point that settler justice could be fair and impartial. Executing Thomas Jackson, Arthur Peach, and Richard Stinnings averted war, and at the same time it signaled that English institutions could serve everyone impar-tially. The trial formed one small part of the larger project of making New England on an English model.

The very name of "New England" heralded that project. John Smith (of early Virginia fame) bestowed that name four years before the first Plymouth settlers arrived. His *Description of New England* (1616) not only coined the phrase, it also included—in some copies of the book—a list of English place names for various locations along the coast. According to Smith, Prince Charles (then the heir to the throne and later Charles I) renamed the major river and two capes,

Becaufe the Booke was printed ere

the Prince his Highneffe had altered the names,
I intreate the Reader, perufe this fche-
dule; which will plainely fhew
him the correfpondence of
the old names to the
new.

The old names.	The new.	The old names.	The new.
Cape Cod	*Cape Iames*	*Sowocatuck*	*Ipfwitch*
	Milford haūe	*Bahana*	*Dartmouth*
Chawum	*Barwick*		*S indwich*
Accomack	*Plimouth*	*Aucocifcos Mount*	*Shooters hill*
Sagoquas	*Oxford*	*Aucocifco*	*The Bafe*
Maffachufets Mount	*Cheuit hill*	*Aumoughcawgen*	*Cambridge*
Maffachufets Riuer	*Charles Riuer*	*Kinebeck*	*Edenborough*
Totant	*Fawmouth*	*Sagadahock*	*Leeth*
A Country not difcouerd	*Briftow*	*Penmaquid*	*S. Iohnstowne*
Naemkeck	*Baftable*	*Monahigan*	*Barties Iles*
Cape Trabigzanda	*Cape Anne*	*Segocket*	*Norwich*
Aggawom	*Southhampton*	*Matinnack*	*Willowby's Iles*
Smiths Iles	*Smiths Iles*	*Metinnicut*	*Hoghton's Iles*
Paffataquack	*Hull*	*Mecadacut*	*Dunbarton*
Accominticus	*Bofton*	*Pennobfcot*	*Aborden*
Saffanowes Mount	*Snodon hill*	*Nusket*	*Lowmonds*

John Smith—best known for his sojourn in Virginia—wrote a detailed description of the
region he dubbed "New England." As part of his project of presenting the area as a great
prospect for English colonization, he gave English place names to various locations. He
claimed to have gotten Prince Charles (son of James I) to choose new names. Here he lists
earlier (usually but not always native) names and the corresponding English terms in *A
Description of New England*, 1616.

assigning names taken from members of the royal family. The cape already known to English sailors as Cape Cod for the plentiful fish in local waters he rechristened Cape James after his father. That new name did not catch on, but other royal referents—Cape Ann for his mother, Charles River for himself—endure. As Smith realized, naming laid claim to a place.

Previously—when England founded two charter companies to divide up the North American coast—each company was designated a Virginia company. One, set in London, had responsibility for the southern region, and it would become known as the Virginia Company, founding the colony of Virginia. The other, set in Plymouth, England, had charge of the northern coast (the area Smith renamed New England), but it never accomplished much. In fact, in the same year that the *Mayflower* sailed, that company was reorganized into the Council for New England, adopting the area's new name to distinguish it from the southern undertaking. The Council produced a promotional publication that cited Smith's naming, endorsing his efforts to reshape the northern region into a linguistically new England. Sir William Alexander soon published a different map, one that showed how elite men in England had hypothetically carved up the area, giving each man his own domain.[4] According to that way of thinking, English names would be followed by English overlords who owned the land and supplied men to work it. This quasi-feudal view of how to manage expansion did not prosper, as new arrivals paid little attention to Alexander's elites, who did less for the region's development than they might have. Smith's vision had more staying power, as the idea of creating English-style towns bearing the names of English places gradually conquered the landscape. Not all the names offered by Smith and the prince remained, but the project itself proved a success.

Plymouth Plantation may have been so named because of Smith's map. The planters apparently carried it and the place-name list on the initial voyage, and their town was founded in the general vicinity of the place marked as Plymouth. For those conscious of earlier English claims to the area, Plymouth had another resonance as well. The English investment company known as the Virginia Company of Plymouth theoretically held the territory, so the planters may have meant to reference the company that they hoped to approach for belated permission to set up on Cape Cod Bay. Plymouth chronicler Nathaniel Morton later offered a third explanation for the name's origins, stating that it honored the city from which they had sailed.[5] However Plymouth came to be so named—in a nod to Smith's map and Prince Charles's naming exercise, in reference to the company, or in memory of the English port city—the planters supported the effort to rename the landscape with English place names.

The naming scheme, from Smith's viewpoint, declared that the region was so similar to England itself that its new residents would be easily able to form it into a new England. He implied that settling in New England would allow English people to replicate their culture in every way, extending England across the Atlantic. Roger Cushman, writing of early Plymouth Plantation, which he had just visited, explained that New England (which he believed might be an island) was so called not just because of Smith's renaming project but also for its similarity to "England the Native soile of English-men."[6] Thomas Morton, an enemy to Plymouth planters with whom he rarely saw eye to eye on anything, nonetheless agreed in praising the region. In Morton's writing, he objected to the men who ran Plymouth but had nothing but complimentary observations about the location. Calling it "The New English Canaan" in a reference to the Old Testament idea of a promised land, he suggested that this promise would be fulfilled in New England.[7] In his view, all the land needed to deliver that promise was to rid it of the pesky Plymouth residents. For English people, then, this land would be a sort of paradise, offering refuge and comfort. Morton even accused the settlers of hiding New England's benefits in order to keep it to themselves.

Like all migrants, the people of Plymouth tried to create a new home that would seem familiar, one that would recreate not only legal institutions but also more basic aspects of life. They measured distance in the English mile. They brought English material culture and foods, built English-style houses, and wore English clothes. When explaining the appearance of the region's original inhabitants, they likened them to a familiar group in England: "they are of complexion like our English Gypsies."[8] Although they quickly learned to subsist on Indian corn, they longed—without notable success at first—to replace it with English grains. They introduced English livestock and poultry so they could eat those animals as well as eggs, milk, and cheese. All these introductions sought to recreate what was known, to make the land more like home. As they experimented with bringing the specifics of English cultural practices to New England, they tried to shape the place into something like what they had left behind. They hoped, in the arrogant terms proposed by William Morrell, "If Heavens grant these, to see here built I trust: An English Kingdom from this Indian dust."[9]

Those settlers who came from Leiden, in the Netherlands, may have been drawn by the opportunity to create a culture more like that of England than what they had known in Holland. According to a later account explaining the reasons for migration, one motive for leaving Leiden had been that their children had begun to assimilate to Dutch culture. The younger generation learned to speak Dutch and entered, as immigrant children eventually do, into the host culture. By moving to New England, their parents hoped to reclaim the English cultural heritage of their children and pass it on. In that respect, Smith's naming practice and the planters' goals (as described later by Nathaniel Morton) were entirely aligned. Although Smith did not much care for those who settled at Plymouth, they very much endorsed his project of a new England.

One of the great ironies, then, in the first years of Plymouth Plantation was that the Leiden migrants traded one foreign language and one foreign cultural context for another. Imagining they were going to a place where they could import English culture unchallenged, they nevertheless entered a world with its own languages and cultural traditions. The residents spoke variations of the Algonquian language. Unlike a handful of other North American visitors (such as Thomas Harriot of Roanoke), no one onboard the *Mayflower* had—as far as we know—learned a Native language in advance of sailing. Over time, a few settlers, particularly those who worked in the fur trade, learned—as Roger Williams put it—"to speak much Indian."[10] The prospect that migrants to Plymouth might learn a different second language rather than going back to using solely English seems not to have occurred to the residents of Leiden who chose migration in part to pull their children away from a foreign language and culture. Other settlers viewed with some suspicion those who mastered an indigenous language, especially if they thought this linguistic accomplishment had been facilitated by too-close contact with Native peoples. William Baker, one man whom Williams identified as having a facility with a local language, was also suspected of entering a sexual relationship with a Native woman. Cultural adaptation in Plymouth, as in Holland, dismayed many leading settlers (even Williams, who himself learned Native languages).

Language learning went the other way as well, a fact that did not bother the English. As is well known, the Plymouth planters found spoken English waiting for them in the persons of both Samoset and Tisquantum. Their writings communicate their sense of amazement when—after months of trying to make contact with the Native peoples—they were greeted by first one and then another English-speaking Native man. Samoset and especially Tisquantum (whose grasp on the language was superior) played important roles in facilitating interaction, although eventually the Plymouth planters realized that Tisquantum also had his own agenda, which did not always align with theirs. With time, communication between Native and newcomer became easier, as more people on both sides of the linguistic divide learned the others' language and the reliance on interpreters declined. Captain Christopher Levett found it quite gratifying that under the circumstances of huge variation in Native dialects and the increased presence of English people up and down the coast, English might serve as a sort of *lingua franca*. He reported that when a Native person from Maine and one from southern New England met, they spoke English as the only tongue they shared in common.[11] If "speaking Indian" revealed acculturation that the people of Plymouth greeted with mixed feelings, the fact that Native peoples learned English implied that the effort to make the region English was bearing fruit.

In remaking this section of North America as an English province, the leaders in Plymouth did not want to replicate England perfectly but rather hoped to avoid what they considered its worst features. Their aim, as Winslow summarized it, was to expand the king's "Dominions, by planting his loyal subjects in so healthful and hopeful a Country" as well as to achieve "the Church of God being seated in sincerity."[12] Setting up an English outpost in America might bring the best of both worlds: they could reaffirm English language and culture but retain control that would have been lost if they had simply returned to England.

At times, the plantation's leaders had to admit that they had fallen short. Bradford's pained reference to the second murder trial in as many decades signaled one area where Plymouth failed. These handful of murderers were not the only causes of embarrassment. Thomas Hunt, who had kidnapped various men off the coast some years before the Plymouth planters arrived, they renounced as "a worthless fellow of our Nation" and "a bad man." They asserted that "all the English that heard of it condemned him."[13] Thomas Morton—who enticed away other men's servants, drank with the Indians, and traded them guns for furs—appeared to be another failure to attract only the best. The thieves among Weston's men at Wessagussett they saw in similar terms. Bradford complained to the Council for New England, in 1627, of the "irregular living" in which some in the area indulged.[14] It might be, as Bradford feared, that the region attracted troublesome men. Yet some of the criticism might have masked real differences of opinion about what constituted Englishness. When Morton raised a maypole and staged a joyous—and alcohol fueled—community celebration, he hosted a festival popular in rural England. Bradford, Standish, and others saw Morton's community sinking into debauchery and crime, but that may have been a matter of interpretation, or so Morton tried to demonstrate when he published about their conflicts later. Murderers, maypoles, and men who not only spoke "Indian" but consorted with Native women gave the leaders of Plymouth pause: a new England it might have been, but not precisely the one they envisioned.

Still, the verdict on how English New England became during the first years in Plymouth was certainly not all negative. James Sherley, after more than a decade of investing in the plantation, gave Plymouth credit for getting the region off to a good start: "For had not you and we joined and continued together, New England might yet have been scarce known, I am persuaded; not so replenished and inhabited with honest English people as now it is."[15] Nathaniel Morton, like many younger colonists, looked back with admiration to the accomplishments of the first settlers. He declared "Our Fathers were English-men, which came over this great Ocean, and were ready to perish in this Wilderness."[16] This imagery of a wilderness that might overwhelm new arrivals but that could host Englishmen who transformed it offered a compelling memorial to the first generation's struggles. The truth lay somewhere between Smith's idea that the region simply awaited the arrival of English people to become a new England and Nathaniel Morton's vision of sacrifice and peril. With the right sort of people, transplanting a version of English culture—replete with institutions of justice and loyalty to monarchy—might succeed, more or less.

In later years the idea that New England was the model for early English America came to be so widely accepted that historians wrote as if it were the only English presence that mattered. Partly the elevation of New England arose because so many excellent records from the colonial period (like the ones on which this book is based) survive. In addition, New Englanders like George Bancroft wrote the first national histories to gain wide currency, and they emphasized New England's role. Finally, compared to the deep engagement of the southern colonies with slavery, New England chroniclers cultivated the (incorrect) impression that their region was never tainted by involvement in slavery or the slave trade. By creating a history that presented New England as quintessentially English and the United States as arising out of New England, nineteenth-century writers offered a version of the past that made the new nation admirable—and English. What began as a promotional device authored by John Smith developed into an idea that has had a significant impact on the region's self-understanding, not to mention the histories written about the early United States.

STOCKINGS

THOMAS HALLOWELL came before the Plymouth magistrates in 1638, in trouble for wearing red stockings. His offense was not that he sported overly flamboyant attire: despite the popular concept of drab early New Englanders, no law prevented the wearing of red stockings or any other article of clothing. Rather Hallowell offended by wearing clothing that his neighbors were certain he did not own. Virtually all clothes or the material to make them had to be imported. Given their scarcity—and the notable nature of red stockings— Hallowell's neighbors recognized his hosiery as an item he had never before worn. No one—not even the men who governed Plymouth— owned an extensive wardrobe. So, when Thomas Hallowell suddenly pulled on red stockings, his neighbors took note. When the grand jury met to list cases of possibly illegal activities that the court justices should consider, they presented Hallowell for his mysterious stockings. When he came before the court, the magistrates learned, probably from the offender himself, that he had indeed stolen his distinctive legwear. He had acquired them on a visit to Boston, where he had snatched them from a windowsill where they had been placed to dry. If Hallowell thought Boston was sufficiently far removed from Plymouth that his theft would never be discovered, he seriously miscalculated the observant nature of his acquaintances. Whatever he had hoped, the Plymouth authorities uncovered his theft and ordered him to take the ill-gotten article back to Boston.[1]

Shoes and clothes or the material to make them had to be imported into the plantation. Without a shoemaker, a tanner to process the leather, and herds of cattle to slaughter for hides, shoes came from Europe. Clothing came ready-made or in the form of cloth. Seventeenth-century English people most commonly wore wool (from sheep's fleece) and linen (from the flax plant). England raised multitudes of sheep and produced a great deal of wool cloth. The multi-stage process began with shearing the sheep, went through various steps preparing the wool, and then turned to the processes of carding (to separate out the fibers), spinning (to form the fibers into yarn), and knitting or weaving. In the absence of sheep, residents purchased yarn or woven cloth. The dye in Hallowell's stockings— assuming they were a vibrant red—came from the cochineal insect, which was harvested in Spanish America, powdered, and turned into dye used throughout Europe. Linen, from the flax plant, undergoes a multistep process required to transform the harvested stalks into a form that can be spun into thread and woven into cloth. Again, the absence of flax plants or the workers skilled in processing it meant that linen too was imported.

Clothing or the cloth to make it was in perpetually short supply. The investors in Plymouth wrote in 1624—in response to repeated requests for more clothes and more cloth—that they were sending cloth, hose, shoes, and leather.[2] When a French ship foundered on the shore two years later, Plymouth got a share of what was salvaged from the wreck. The residents were pleased to be able to use the unexpected windfall to pay off debts and "Get some clothing for the people."[3] A year later, when a Dutch merchant in neighboring New Netherland sought to entice Plymouth into a commercial relationship, he brought "cloth of three sorts and colors" as an inducement.[4] Clearly, although Plymouth lacked ready access to even the most basic articles of attire, it was becoming something of a crossroads, with a French ship and Dutch traders frequenting the neighborhood.

This family group walking down the lane of a modern recreation, Plimoth Plantation, is made up of reenactors who interpret Plymouth life for the public. Given the attention to detail at work in this living history museum, their attire offers a good approximation of the clothing that would have been worn in 1627. Although only his are visible, both the man and the woman would have worn stockings.

Early arrivals urged those who joined them later to come equipped with a "good store of clothes, and bedding."[5] Despite such advice, new arrivals often lacked essentials. A large contingent coming from Leiden in 1629 landed without many necessities, and had to be supplied with Kersey (a woolen cloth), linen, and sixty-six pairs of shoes, not to mention hats and other essentials.[6] Also in 1629, James Sherley, London merchant and supporter of the outpost, enclosed in his letter to William Bradford a pair of stockings that his own wife sent to Alice Bradford, as a "token."[7] A token it may have seemed in London, but in Plymouth, new stockings represented a rare and highly desirable item.

Given the need, masters who employed servants with long-term indentures faced a legal obligation to supply their servants with clothing. Contracts routinely guaranteed that those in service to a Plymouth master would be clothed adequately during their terms. At the end of their time, masters further promised to supply suits of apparel. Ideally, they left service with at least the basic clothing "competent for a servant," as Alice Grinder's contract with Isaac Allerton declared, or "fit for such a servant," according to William Shetle's agreement with Thomas Clarke.[8] Such agreements guaranteed that newly freed servants would not immediately need to find funds to buy clothes and shoes but would enter their new lives clad. Clothes as payment for years of labor might seem stingy to us, but the distance to supplies made these essential items hard to get and the need to acquire them a possible hardship for newly freed servants. In one odd case, the court sentenced Web Adey to be placed in service as a punishment for "disorderly living in idleness & nastiness." Rather than supply him with clothes, the master who took him on was relieved of that duty when the court ordered that Adey lease or sell his house in order to pay for proper apparel.[9] Perhaps Adey's "nastiness" extended to wearing inadequate clothing. In any event the magistrates believed Adey should take some responsibility for covering himself rather than relying entirely on his new master.

Clothing mattered not least because it served as a mark of European identity. To dress as befit a European demonstrated proper civility, which the first migrants believed important for signifying participation in European Christian society. Those who failed in this regard joined Web Adey in nastiness or suggested they had more in common with the Natives than with their fellow English people. When the settlers first arrived and began exploring the Cape Cod region, they dug up a grave. In it, to their surprise, they found a man and a child, the former wrapped in a hemp canvas of the sort used to make a ship's sails, with light hair still visible on his scalp and wearing "a pair of cloth breeches."[10] The breeches as much as the blond hair indicated European identity. They wondered how a blond man in

European attire came to be so respectfully buried in what appeared to be a Native-style grave. The solution to the mystery of the buried European man, if it was ever discovered, was not recorded. The incident clearly demonstrated, however, that clothes identified a European.

Clothes became a kind of currency. Once they began meeting with local leaders, the first residents of Plymouth Plantation gave them gifts of European clothing. Sending Samoset, a local man who spoke some English, to parlay with others, the Plymouth leaders attired him in "an hat, a pair of stockings and shoes, a shirt, and a piece of cloth to tie about his waist."[11] Perhaps Samoset, so attired, advertised what an alliance with the new arrivals might provide the residents in terms of material goods, or perhaps the unusual apparel simply marked him as their agent.

Native clothing, different as it was, earned repeated comment. Because English writers understood their own attire to be a sign of their social organization and cultural position, Plymouth people read Native attire as a clue about their society too. That the Native peoples did not arrive naked was a mark in their favor, since nudity (or scanty attire) signaled primitive social organization. The settlers would have known that Americans had been depicted as near-naked savages, so the fact that the people they encountered wore clothes spoke well. One description of an important early meeting noted that "On this day came again the Savage, and brought with him five other tall proper men, they had every man a Deer's skin on him, and the principal of them had a wild Cats skin, or such like on the one arm; they had most of them long hosen up to their groins, close made; and above their groins to their waist another leather, they were altogether like the Irish-trousers."[12] Embedded in this description was an English desire for furs, to which they hoped to gain access through trade. Hence the clothes worn interested them generally, but the materials drew their attention as prospective traders. Eventually the materials used to make Native clothing—especially pelts—would be shipped to England (there to be turned into more suitably European articles of attire, including hats), and the resulting income from the trade would be used to purchase many things, including English-style clothing.

The description's odd reference to Irish legwear pointed to another issue attached to clothing; it was seen as a useful indicator of larger cultural issues. At its most basic level, Irish trousers offered a more familiar example for the benefit of readers who tried to envision this first encounter. Unfamiliar with Native clothing, readers might be able to picture an article typically worn by the Irish. At the same time, the reference hinted at a way to judge the larger meaning of Native clothing. Similarity to the Irish also implied that the resident "savages" were not as civilized as the English but rather had more in common with the wild Irish. Wearing clothes at all was promising, but clothes like those of the Irish suggested limits to their achievements.

Given the shortage of European-style clothing in Plymouth, adopting Native attire might have seemed an obvious solution, except that its cultural meaning dissuaded most Plymouth people. When considering whether to employ Edward Ashley as a trader, Bradford noted that they worried because "though he had wit and ability enough to manage the business, yet some of them knew him to be a very profane young man, and he had for some time lived among the Indians as a savage and went naked amongst them and used their manners, in which time he got their languages." Ashley had not gone literally naked, but had in fact adopted Native attire. This move, along with using their manners and speaking their language, made him a better agent but also the object of some suspicion.[13]

In a relatively short time, it became more difficult to maintain sharp distinctions between Europeans and Americans on the matter of their clothing. Native peoples donned the clothing they received as gifts. An early account describes Massasoit, upon receiving a coat and a chain, "not a little proud to behold himself, and his men also to see their King so bravely attired."[14] On another occasion, a colonist described the impulse to clothe a Native man—while also evidencing an interest in his usual attire: "we cast a horseman's coat about him, for he was stark naked, only a leather about his waist, with a fringe about a span long, or a little more."[15] As the Plymouth planters created trading networks linking their town with Native hunters who brought beaver and otter pelts, woven cloth imported from Europe quickly entered the mix as an object of exchange. Edward Winslow conducted much of the trade for the Plymouth leadership cadre trying to pay off its debt to the investors, and he used cloth as a trade item with some success. When John Winthrop, Jr., later began trading along the Connecticut River, his agent bought cloth "such as master Winslow did buy here to truck with the Natives."[16] Although the original residents continued to wear deerskin and furs, as they had when the English first arrived, their clothing became intermixed with cloth imported from Europe. The circulation of clothing reached far into the Native interior, as beaver skins came down river and European cloth traveled upstream.

As clothing and shoes came from Europe at great expense, those who resided in Plymouth realized that making clothing locally would increase the supply and relieve some of the financial strain of acquiring it. One settler composed verse bemoaning how the expense of cloth made it out of reach for some consumers.

> But now most begin to get a store of sheep,
> That with their wool their bodies may be clad;
> In time of straits, when things cannot be had;
> For merchants keep the price of cloth so high,
> As many are not able the same to buy.
> And happy would it be for people here,
> If they could raise cloth for themselves to wear;

And if they do themselves hereto apply,
They would not be so low, nor some so high.[17]

As the verse declared, the cost of cloth was prohibitive for some, affordable only to those of high status. Better, the writer thought, to produce it locally so that all could be attired in proper European-style clothes. Local production would give residents greater access to clothes, although unexpected red stockings would still draw attention for some time.

The idea that clothes made the man—as the old proverb states—was fully endorsed by the people of Plymouth. To them, clothing had practical uses, covering the body to protect it from the elements, but also deep cultural meanings too. Clothes meant not just warmth and modesty; they also marked their wearer's social station and even, in the context of New England, their particular culture. While New England began to produce clothing and shoes as time passed, and the dearth of apparel that gave away Thomas Hallowell's act of theft lessened, area residents still sought English-made clothing as a sign of their civility and social status. In the years before the American Revolution, when Americans decided to boycott English goods to show their hostility to British policies, a movement arose to wear only locally made clothes. Patriotic women held ritual spinning bees in public spaces to show their support and wore only the homespun cloth produced locally. This politically inspired move to produce cloth had very different sources than the Plymouth poet's reasons for supporting local industry, but the symbolic nature of clothing spanned the decades.

5

CREATING
A COMMUNITY

SERVANTS

SEPARATISM

FURS

SERVANTS

In 1642, William Bradford worried that New England attracted particularly sinful people. Amidst news from Massachusetts of a sudden spate of cases of sexual "uncleanness," Plymouth uncovered its own act of "buggery." Thomas Granger (a sixteen- or seventeen-year-old servant in the Plymouth town of Duxbury) came before the court charged with having sex with animals. Magistrates in neighboring Massachusetts as well as Plymouth agreed that this act constituted a crime that deserved death. Although they were inspired by the Old Testament prohibition in Exodus 22:19 and Leviticus 20:15, they followed an elaborate ritual not described there, one that apparently had deep roots in European practice. The first phase of this punishment involved making Granger watch the slaughter of the animals in question.[1] The authorities, finding that "some of the sheep could not so well be known by his description of them," asked Granger to identify the specific animals. Once killed, the sheep were not consumed but were thrown into a pit—"no use made of any part of them." This ritual having been followed, the Plymouth executioner then hanged Granger. Afterward, Bradford and others wondered how it happened that Plymouth came to house such a dissolute individual. Considering Granger's case and that of another man who had previously made "some sodomitical attempts upon another," Bradford debated whether such sinful inclinations originated in England or had been picked up in New England. The answer appeared to be both, and Bradford dedicated a long passage to analyzing the problem.

He thought servants represented a special danger. Planters, overwhelmed by work and desperate for help, hired anyone they could. The plantation was thereby inundated with "many untoward servants." Those in England who supplied servants for the transatlantic trade cared little for the character of individual recruits. By the time Bradford wrote, a vigorous market in servants existed, as some of England's many unemployed put themselves forward as prospective servants. Others filed onto American-bound vessels in English ports straight from jails, where they had been held for vagrancy, theft, and other minor crimes. The rising demand for servants throughout the English Americas even led to a practice of kidnapping potential servants; plied with alcohol in port cities, they awoke from their stupor onboard ships sailing west. "And by this means the country became pestered with many unworthy persons who, being come over, crept into one place or other." Bradford strongly urged masters to take special care in determining "what servants they bring into their families."[2] Servants, in other words, were both essential and potentially dangerous.

Service was part of life in England as well as New England, but the institution of service altered as a result of the journey to American shores. In England, more people sought positions than there were places to fill. As a result, contracts were renewed yearly, which allowed masters latitude to replace unsatisfactory servants. Although some people spent many years—indeed in some cases their entire working lives—as servants unable to marry, the annual contract renewal allowed an escape to anyone who did not want to continue in service. Servants in England worked for wages as well as room and board. On rare occasions Plymouth servants signed similar, short-term contracts, for which they received wages. William Baker signed a contract with Richard Church, promising to work for seven months sawing boards. In payment, Church committed to give Baker four-teen bushels of corn and twelve shillings as well as to continue feeding him for one month after the contract expired. This contract bore some resemblance to the English practice of annual hiring, but it was the only one of its kind recorded in Plymouth in that decade.[3]

Far more common were longer terms, which made sense in a con-text of labor scarcity. Labor practices attempted to bind workers to masters, using the need to pay off the debt owed for the cost of the transatlantic passage. As Edward Winslow explained in his 1624 pub-lication, *Good Newes from New England*, a difference between living in London and in Plymouth Plantation was the work needed to sus-tain life in the latter. While the ready availability of land and of wood for fuel made New England appear a paradise, this bounty nonethe-less required labor to reap its benefits. Winslow observed of the pro-spective settler "as he shall have no rent to pay, so he must build his house before he have it, and peradventure may with more ease pay for this fuel here [in England], then cut and fetch it home, if he have not cattle to draw it there; though there is no scarcity, but rather too great plenty."[4] Winslow did not address the connection in this pas-sage, but his description implied the need for servants who could be made to do that work of cutting and fetching home. Servants, what-ever drawbacks they introduced, meant masters could escape or at least share the more gruelling work.

With servants in Plymouth fewer and harder to get, masters gen-erally sought to bind them with longer contracts, a desire often grat-ified by servants whose transatlantic travel left them in debt. Mas-ters got laborers, and migrants worked off the cost of their transport. The migrant servant left England, where he (or more rarely she) had been unable to find employment, and came into a labor-poor envi-ronment where masters eagerly sought their services. In England, only apprentices signed long indentures, with the understanding that their masters would teach them a skill over the term of their service. A few

Plymouth contracts—especially those signed with people already resident in the colony—worked like English apprentice indentures, promising skills training. For instance, Robert Barker "bound himself" to John Thorpe in order to learn the trade of carpenter. Unfortunately, Thorpe died before the contract was completed, and his widow turned over Barker's time to William Palmer, who worked as a "nailer" (that is, a maker of nails). Under the new agreement, Barker would learn that trade instead, and at the end of his time, in April 1637, Palmer owed him only two suits of apparel.[5]

Many other contracts make no mention of skills, promising the servant only something in payment at the end of the term, as well as bed and board during it. John Harmon, son of Edmund Harmon, a London tailor, contracted to work for Francis Cooke of New Plymouth for seven years; at the end of that period, he got apparel and corn.[6] William Snow traveled to Plymouth in 1637 in the company of his master, Richard Derby. In Plymouth, Snow agreed that his contract would be sold to Edward Dotey and extended from five to seven years. At the close of that time, Dotey owed Snow more than the usual freedom dues, as he was to receive "one lively cow calf of two months old, and eight bushels of Indian corn, and a sow pig of 2 or 3 months old, with two suits of apparel." The agreement also spelled out that Dotey was responsible for Snow's "meat, drink, & apparel during his term."[7] William Shetle agreed to work for Thomas Clarke for eleven years in exchange for two suits of clothes and eight bushels of corn.[8] One particularly odd case bound Mary Moorecock (with consent of her father-in-law—which might in this case mean stepfather) for nine years to husband and wife Richard and Pandora Sparrow. If the couple died before the nine years expired, Mary would be free. If she desired to marry before her term ended, two men with no stake in the agreement would arbitrate the terms of payment for her freedom.[9] This language of freedom revealed the difference between an annual servant contract and the sort of indentured servitude that many accepted in Plymouth. In Mary's case, it offered her a way to enter a household where she would be supported until she married, but the fact that she was to work nine years and needed to negotiate her freedom suggested a debt as well.

Masters and the magistrates held responsibility for regulating servants and the trade in them. No one was to take a person into service unless they knew that person was free to enter into such a contract. Especially after other colonies had been launched in the neighborhood, the potential for runaways' success grew. Trying to forestall the practice of fleeing in search of a new place in a different colony, Massachusetts and Plymouth created policies to ensure the return of absent servants.[10] In 1636, a man listed only as "Whitney" sat in the stocks for detaining another man's servant.[11] Stephen Hopkins and other men who had licenses to retail alcohol from their homes were ordered to keep local children and servants from lingering. When Hopkins nevertheless allowed a group of servants and others to drink and play shuffleboard on the Sabbath, the grand jury charged him.[12] The leaders of Plymouth loathed Thomas Morton, who founded a nearby trading post, for many reasons, but his transgressions began with tempting servants away from their masters. As Bradford and others worried, no master would ever be able to keep a servant if Morton entertained them without question, providing alcohol and other diversions. The long-time Plymouth governor flatly referred to the Morton affair as a servants' revolt.[13]

Unfortunately, we have no specific information about how servants for Plymouth were recruited. In the very early years, the investor group fitted out the ships and presumably collected servants from the pool of London laborers. Once the team of investors fell apart and only a few London merchants remained in partnership with Plymouth, those men may have carried on with finding prospective servants to dispatch to the settlement. Once Massachusetts Bay Colony was founded, many more ships and people traversed the Atlantic to

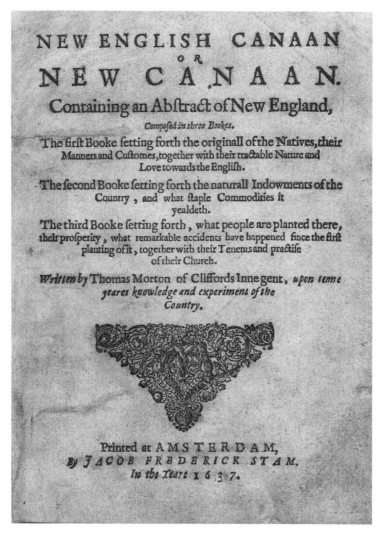

NEW ENGLISH CANAAN
OR
NEW CANAAN.

Containing an Abſtract of New England,

Compoſed in three Bookes.

The firſt Booke ſetting forth the originall of the Natives, their Manners and Cuſtomes, together with their tractable Nature and Love towards the Engliſh.

The ſecond Booke ſetting forth the naturall Indowments of the Country, and what ſtaple Commodities it yealdeth.

The third Booke ſetting forth, what people are planted there, their proſperity, what remarkable accidents have happened ſince the firſt planting of it, together with their Tenents and practiſe of their Church.

Written by Thomas Morton of Cliffords Inne gent, *upon tenne yeares knowledge and experiment of the Country.*

Printed at AMSTERDAM,
By JACOB FREDERICK STAM.
In the Teare 1 6 3 7.

Thomas Morton gathered other men's servants to live and work at his trading station, dubbed Merrymount. His feud with others in New England was partly behind his publication of this work, *New English Canaan*. Interestingly, despite the fact that he wanted to garner the support of the archbishop of Canterbury in England, his tract was published in Amsterdam. It is unclear whether his targets who lived in New England ever read the work.

New England, which brought more servants but also created competition for those who came. Complaints about the lack of servants
could be heard throughout New England by 1640. Such was even the
case in Massachusetts and Connecticut, where colonists had divided
the Pequot War captives, distributing enslaved Native women and
children into English households. (The men were generally sold to
other colonies.)

Not a party to that military engagement and therefore not included
in the distribution of slaves, Plymouth continued to look to Europe
for servants to solve its recruitment problems. Plymouth masters did
not in this period turn to the other option for fulfilling their labor
needs, African slaves. Their failure to tap the burgeoning transatlantic
slave trade arose from lack of opportunity rather than principled opposition to slavery. Later Plymouth households would include a
smattering of Africans purchased through that trade as well as a far
greater number of Native slaves, the latter drawn from the vanquished
in King Philip's War. In the first decades of the plantation, however,
residents relied solely on English servants.

In the first years, many male servants received land at the end of
their terms, giving them a foothold for establishing their own
households. The plantation government itself—or rather the Undertakers, who undertook the debt to the Adventurers and controlled
land distribution until the debt was paid—initially provided land
rights, parceling out unclaimed territory within Plymouth's bounds
to freed male servants. In 1636, they limited the amount the central
authority would give to each former servant to just five acres. In theory,
masters could offer more, but they would need to provide any additional acreage themselves. Finally, in 1639 the plantation stopped
giving land to ex-servants in payment of their dues, transferring responsibility for the necessary arrangements to masters themselves.
After 1639, masters had to hand over a portion of their own property in payment, the government declaring itself "free from any such

Covenant."[14] By this time, much of Plymouth's land had been distributed, and the Undertakers were nearing the end of their term of responsibility; soon, the debt to the Adventurers would be paid, and they would no longer manage the plantation's land.

Although centralized land distribution took the burden of funding servants partially off the shoulders of individual masters, the practice also led to some controversy. Undertakers increasingly gave away unclaimed lands in clusters to recently freed servants. These lands were usually in outlying locations newly opened to settlement. In 1633, the court ordered that ex-servants would get allotments in the new town of Scituate in the northern reaches of Plymouth's territory, or otherwise in "some other convenient place where it may be useful." Quite possibly, the magistrates' new focus on distributing Scituate land had been prompted by fears that Massachusetts Bay, recently founded to the north, would encroach on Plymouth's claim. If so, the magistrates' concerns were well founded, since the two governments would soon debate their respective boundaries. Having Plymouth people in Scituate supported the southern settlement's claim that the land there fell within its jurisdiction. Duxbury was also a site for these land distributions. Duxbury men complained that their town land was being given too often to unattached young men and former servants. Rather than the poor and the young, they wanted men able to settle—by which they meant those in a position to begin a household.

Servants posed no end of trouble to the masters and magistrates of Plymouth. Held to labor for a period of years, they occasionally absconded. In 1633, Thomas Brian ran from Samuel Eedy. Trying to escape his servitude, he became lost in the woods, where an unnamed "Indian" found him and returned him to Plymouth. The court ordered Brian whipped.[15] In another case that summer, William Mendloue fled, apparently to escape punishment for his attempted "uncleaness" with his master's maidservant. Penwatechet, identified as a Manomet Indian, returned him to his master, William Palmer,

and the court ordered Mendloue whipped as well. Possibly to separate Mendloue from the maid, Palmer sold his contract to Richard
Church. Late in the same decade, James Bishop absented himself
from his master Thomas Farrell for over a year. Once he was caught,
the court extended Bishop's term of service. With ready access to his
masters' property, James Till had been "purloining" corn as well as a
shirt from two different men who had held his contract. He had to
repay one of them, John Emerson, "in service, corn, or otherwise," according to the court's order. Widow Warren reported trouble with
her servant Thomas Williams. The court declared him guilty of "profane & blasphemous speeches against the majesty of God" made in
an argument with "his dame" who called on him to fear God. To their
shock and hers, "he answered, he neither feared God, nor the devil."
Although Governor Bradford urged "a bodily punishment" for these
offenses—whether branding or whipping, the record does not
state—the court only gave Williams a "reproof."[16]

Sex proved a particularly fraught issue with servants, who were
expected to avoid it. Although later commentary has accused New
Englanders of being sexually repressed and repressive, they in fact
enjoyed sex and thought it a generally positive and healthy aspect of
life. They did, however, aim to limit sexual activity to married, het-
erosexual couples. Sex before marriage, as long as the couple married
prior to any resulting child's birth, was punished, but only moder
ately. Sex in other circumstances was forbidden: certainly when it involved animals, as in the case of Thomas Granger, but also if it occurred between unmarried people, those of the same sex, or those
who were already married to other individuals. All of these forms of
sexual activity were punished, and in all save the case of premarital
sex, death was a possible penalty. Unable to marry, servants were
forbidden to have sex. Marriage required having a household and
resources of one's own, which servants lacked. The prohibition
meant that servants were expected to endure an extended period of

abstinence. Servant contracts lasted as long as eleven years in some cases, while seven years was common. Hence Plymouth housed many teenagers and young adults who were expected to be chaste, potentially over a term of service that could last years.

As a result, servants frequently courted trouble by indulging anyway. Thomas Morton recruited runaway servants with offers of freedom and alcohol, but also—Bradford and others thought—the opportunity to have sex with Native women. In August 1637, two men—John Alexander and Thomas Roberts—came before the court guilty of "lewd behavior and unclean carriage," not with each other but instead toward a serving woman. One of them, deemed the more culpable, was whipped, branded, and banished. The other—a servant—was ordered whipped and returned to his master to finish his time. He, however, was disqualified from receiving land in Plymouth after his term expired, unless he proved deserving based on subsequent good behavior.[17] The woman went unpunished, since the court apparently saw her as a victim rather than a willing participant. Servant Dorothy Temple and Arthur Peach, who was not a servant, had sex that may have been consensual. His execution for another crime left Dorothy, then pregnant, to deal with the consequences alone.[18] Servants, whether sexually active themselves or unwillingly targeted by others, often came before the court over sex.

In Plymouth, service underwent a process of degradation, a fact that put Plymouth in company with other Atlantic locations. In contrast to England, where servants worked for wages on annual contracts or else signed for a longer period with masters who committed to train them in a skilled trade, in the Plymouth setting individuals worked for long periods without respite and with nominal instruction. People who went into service overwhelmingly used that option to pay off a debt, usually one they incurred getting to Plymouth in the first place. Having already gained the benefit of their transportation, they received less and served long terms. Many people who crossed the Atlantic from Europe did so with financial obligations hanging over them, and they had to work for another before they could begin a life for themselves. Their circumstances—especially in a place like Plymouth—were vastly better than those of enslaved people from Africa, who had no say in their transportation and no promise of freedom. But, at least for a time, Plymouth servants too were not free. Their penchant for running away indicated as much.

Sir William Alexander bemoaned the idea that planters would be beholden to investors for the funds to journey to New England. In *An Encouragement to Colonies,* he decried an English financing practice that forced the planters to work as servants to their investors rather than as "Fathers providing for their Family and Posterity."[19] In his view, Plymouth leaders Bradford, Winslow, and the rest—the Undertakers—also suffered under a sort of servitude, laboring for over two decades to pay off the obligation to investors. Those same men also held the position of master and of magistrate, commanding labor, controlling land distribution, and deciding the fates of others. Had planters taken Alexander's observations to heart and compared their difficulties to those of their servants, they might have understood the resentment of servants who ran away and entered into forbidden sexual liaisons.

Although enslaved laborers would eventually work in the plantation, servants remained an important source of labor in Plymouth and many other locations. In 1620, the transatlantic slave trade was already exactly a century old, but ships carrying enslaved Africans did not visit such small, poor ports as Plymouth. Slave ships followed demand (of which there was plenty in Plymouth) but also potential for profit (which Plymouth decidedly could not provide). Native peoples entered the ranks of the enslaved too, usually after wars that periodically rocked the region. Plymouth did not receive any of the captives taken in the first war, the Pequot War in the 1630s, but it did after King Philip's War in the 1670s. On one occasion late in the history of Plymouth Plantation, the court sentenced Thomas Wappatucke to perpetual servitude after he was found guilty of burglary; this extreme penalty was never meted out to an English thief.[20] Service for English transplants could be onerous, but none of them faced perpetual service. In the absence of a sufficient supply of potential slaves, Plymouth largely continued to rely on servants with temporary terms. Like slavery, these indenture contracts, as they played out in America, represented a new variation on older practices for organizing and even coercing labor.

SEPARATISM

EARLY IN 1625, William Bradford, Isaac Allerton, William Brewster, and "the rest of the general society of Plymouth in New England" received a letter. Written by four of the many investors who had first funded the new plantation, the letter announced that the group—known as "Adventurers" for having adventured (or invested) their money—had dissolved. The planters learned that they could no longer rely on the financial backing of this group. Their four correspondents communicated their view of the situation: the other men withdrew largely because they had no more money to invest and were disappointed by the returns they had received, but they claimed to have done so for other reasons. The majority had declared that the settlers were "Brownists," by which they meant followers of Robert Browne, a man infamous for supposedly urging the utter rejection of the Church of England. According to the disgruntled majority, the Plymouth people condemned every church but their own and dismissed anyone who did not follow their narrow way. In addition, the letter went on, their critics thought them "contentious, cruel, and hard hearted." They alleged that the Plymouth planters only cared for those who agreed with them in matters "both civil and religious," and treated poorly those who "jump not with you."[1] The men who described these criticisms did not agree, believing instead that the Plymouth people were neither Brownists nor cruel. They did, however, advise their friends to avoid giving offense that could elicit such criticisms. James

Sherley and the letter's other authors had decided to stick with Plymouth and do what they could to help, even as the majority of investors abandoned the enterprise.

The charge of being "Brownists"—or separatists—followed the Plymouth Plantation through its history, with its enemies and detractors making the accusation and the planters themselves denying the claim. Robert Browne had briefly advocated sidestepping the Church of England if it refused to be reformed. In some important writings, Browne responded to the frustration that some reformers felt with the English Church by advocating that they simply make the changes they sought in their local churches, without permission if necessary. His views—published in the 1580s—were controversial, and his name became associated with the idea of complete rejection of the Church of England. The use of his name continued even though he soon renounced his ideas. Those who embraced separation as a way to achieve reform became known as Brownists or separatists. Plymouth's enemies smeared their church with this accusation, using the "scandalous manner of the Brownists" as a way to discredit it and, in the case of the investors, to back out of a financial arrangement.[2]

Numerous detractors attacked Plymouth as Brownist. When making the case against the Plymouth church in England, the disgraced clergyman John Lyford emphasized this criticism, alleging that the church had demanded that he renounce the Church of England and that they had disliked him for his refusal to do so. (No evidence exists to corroborate Lyford's claims, which appear to be at least an exaggeration and perhaps an outright lie.) John Smith, the early Virginia colonist who eagerly observed the establishment of English settlements in New England, referred routinely to the Plymouth settlers as Brownists. He also erroneously believed that the Massachusetts government was praiseworthy for blocking all "discontented Brownists, Anabaptists, Papists, Puritans, Separatists, and such factious Humorists" from its settlement. He asserted that if John Winthrop found any Brownists in Massachusetts, he packed them off to neighboring Plymouth to keep his own colony orthodox. Yet Smith also admired the Plymouth people, who "by accident, ignorance, and willfulness, have endured with a wonderful patience, many losses and extremities."[3] Thomas Morton—briefly Plymouth's neighbor and consistently its critic—had nothing good to say of either Plymouth or Massachusetts after he tangled with the authorities in both governments. Back in England to campaign against them, he scorned both as Brownists and separatists.[4] All these men used the term to insult and undermine.

The accusation of being a separatist could have political consequences. In 1630s England, Charles I pursued a policy of religious repression, forcing conformity to a narrow definition of what it meant to be a loyal member of the Church of England and punishing those who refused. Charles appointed Archbishop William Laud to put this policy into effect. Those who attacked Plymouth appealed to Laud's hostility toward religious dissent. When they characterized the plantation as separatist, they implied it was a stronghold of disloyalty and radicalism. Morton found an ally in Sir Ferdinando Gorges, who sought an appointment as governor general over all New England. It behooved both Morton and Gorges to attack the New England colonies, since they hoped to encourage Laud to send Gorges to discipline them. For this reason, Morton emphasized the hostility of the Plymouth planters to the Church, even suggesting that of all the many things he had done to enrage his neighbors it was his support for the Church of England that most upset them. None of the Plymouth records—even those private writings like Bradford's narrative—ever mentioned Morton's alleged dedication to using the Church's Book of Common Prayer, which suggests that it was not his purported attachment to the Church of England and its liturgy that set them against him. Casting himself as a very unlikely defender of the Church, Morton castigated the Plymouth people. Laud used

Morton's information to present Plymouth's agent Edward Winslow as a rigid separatist and got him thrown into prison for seventeen weeks as a result.[5] To be a "Brownist" was to court condemnation and even, in special circumstances, imprisonment.

The Plymouth leaders denied that they were "rigid" separatists. William Bradford explained the history of the church that gave birth to Plymouth in his "Of Plimoth Plantation." Some Christians in the town of Scrooby, in Nottinghamshire, followed Browne's advice, worshipping as they pleased rather than adhering to the practices dictated by the Church. Later, they chose to remove to the Netherlands with the aim of forming their own church. Once in Leiden, however, the church they gathered pursued a less rigid form of separation, and their pastor, John Robinson, eventually concluded that limited relations with those of the established English Church were acceptable. These principles, as laid out by Robinson, guided those of his flock who migrated to Plymouth. Although Americans think of the Plymouth migrants as coming to New England for religious freedom, those who left Leiden already enjoyed that freedom. What united all those who came to Plymouth, whether from Leiden or England, was a general commitment to Reformed Protestantism. They were not united by a desire for separation, and that principle never became an acknowledged basis for their church.

On various measures of strict separation, Plymouth failed. One measure—requiring a minister to renounce any previous ordination at the hands of the bishops of the Church of England in order to serve them—Plymouth never required. Roger Williams, who served the church briefly, advocated for such a renunciation but could not gain the support of his Plymouth congregation for the policy. The church did require a prospective minister to accept that he did not become their pastor as a result of an appointment from a bishop but rather when the church itself called him to the post. On a second measure of separatism, the Plymouth church took a similarly mild stance. Following the dictates of John Robinson, they agreed that they could enter into fellowship with Church of England members through such actions as listening to one of its clergyman preach, although the occasion did not arise in Plymouth. Neither of these policies—seeing no need to renounce the Church or avoid its clergy—were consistent with strict separatism. When their enemies described them as rigidly separating, they mischaracterized Plymouth's position and sometimes even lied about its practices. For instance, Lyford claimed that he had been promised the post of pastor (which all parties denied) and that he had been blocked from taking up the duties because he would not renounce his episcopal ordination. In fact, he was never offered the post. Thomas Morton did much to promote Lyford's allegations, falsely describing the situation so as to anger Archbishop Laud.[6]

In defending themselves against such accusations, the Plymouth people walked a fine line. They flatly denied that their church order was radical in the way that their detractors claimed, instead presenting themselves as dedicated to the tenets of Reformed Protantism. Their critics asserted that they had lied in stating before they migrated that they adhered to the version of Reformed Protestantism advo cated by French Huguenots, an accusation which church leaders in Plymouth rejected. They instead asserted that "we both hold and practice the discipline of the French and other reformed churches, as they have published the same in the Harmony of Confessions." The Harmony was a 1581 effort to lay out a shared faith among all Protestants. At the same time, Plymouth's leaders refused to swear that they would follow "the French discipline in every circumstance," because they believed all Christians needed the liberty to follow Christ alone, and to consider for themselves "the infallible Word of God, and pure Testament of Christ . . . as the only rule and pattern."[7] They even taught that bishops—assuming they functioned as described in the New Testament (which the too-powerful Church of

England bishops did not)—were acceptable. Willing to accept bishops in theory, they argued that bishops ought not to be considered spiritual lords with "sole authority, power, and government over the churches."[8]

If objecting to any aspect of the Church of England made one a separatist—as some critics claimed—then the Plymouth church (along with the other churches founded in New England, not to mention many parishioners worshipping in English churches) were guilty as charged. The Plymouth people preferred a more refined definition: rigid separatism required that separatists renounce the established church and its practices. They asserted that differing with the church was acceptable, but only up to a point. Roger Williams, when he pushed the church in Salem, Massachusetts, to take a strongly separatist stance, departed not only from the prevailing practice in Massachusetts Bay Colony but also from that in Plymouth Plantation, where he had recently given up his post as minister over just such differences. Hence Nathaniel Morton, Bradford's nephew, using the late governor's own account and other information to compose a history of early New England, deemed Roger Williams "a rigid separatist." Morton placed Williams outside New England mainstream opinion and Plymouth as well as the colony of Massachusetts within that mainstream.[9]

Nathaniel Morton's characterization of the Plymouth church as closely allied with the region's other churches was not far from the mark. The well-known prehistory of the Plymouth church—its start in England, its dramatic migration to Holland, and its collective decision to migrate to America—treats the experience of Plymouth as unique and suggests that its religious orientation differed from that of other reform-minded Christians in England who would migrate directly to New England without an intervening stay in Holland. That impression masked similarities that bound together most of the English Christians who came to New England, not to mention others who migrated to other colonial regions. Despite the way Bradford narrated the story of Plymouth as moving from Scrooby to Leiden to New England, very few residents of the plantation actually experienced that trajectory. Most people in Plymouth by 1640 had no connection—personal or familial—to the Leiden church. They came instead from parish churches in England. Of those who migrated from Leiden, only a few had been in Scrooby. The arc that Bradford gave the story followed the experiences of the church elder William Brewster and a few others. That story did not capture the dominant experience of those who peopled Plymouth. Brewster, who served as the church's sole leader for almost a decade, maintained the link to Leiden and Scrooby. Yet that history did little to create a worship experience that separated the church in Plymouth from those churches founded nearby, beginning with Salem in 1629. Separatist roots or not, no New England church used the Book of Common Prayer initially, and every church called its minister to serve without making him renounce any episcopal ordination he had previously accepted. Plymouth's first minister (hired only after migration into Massachusetts started to bring clergy to the region) may have chosen Plymouth as more amenable to his separatist inclination—as some historians have suggested—but his experience as a clergyman in Plymouth or in Salem would have been largely indistinguishable.

The supposed separatism of Plymouth Plantation has been overemphasized. William Bradford's great account of the plantation's origins—an incomplete English Reformation and a refugee church in Holland—goes a long way toward explaining why that is so. The insults that Bradford's enemies hurled at the plantation helped too. Yet the commitment to separatism as a political principle became less pressing even before some of the Leiden church members migrated to Plymouth. As an independent English church in Holland, Robinson's congregation enjoyed the freedom to worship as they chose without having to consider their relation to the Church of England.

Under those freer circumstances, Robinson increasingly counseled moderation, instructing church members that it was acceptable to treat members of the Church of England as brethren rather than to emphasize their differences. In that regard, they became much like any reform-minded member of a parish church in England who worshipped within the church but at the same time sought out godly preaching and hoped to see the established church become more vigorous in its prosecution of sinners. Those reform-minded Christians who stayed in England found a way to make their peace with the Church of England until Archbishop Laud began to suppress godly preaching and to enforce conformity. Whether they migrated directly from England to live in Massachusetts or Plymouth, they found in both places churches that suited their views. Plymouth's separatism became an origin story—part of the heroic history of (some of) the first settlers' past. Separatism was not, however, a directive for organization of their church. The early Leiden history did not set Plymouth on a path that divided it from the region's other churches in any important way.

In 1641, James Sherley wrote to Bradford, crowing that the people of Plymouth (and elsewhere in New England) could "return to your Native country again and have such freedom and liberty as the Word of God proscribes." Interestingly, at least one Plymouth leader would take advantage of this changed religious situation: Winslow returned to England on business and remained to support the revolution unfolding there. Sherley expressed his joy that the bishops of the Church of England "were never so near a downfall as now." A longtime ally and supporter of Plymouth, Sherley had never embraced separatism. He had maintained his investment in the colony when others decamped, and he had defended his friends against accusation that they were rigid separatists. He had remained in England and worshipped there, despite what he saw as the bishops' "popish and Machiavellian plots and projects."[10] The common ground between him

Plymouth planters' religious commitment became important to the understanding of the United States' colonial heritage, so much so that Congress commissioned Robert Weir to paint this imaginative scene for the U.S. Capitol building in 1836. Subsequently, the Pilgrim Society commissioned another artist, Edgar Parker, to reproduce the image, *Embarkation of the Pilgrims* (1875), for its own collection. The artist imagines a rather well-dressed group of prospective migrants taking over the ship's deck to hold a religious service prior to the departure from Holland to England.

and his friend Bradford demonstrated how little the historic separatism of the Scrooby church mattered. Far more important, both men knew, was the freedom to practice as they saw fit. They agreed that it did not matter whether Christian liberty had been achieved through separation and migration, or through perseverance in the face of Machiavellian and overly powerful bishops.

Thinking about separatism gets us into the minutiae of religious debates unfamiliar to most modern Americans. Although historians and scholars of religion might care whether and to what extent the Plymouth church was separatist, for the rest of us such disagreements only matter as a general indication that these people were persecuted for their religion. Accepting the idea that the *Mayflower* passengers came to practice their religion, we fail to consider the details of that religion. What set the Plymouth people apart was less a fundamentally different faith as the perception—based on the fact that some in their church fled to Leiden—that they were religious rebels. Their enemies exploited that view, certainly, but they did so by exaggerating and misrepresenting. Separatism was an idea that circulated, but less because the planters brought it with them and more because their detractors used it to renege on financial obligations or to avenge a wrong they felt had been done to them.

FURS

In 1634, William Bradford reported "the saddest thing that befell them since they came," a double murder involving a Plymouth man. John Hocking, sent by two English noblemen (Lord Saye and Sele and Lord Brooke) to trade in the Kennebec region, intruded on a Plymouth claim. He traveled upriver beyond Plymouth's trading station, intent on intercepting any Native hunters who were then heading downriver with furs. The men stationed at the Kennebec outpost followed him to put a stop to his scheme. An altercation ensued. John Howland, the leader of the Plymouth station, ordered three men to take a canoe alongside Hocking's ship, to cut his anchor cables so that his vessel would drift downstream. To stop them from completing their task, Hocking shot and killed Moses Talbot, one of the three. A friend of Talbot's "(which loved him well)" then killed Hocking. Bradford expressed great dismay that Plymouth was implicated in these deaths, all the more so because the fighting occurred between English men rather than with the French, who also menaced the trade. That Hocking was employed by noble lords complicated matters, creating the potential for a political crisis. The men who had sent Hocking to New England declared "that howsoever they might have sent a man of war [meaning a private ship fitted out to wage war], to beat down the house at Kennebec for the death of Hocking," they would agree to a mediated settlement instead.[1] Massachusetts

Bay oversaw the negotiations, which concluded that Hocking had caused his own death by firing the first shot.[2]

That men killed over rights to the fur trade demonstrated the high value Europeans placed on the acquisition of pelts. As the Plymouth men reasoned, "now was the season for trade to come down"— meaning that hunters would be bringing furs downriver—and if they allowed a rival trader access to an upriver location, he would intercept the supplies of beaver and "take it from them," so that they would lose their investment.[3] Plymouth Plantation desperately wanted access to furs, even if its leaders concluded that killing to maintain it went too far.

Furs—or skins as they were often called—appeared to be one locally available item that could be readily turned into money. Even before settlement had begun, John Smith identified furs and fish as the best prospects for New England's economic future.[4] Although he was particularly enamored of fish, he also noted his hopes for furs. He advised that the English drive the French out of the region in order to crush the competition, since their rivals often "afford them better" trading terms.[5] When the Plymouth men finally met some Native inhabitants—after months of wary glimpses and near encounters— they carefully noted what furs the Natives wore.[6] With alacrity, they distributed a few gifts and asked to establish a trade in pelts. After that, everywhere the Plymouth men traveled around the region, they greeted all new peoples with questions about furs.

Animal pelts became the symbol of Plymouth's desire. When meeting an elderly woman whose three sons had been among those kidnapped (along with Tisquantum) by the notorious Thomas Hunt, the settlers took pains to dissociate themselves from Hunt's activities. They used their hankering for furs as a measure of their disdain for Hunt's actions toward the Natives he encountered: "we would not offer them any such injury, though it would gain us all the skins in the Country."[7] On a journey through the countryside, they met numerous

"Sachems, or petty Governors" and joined in gambling games. Tellingly, what the Native gamers sought were metal knives to replace the
bone cutting tools they made; what the English winners desired were
furs.[8] Getting animal pelts, which they had little facility for acquiring
on their own, required relations with skilled and wide-ranging Native
hunters.

Plymouth shared with every new settlement the need to generate
income. Across the Atlantic basin, choices were basically two: extract
or grow something that could find a market. The Spanish, the first
Europeans in the Americas, took mountains of mineral wealth. The
English never found mines of any note—although they kept searching.
The first success the English gained came instead via a plant: tobacco.
Planters in Virginia learned to cultivate this Native crop, tapped a
growing market, and grabbed more land in order to increase their
acreage. Although New England also supported tobacco cultivation
and Natives grew it for their own use, the Plymouth settlers quickly
rejected that option: the lesser quality of the local variety made it an
infeasible export. They relied instead on other local resources: fish—
which had for over a century been pulled from North Atlantic
waters for consumption in Europe; the much sought-after furs of
both beaver and otter; and timber, along with other forest products.
In early Plymouth, planters focused especially on fish and furs. The
first they could theoretically take on their own, although they needed
boats, tools, packing barrels, and salt (not to mention some skill). Acquiring the second, pelts, required trading partners.

Relying on this trade, Plymouth might have pursued an economic
model that was used in many locations: the trading post. Europeans
in Africa and Asia set up outposts—often called factories—that provided shelter to traders, a meeting place for transactions, and storage
for trade goods awaiting ships to carry them off. Such outposts did
not necessitate actual colonization in that the European traders
tended to be temporary residents; in addition, they were present only

with the permission of the local ruler and were often constrained in their movements. Dutch trade on the Hudson began along these lines, with traders traveling upriver to meet Mohawk hunters to bargain for pelts. Only gradually did New Amsterdam develop economic functions beyond supplying traders and storing pelts. Even though the Plymouth fur trade resembled such factory outposts in its aims, the settlers clearly meant to remain in New England. For them, furs offered a hoped-for income to buy what they needed from England and, especially, to pay off the debt incurred in establishing the settlement.

Such a trade proved difficult to organize, as the Plymouth leaders quickly learned. As soon as Massasoit and Plymouth established an alliance, the plantation received a continual flow of visitors who came to check out the new settlement, share a meal, and trade a pelt or two. This stream of prospective traders proved disruptive and expensive, and the planters asked Massasoit to put an end to it. Instead of receiving one or two furs at a time, Plymouth wanted them to arrive in bulk. They wanted to negotiate a single price for a lot.[9] This plan assumed a level of organization within Native communities around servicing the trade that did not yet exist. Hunting was an individual activity, and the mechanisms for collecting numerous pelts and trading for a bulk shipment did not fit well within Native practices. Getting hunters to join together to trade represented just one hurdle.

Another challenge involved settling on an item that could be given in exchange for the furs that Plymouth so eagerly sought. At first hunters accepted novelty items of European manufacture, valuable because rare: beads or similar "trifles." As the trade grew, however, and hunters became accustomed to having access to European goods, they demanded more: metal tools, European cloth, or even guns. As a result of this trade, wampum (clam shells formed into small beads) circulated more vigorously, and Plymouth then sought access to those from the Narragansett Bay where they were harvested and manufactured. Competitors for the trade began arriving soon after the *May-flower*, so that Plymouth found itself vying not only with the French to the north and the Dutch to the west but also with other English men in their immediate area. More traders gave local hunters the power to pick their partners, which in turn placed demands on Plymouth to supply appealing trade items. For all their confidence that they dealt with a primitive people, Plymouth traders quickly found local people engaging with increasing sophistication in this burgeoning market economy. In such ways, Atlantic networks reached into Native America.

In organizing trade, location mattered. Bulky items (as well as people) moved with the greatest ease via waterways, and so trading stations set on a river—like the Plymouth trading house in Kennebec— were most likely to succeed. Plymouth, however, did not boast a sizeable river system, and the plantation's leaders soon looked farther afield, both to the west and the north, in search of workable locations. Plymouth tried to parlay the fact that it had arrived first in the area into claims that reached beyond the limited land grant they eventually held from the Council for New England. They moved into the Connecticut and Kennebec river regions, in the former case at least claiming a right to the trade as a result of having "discovered" (by which they meant "explored") the river. In the Kennebec case, they went back to the council to get the rights to the trade there. By the middle of its second decade, Plymouth had two remote trading stations, one of which was threatened when Hocking moved in on its claim.

Despite Plymouth's diligent and sometimes fatal efforts to command the fur trade, its ability to do so proved limited as well as short-lived. With the goal of retiring the colony's debt through the trade, Plymouth prohibited any resident from trading independently. A 1637 notation in the court record book continued the same few men in the management of all the trade (listing beaver as well as beads and corn as the items being exchanged).[10] Just as they wanted their Native

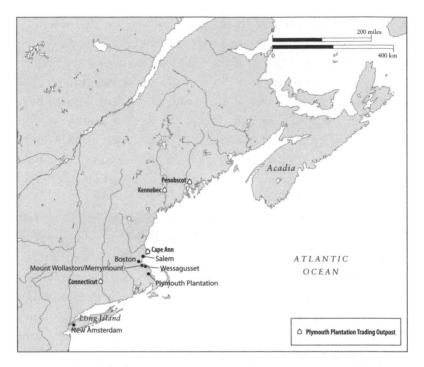

Plymouth, although the first European settlement in the region, was soon joined by the Dutch to the west and a smattering of small and often temporary English outposts in their general vicinity. To further their trade with Native hunters, residents established outposts around New England, fending off both English and French competitors. In 1629, Massachusetts Bay was founded, with its initial settlement at Salem.

trading partners to organize the trade on their end, sending furs in bulk and deputizing one trader to deal with them, so too they wanted to organize their end of the trade. Bradford praised the Dutch for blocking interlopers and funneling all pelts through its company, clearly desiring that Plymouth would similarly control all English trade. In 1626, eight men known as the "Undertakers" accepted personal responsibility for Plymouth's debt and took control of the trade. One of them, John Howland, commanded the Kennebec station at the time of the confrontation that killed Hocking and Talbot.

In addition to rivals for the trade, Plymouth planters faced all the usual tribulations of transatlantic trade in the early modern era. One ship sunk with their goods on board while another was taken by a "Turkish man-of-war," a ship fitted out for warfare.[11] Another shipment arrived in London during an epidemic, when trade was at a standstill and the price offered for the pelts was far below expectations.[12] Even had Plymouth commanded the trade as Bradford and others wished, unforeseeable setbacks were a routine part of doing business. Furs held out the prospect for financial solvency, but they also brought frustration and disappointment—as well as murder.

They never succeeded, save for largely within Plymouth itself, in limiting the trade. Bradford complained of men who came to fish but turned to trading for furs as only one of many threats to their business.[13] Thomas Weston, a former Plymouth investor, established a rival outpost in 1622. It soon collapsed, but before doing so it prompted many complaints for its "injurious walking" toward the neighboring Native communities. Winslow blamed Weston's men for damaging the trade in both furs and corn; in their hunger—the result in his view of laziness—they gave "as much for a quart of corn, as we used to do for a Beavers skin."[14] When that outpost broke up, some of Weston's company joined another enterprise under the direction of Thomas Morton. He angered Winslow and his companions even more by trading guns for furs. This scheme was not original with Morton, as Bradford blamed English fisherman, as well as the Dutch and the French, for initiating it; still, Morton—nearby and irritating for a whole host of reasons—earned their special ire.[15] They eventually arrested him and returned him to England, but competition for the fur trade continued.

Matters only worsened in the 1630s, as thousands of other English people arrived in New England, threatening Plymouth's access to both Connecticut and Kennebec. By 1642, Bradford was grumbling that the trade had decayed.[16] The demand for pelts led to overhunting, and the beaver and otter populations declined dramatically. The elimination of beaver in particular drastically altered the landscape, bringing changes to the land when spring dams no longer held water back, as the environmental historian William Cronon has noted.[17] The decline of the beaver also dashed Plymouth's hopes for profit. It had taken the Plymouth Undertakers more than two decades from the time of their arrival and a decade and a half from the date they initially expected to have repaid their investors for them to retire the debt. They had been hampered by the vagaries of the trade in general but more so by the rising competition to exploit what proved to be—under the pressures of English, French, and Dutch demand—a finite resource.

The fur trade in southeast New England was minor and soon exhausted. For that reason, Plymouth leaders quickly saw the need to establish outposts elsewhere, but even those trading stations had limited prospects given the rapid increase in competition. Plymouth, in participating in and for a time heavily depending on the trade, partook in a larger process in which Native hunters were drawn into transatlantic trade networks, and local resources were exploited at an unprecedented rate. The fur trade would continue long after it dried up in Plymouth, especially trade managed by the French to the north and west, but everywhere it would prompt competition, conflict, and poor resource management. Extracting American resources became a way to gain a profit, and men exploited it aggressively.

6

CONNECTING TO
THE WIDER WORLD

PRIVATEERS

KINGSHIP

BOOKS

PRIVATEERS

IN SPRING 1646, a group of seamen in Plymouth began to squabble. When their captain ordered them to stop, one of them—"a desperate fellow" who was frequently "quarrelsome"—refused. He proceeded to revile Captain Cromwell, eventually brandishing a rapier (a thin, light sword). Even when Cromwell disarmed him, the man persisted. Using his own weapon against him, the captain hit him over the head with its hilt. The blow must have been remarkably well placed, as the "desperate fellow" died a few days later.

The Plymouth court did not take up the case, but rather left the crew to mete out its own justice in a court martial. The crew's judicial proceeding exonerated the captain, and having completed a month's stay in Plymouth, he and his men—eighty strong and young—departed in their three ships. During their stay of more than a month, they spent a good deal of time drinking. In fact, Bradford said they "so distempered themselves with drink that they became like madmen." This time, Plymouth's magistrates did not rely on the sailors to handle the offense; they punished and imprisoned some. Eventually order was restored; they "became more moderate and orderly." During that time, they scattered "a great deal of money among the people,—and even more sin than money . . . notwithstanding all the care taken to prevent it."[1] In the extended visit of these three ships, Plymouth experienced the danger and appeal of playing host to a crew of privateers. The privateers, for their part, experienced life in a small

New England seaside town, one that had few amenities or entertainments catering to seafaring men with prize money to spend.

Captain Cromwell's visit proved Plymouth's most sustained and direct encounter with privateers. Privateers (generally referred to as private men of war) and their privately owned ships fitted out for war carried government-issued commissions permitting them to attack other ships. Licensing private ships allowed authorities to pursue naval warfare with a minimum of direct expense, as the privateers provided their own ships, men, and provisions. Their reward came when they seized wealth, a portion of which they were permitted to keep. When a voyage failed to take a prize, the men went unpaid. Cromwell carried a legal commission to seize ships and attack towns, and he commanded three private ships sent to attack the Spanish settlements further south on behalf of England's Lord High Admiral, the Earl of Warwick.

The earl served as the admiral not at the command of the king but instead by an unprecedented appointment from the English Parliament. With civil war then dividing England, Warwick supported Parliament against the king, and Parliament had gained control of the Admiralty and appointed its head. Hence Plymouth risked the appearance of making a political statement in welcoming Cromwell, by accepting him and his commission as legitimate. Yet Plymouth had little choice in the matter, given its inability to stop three "men of war" from sailing into its harbor. Although most colonies tried to avoid taking a decisive stance on the divisions tearing England apart, they often found it difficult to remain aloof. Even a small settlement on a mediocre harbor such as Plymouth, a place of little wealth and less consequence, could not avoid the implications of civil war in England. Nor could it remain untouched by the fighting ships that sailed American waters during these years.

In any event, the settlement's leaders were familiar with Warwick. Long interested in colonization, he had been a member of the Council

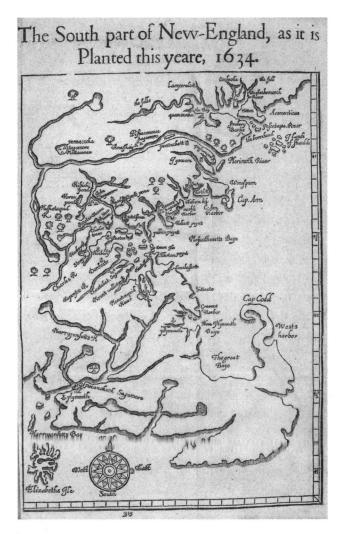

The South part of New-England, as it is Planted this yeare, 1634.

William Wood's map—which served as a frontispiece to his 1634 book, *New Englands Prospect*—was the earliest published map of the region showing the place names that the English residents had assigned (as opposed to Smith's map, which made up English names in the absence of English people). Wood both charted the new attention being paid to the area by English people and encouraged further awareness of it. Under such circumstances, Captain Cromwell would have been aware of New England certainly and possibly even of Plymouth in particular. It was nonetheless an improbable location for privateers to shelter.

for New England, and he had helped Plymouth get a grant to set up a fishing station on Cape Ann. Hosting Warwick's privateers, though exposing Plymouth to charges of choosing Parliament over the king and risking the sinful behavior Bradford feared, gave Plymouth its first opportunity to appreciate how privateers could infuse money into a local economy.

The visit of Cromwell's crew to Plymouth Plantation was not the only such encounter. On at least one other occasion, Plymouth hosted men who were—or at least aspired to be—privateers. In 1623, Plymouth's investors in Europe sent over the *Little James*, which carried a commission permitting it to take ships. The seamen who signed on for the voyage expected to receive a share of any prize seized in accordance with that commission. When the ship arrived in New England, it was not sent out on a privateering voyage but instead fitted out to sail up the coast to fish. Some of the men, disappointed about the change, resisted. They declared "they were fitted out for a taker, and were told they might take any ship whatsoever that was not too strong for them." If the ship had been legitimately fitted out to take other ships, it would have needed a license that either deputized it to make war or permitted it to seize a vessel in retribution for a previous wrong; since England was not then at war, the latter explanation— peacetime retribution for a previous seizure—would have been most likely.

Faced with the crew's recalcitrance, Bradford had to promise the seamen wages for their work in lieu of the anticipated share in prize ships. Some of them, enraged by the transformation in their status and prospects, tried to convince others to join them in a mutiny against the leaders of their expedition. Emmanuel Altham, the investor assigned to oversee the voyage, reported that one of the men threatened "to kill us or to blow our ship up."[2] The problem was resolved in a way that satisfied no one: the *Little James* wrecked on rocks off the coast, causing a great loss to the investors, and among those drowned was the leading troublemaker. These would-be privateers had been willing to defend their right to spoils with violence and, despite the difficulties arising from the loss of the *Little James*, the Plymouth Undertakers felt relieved that the wreck had forestalled mutiny.

On another occasion, then-governor Bradford used the threat of hypothetical privateers in the region to warn the neighboring Dutch against intruding on English territorial claims. In 1627, Plymouth cautioned the Dutch in New Netherland from coming into waters claimed by the English along the coast. Although it had no capacity to seize foreign ships illegally trading, Bradford advised the Dutch merchant factor for the Dutch West India Company that ships from Virginia or the fishing ships that visited the local waters would certainly seize them "if they find you trading within those limits." He recommended that their masters make an agreement with the English king to avoid such troubles.[3] Privateering seizures were a standard way for early modern states to enforce their claims, and Bradford wielded that threat while at the same time working to open a trade relationship with the Dutch.

Besides hosting privateers—whether willingly or not—Plymouth also suffered from their attacks. No warship ever attacked Plymouth, a small, remote, and relatively poor settlement with little to offer. Some English people thinking of taking up residences in the region worried that "the Spaniard" would come "thousands of miles with a great Navy to [assail English] plantations," but William Wood assured his readers that they were "as yet not worth the pillage."[4] Located too far north to receive a Spanish attack, Plymouth did fear French crews that came down, not as far as their town, but to the fishing outposts they held nearer to French Acadia (today, Nova Scotia). Indeed, French ships did assault fishing camps that Plymouth owned and ran, contributing to the eventual end of Plymouth interests in that northern region.[5]

More seriously, privateers took ships carrying cargos from their settlement. The *Fortune* proved unfortunate in that regard. Sailing back to England from Plymouth, it was seized off the western coast of France. Thomas Barton, the shipmaster, sailed into a patrol set to stop the resupply of the French Protestant coastal city of La Rochelle, then under blockade. Although the *Fortune*, returning from Plymouth with beaver skins and timber, clearly did not intend to aid La Rochelle, a dishonest privateer captain laid claim to the ship and its cargo nonetheless.[6] Once they finally got back to England, the Plymouth investors and leaders filed a complaint with the Admiralty. If they then received a license to take what was stolen, that would explain why the *Little James* was fitted out as a "taker" the following year.

A few years after the French seizure, "Turkish pirates" patrolling off the coast of England snatched another vessel returning with Plymouth's trade goods. The investors sent the *Little James*—which had been salvaged and rebuilt—and the *White Angel* to New England. Both were to fish, the larger of the two taking its catch to sell in a Spanish port and the smaller to return fish and beaver pelts to England. The two separated in sight of the port of Plymouth, England, but before the *Little James* could get to safety, a "Turk's man of war" snapped it up. The North African crew sailed the ship to Morocco, "into Salé, where the master and men were made slaves." Seamen captured in the Mediterranean faced enslavement in North Africa, or if they were North Africans, in southern Europe. That an English ship's crew sailing in home waters was taken was not unprecedented, although men who sailed the North Atlantic met that fate far less often than those on more southern routes. In addition to the crew, the fish, 800 pounds weight of beaver pelts, and the ship were also lost.[7] Although the *White Angel* made it to port on that occasion, it would be stopped on another voyage in the next decade by Irish raiders who took its best sails as well as provisions.[8] The seas were full of lurking maritime predators ready to seize cargos, ships, and even crews, making transatlantic trade difficult, as the Plymouth planters came to understand.

As a small commercial and settlement venture, Plymouth was dependent on transatlantic shipping as well as on the ability to navigate New England coastal waters to collect fish and furs to use in discharging its debts. The connection to Europe and to its fishing and trading outposts could be disrupted by maritime predators—privateers licensed to attack shipping or pirates who operated on their own account without regard for proper license. Most of the ships that pestered Plymouth and its cargos were not pirate vessels. The Irish who robbed the *White Angel* were probably an exception, and the Moroccans who seized the *Little James*, cruising English waters out of the unregulated port of Salé, may have been another. Otherwise harassment came from more official quarters, especially from the French, who tried to defend their fishing rights and their own coasts. Losing a ship full of furs, fish, or timber hampered Plymouth's ability to repay its investors. Privateers could mean revenge and protection or danger and loss, and Plymouth, connected to England by the ships that sailed the Atlantic, contended with that uncertainty.

Such was the price of doing business in the early English Atlantic, as Plymouth settlers learned and ships' captains and crews well knew. Even a minor, somewhat remote, and relatively modest undertaking such as New Plymouth proved vulnerable, if not to direct attack, at least to having its sources of profit and repayment taken. Far from the major cruising grounds in the Caribbean, Plymouth nevertheless faced maritime predation. In addition, as with Captain Cromwell and his crew, they also occasionally received the benefit of privateering largesse strewn around their community. Years later when they heard that Cromwell died falling onto his rapier, New Englanders recalled the fact that he killed a crewman in Plymouth with the same weapon. His end seemed divine justice. Still, in the moment, Bradford and the others had been willing enough to host him and his men—despite the danger represented by their lax conduct—and to enjoy the much-needed infusion of cash that they brought. Privateering conveyed both advantages and disadvantages, and Plymouth had occasion to experience both.

KINGSHIP

IN 1621, the leaders of Plymouth negotiated a treaty of amity and friendship with local leader Massasoit Ousamequin. After carefully orchestrating a meeting—through messengers who passed back and forth—the leaders of both communities met to hammer out the terms of their relationship. They agreed to offer mutual aid and support. Entering into these diplomatic negotiations, the men of tiny Plymouth drew upon the ritual forms of their European culture. They characterized themselves as representatives of the monarch James I and VI, king of England, Ireland, and Scotland. Their messenger relayed to Massasoit "that King James saluted him with words of love and Peace, and did accept of him as his Friend and Ally, and that our Governour desired to see him and to truck [meaning to trade] with him, and to confirm a Peace with him, as his next neighbor." During the meeting that brought the English governor and the Wampanoag leader together, the English assured Massasoit of King James's esteem. They interpreted the reaction of the Wampanoag men in the best possible light, noting "all which the King seemed to like well, and it was applauded of his followers."[1] In making this overture, the Plymouth people confidently depicted themselves as the emissaries of a monarch who had most certainly not deputized them to act on his behalf. Considering their previous relationship with the king, their assertion that they represented the monarch was nothing short of remarkable.

The leaders of Plymouth Plantation, although they presented themselves as the king's emissaries, actually had a rather fraught relationship with the monarchy. Some of the people residing in Plymouth, and most of the community's leaders in 1621, had fled England rather than live under the religious establishment which James headed, the Church of England. Once in the Netherlands, the future religious leader of the plantation, William Brewster, launched a printing press that lobbed criticism at the English Church. The press eventually employed a young Edward Winslow as well, and he would go on to be involved in the negotiations with Massasoit (and to serve repeatedly as governor of Plymouth). This press was sufficiently critical of royal policy that the English authorities arranged to have their counterparts in Holland shut it down. Unwilling to live under direct royal rule, the Plymouth leaders took advantage of their distance from crown authorities to criticize James's policies. Nonetheless, they displayed no qualms about later depicting themselves as having come to New England specifically on James I and VI's behalf.

This interaction with Massasoit, with its invocation of the monarch, was far from an isolated incident. In later encounters with other Native neighbors, the Plymouth men made similar statements. They asserted that they represented James and that their king would be pleased to enter into any alliance they arranged. On various exploratory excursions around the area, they collected pledges of allegiance to King James. As some of them related to another Native leader, "divers Sachems [or Native leaders] . . . had acknowledged themselves to be King James' men, and if he also would submit himself, we would be his safeguard from his enemies." Robert Cushman, who visited briefly during Plymouth's first year, was impressed by the success of these diplomatic efforts. Without "threats and blows, or shaking of sword and sound of trumpet," but rather by "friendly usage, love, peace, honest and just carriages [or actions], good counsel, &c" the

The Netherlands, as depicted in this 1611 map, housed many English men and women. They moved there for many reasons, setting up churches that allowed them to worship in English. Even though the removal of the English church led by John Robinson to the small Dutch city of Leiden could be seen as a rejection of James I's rule, when some of the church's members moved to North America, they referred to themselves as loyal subjects to their king.

settlers had gotten many of their neighbors to acknowledge the king of England's authority.[2]

Whether the Native peoples who received these overtures understood their relationship to a distant monarch as the settlers hoped they did is doubtful, but Plymouth men remained confident that their efforts were both comprehensible and fruitful. Not only did they offer an alliance with England's king, but they also promised protection—and seemed to imply that Plymouth Plantation would provide it. Even though they made this offer at a time when they were confident that their firearms made them all but invincible against any local enemies, this claim was bold, given their general lack of martial skill and their comparatively low numbers. Perhaps they imagined James sending protection, a hope that had no precedent and would never be fulfilled. Framed in familiar European terms—allegiance and protection—their efforts to use their relationship to the king continued to yield results, to their minds. They proudly reported that, with all the local residents desiring alliance and royal protections, numerous communities had become "subjects to our sovereign Lord King James." That fact, they were certain, explained peaceful relations.[3] Regardless of their own history with King James, they considered themselves tied to him by bonds of allegiance. Like many English people who ventured into the world away from their native shores, these people imagined themselves going as subjects of their monarch. In Plymouth's case, they boldly cast themselves as emissaries as well.

Allegiance to the monarch did not simply serve as a convenient façade which the Plymouth people donned when presenting themselves to their neighbors. It appeared to be a deeply held idea. The title of Robert Cushman's lay sermon, preached in December 1621 and published thereafter, declares as much: *A Sermon Preached at Plimmoth in New-England In an assemblie of his Majesties faithfull Subjects.* Whenever the Plymouth people had occasion to explain why they were in New England, they framed their effort in terms of the monarch, often mentioning him along with his divine counterpart; the twin sources of authority were the king and God. Narrating the history of their settlement in their own court records, the Plymouth magistrates declared they undertook the voyage to glorify God and extend the dominion of the English king.[4] Edward Winslow, addressing the plantation's "well-wishers," commended them for helping to enlarge the king's "Dominions, by planting his loyal subjects in so healthful and hopeful a Country."[5] That they were loyal subjects was a point of pride. Phineas Pratt, who joined the plantation after the collapse of Thomas Weston's investment venture nearby, much later claimed that the migrants leaving Leiden to journey to America wanted to reside under English rather than Dutch authority because of "the entire love they bore to their King and Country; for in them there was never found any lack of loyal obedience."[6] Numerous people repeated the idea that the settlers planted Plymouth thinking of God and the king.[7] While we anticipate that those who lived in Plymouth Plantation saw God motivating their undertaking, the fact that they gave equal weight to the need to serve the king—whose authority they had previously fled—contradicts the common understanding of their goals and attitudes.

In that iconic moment when the men on the first ship entered into a "civil combination" (as they called it), better known today as the "Mayflower Compact," they used the language of kingship and affirmed their loyalty to the monarch. The agreement set up government among the disparate group of men who sailed on the *Mayflower*. Women were excluded as they generally had no role in governance. These arrangements were made only off the coast of Cape Cod because their intention to land in Virginia would have put them under the already-existing government of the Virginia Company. Landing unexpectedly farther north, they suddenly required some basis for organizing their affairs.

The agreement repeatedly invoked God and the king. They prefaced their agreement with formulaic language that lent solemnity to the occasion: "In the name of God, Amen. We whose names are underwritten, the loyal Subjects of our dread sovereign Lord King James, by the grace of God of Great Britain, France, and Ireland King,

Defender of the Faith, &c." The mention of James's claim to rule France dated back to the days when the English monarch had, in fact, controlled part of northern France. The text then proceeded to explain the reason they had come to America, attributing their effort to their concern for "the glory of God, and advancement of the Christian Faith, and honor of our King and Country." Their very purpose, in other words, was twofold: to support their Christian faith and to honor their king and their native country of England. They concluded quite formally with what is known as regnal dating—calculating the length of a monarch's reign to date a legal document: "Cape Cod. 11. Of November, in the year of the reign of our sovereign Lord King James, of England, France, and Ireland 18. And of Scotland 54. Anno Domino 1620."[8] A royal charter would have been the best possible foundation for a new settlement, but in its absence, Plymouth's leaders asserted their allegiance to their king as a basis for their government.

In the early years at Plymouth, their status as subjects to their king earned mention in various contexts. If other English people entered the area and caused problems, Plymouth cited the king's authority to curb their excess. Whether the offenders were members of the unsuccessful encampment at Wessagussett or the irksome group at Thomas Morton's trading post, Plymouth warned that the king would punish those who displeased him.[9] William Bradford alleged that Morton dismissed this warning, stating "that king was dead, and his displeasure died with him." This allegation of disrespect to monarchy was intended to undermine Morton's reputation. Bradford's nemesis adopted similar tactics: Morton depicted himself as far more loyal than the Plymouth people.[10] In diplomatic dealings with the neighboring Dutch colony of New Netherland, the Plymouth governor and his council reminded those in the nearby jurisdiction that they operated under the authority of England's new monarch, Charles I.[11] When they sat down to make a permanent record of lands granted in Plymouth since its inception, they formally cited their status as "the Kings subjects inhabiting within the Government of new Plymouth" to justify the grants.[12] Their personal relationship to the monarch and their status as his subjects supported their entire undertaking.

Thinking in terms of monarchs and subjects was so ingrained that the Plymouth people—like many early European sojourners in America—imposed those familiar categories on the people and societies they encountered. The language of kingship permeated their descriptions of Native political organization. As they traveled around, opening diplomatic relations and trying to build alliances, they categorized every Native leader as a king (or, in one case, a queen).[13] Massasoit was the first, and although one author elevated him to the status of an emperor over various other kings, the title usually bestowed on him was that of king. This tendency to impose European categories on Native society was pervasive and unthinking. In a rich moment, Christopher Levett (a visitor to New England) remarked dismissively when Natives he encountered found some aspect of English cultural practice odd, "You may Imagine he thought their [Native] fashion was universal."[14] For their part, Levett and all the other English in the region did precisely that—assumed European practices were universal—when they equated Native and European political structures. All across the English Atlantic (and indeed everywhere seventeenth-century Europeans interacted with varied cultures), English people assumed cultural equivalences that did not exist. Thinking of Massasoit as a king who could form an alliance with James I and VI appealed to Plymouth leaders because it rendered Native culture comprehensible. Kingship was ingrained in their own world, and therefore they expected to find it everywhere.

Knowing about their differences over religion and looking (far) ahead to American independence, we might think of Plymouth planters as holding the king at arm's length. Yet they embraced the relationship, even if they found it easier to be loyal subjects on the other side of the Atlantic where the details of their church order were not regularly scrutinized. That did not mean that their expressions of loyalty were false. They lived in a world that was largely organized around personal loyalty to a monarch. Despite their brief residence in the Dutch Republic, they gave no indication of wanting to escape their status as the subjects of a king. Even their willingness to host Captain Cromwell's privateers cannot be read as an indication of disloyalty to the king or to the idea of kingship. The break between colonists and the British crown that occurred a century and a half later was not anticipated by the first men in Plymouth. Their descendants posthumously recruited them into the American patriot cause, declaring the Mayflower Compact an early expression of democratic striving—without the permission of their ancestors.

BOOKS

In 1631, when native men brought before Governor William Bradford a fugitive from Massachusetts justice, Sir Christopher Gardiner, the governor discovered that the prisoner carried a little book. This otherwise unremarkable occurrence caught Bradford's attention because the booklet "was a memorial what day he was reconciled to the Pope and Church of Rome, and in what university he took his scapula, and such and such degrees." The volume indicated that— besides his other offenses—Gardiner adhered to Roman Catholicism, a faith that made him unwelcome in New England. Knowing that his religious views would win him hostility, Gardiner had previously kept this fact (and his little book) a secret.

Gardiner came into Bradford's hands after he fled Massachusetts, escaping an order for his arrest and deportation. John Winthrop, governor of Massachusetts, had received complaints from two women in Europe who accused Gardiner of bigamy and (in one case) theft. This tale seemed entirely plausible: gossip in Massachusetts had already questioned his assertion that his young female companion was his cousin. Rumor had it she was in fact his "concubine." Gardiner had been beaten by the Native men who captured him, so Bradford had his injuries tended to and then sent him (along with the book) to Boston. Winthrop then wrote to Bradford, asking that he refrain from mentioning the book or Gardiner's Catholicism. The Court of Assistants ordered Gardiner sent back to England to face charges of bigamy, even though he was the protégé of Sir Ferdinando Gorges of the Council for New England.[1]

Books of almost all sorts circulated in Plymouth Plantation. The one exception (besides Gardiner's little volume) was Catholic texts. Inventories enumerating the possessions left at the time of death indicate that none of the earliest arrivals owned such books, not even for the purposes of study. Early Plymouth valued books: planters brought them when they migrated; they got people to send or bring them to add to their collections; they lent them and bequeathed them; and some settlers wrote them and sent or carried them to England to be published. Those who came from Leiden had enjoyed the benefit of life in a university town, where their pastor was a renowned theologian and where some of their number briefly ran a printing press. As one nineteenth-century New England historian observed, Plymouth in its first generation was "a place of books."[2]

Books came with the migrants. Francis Higginson listed books among those essential items that settlers ought to bring.[3] Numerous Plymouth men anticipated Higginson's advice, packing books among their other possessions for the sea voyage. William Brewster brought an extensive personal library. Others who transported books included William Bradford, Samuel Fuller, and Miles Standish.[4] Presumably so did the young Edward Winslow, who had worked in Brewster's Leiden print shop after apprenticing to a London printer. William Wright, arriving in the plantation's second year from Leiden, brought a small library of his own, which included two Bibles and various other books.[5] Many families no doubt had Bibles, the most commonly owned book among Protestants traversing the Atlantic.

Someone on the first ship carried John Smith's account of New England and the map printed with it. To the author's disgust, they thought the book could stand in for the expertise of the man, and they declined his offer to accompany and school them on how to set up a plantation. The never-modest Smith blamed all their troubles on this failure: "having my books and maps, [they] presumed they knew as much as they desired." As a result, he opined, "most vanished to nothing, to the great disparagement of the general business, therefore let them take heed that do follow their example."[6] Smith clearly hoped his books would advertise his expertise and availability as a guide, leading to additional employment.

The bookish settlers, valuing these possessions, circulated them within the migrant community. Bradford borrowed Brewster's copy of a translation of Seneca's *Moral Epistles* (authored by a Roman Stoic philosopher who died in the year 65). He had it in hand when he wrote the first part of his manuscript account "Of Plimoth Plantation," quoting it at a key moment in that narrative. Years later, when he resumed his writing, he had to borrow the same copy from a different owner, Alexander Standish, who had acquired it out of the Brewster estate from one of the ruling elders' less scholarly heirs.[7] Only the fact of Bradford quoting this work, which he did not own, made it possible for scholar David A. Lupher to postulate that this sharing had taken place. Generally, the practice of lending books, an activity that occurred casually among friends, would not have been recorded, and so would have remained hidden from modern view. One case of sharing was explicitly recorded, however, because it represented an odd incident in which one of Bradford's own book recrossed the ocean. He lent his copy of Henry Ainsworth's *Annotations upon the Fourth Book of Moses* to John Pory. On his way to England from Virginia, Pory faced a long voyage and asked to borrow the book when he stopped in Plymouth. This learned work compared different versions of the fourth book of the Old Testament, Numbers, and had been written by a theologian who had led another of the English churches in Holland.[8] Most book borrowing remained local and so did not garner such notice.

Books also circulated as a result of deaths—such as Brewster's in 1644—when libraries were dispersed. Brewster's own collection passed to his two sons, Love and Jonathan. They then sold some of his books to others. Love, for instance, sold the *Almanac* (produced on a press in Cambridge, Massachusetts) that had been put together by Plymouth's sometime champion, mariner William Peirce, to Alexander Standish, a book-loving son of Miles.[9] Brewster, prior to his death, might have passed his copy of *Chrysostom*, printed in Basle in 1522, to his grandson Thomas Prence. Not listed in his inventory, the volume bears Prence's inscription, which notes it had been Brewster's. This indicates that he received it before the inventory of Brewster's possessions at death was made. Other books dispersed in this way. Some were kept by heirs but others were passed along as gifts or through purchase to those in the community most likely to appreciate them.

William Brewster owned one of the most extensive personal libraries in the early English Americas before its dispersal. The church's original ruling elder and briefly a partner in a Leiden printing business, Brewster died owning over 400 books. With that many volumes, Brewster's library rivaled that which John Harvard had bequeathed six years before Brewster's death, in 1638, to the newly founded college at Cambridge, Massachusetts. Brewster both brought books with him and acquired them later. Some of the books listed in his inventory had publication dates after he sailed on the *Mayflower* in 1620, and therefore they must have been purchased for him and sent (or carried) to Plymouth. This transatlantic transmission of print material allowed Brewster to remain current by reading in his own broad areas of interest.[10] The books no doubt supported his work as ruling elder, which required that he teach and preach. He also lent his books to others, thus spreading the benefit of his magnificent library.

Brewster's large book collection was the work of his long life: he died at age eighty-six. His library inventory listed 393 titles, of which most have been identified. Some, listed only as a "bundle of small books and papers," will never be known. Most were in English, although sixty-two were in Latin. He also owned eleven books off the press he briefly ran in Leiden. Brewster acquired at least eighty-nine of the titles after he migrated to Plymouth. One can well imagine his one-time protégé Edward Winslow bringing him items that had been issued by one of the London presses on his return from a transatlantic journey. Interestingly, Brewster himself apparently did not bother to acquire any works about Plymouth, including those by Winslow himself. The volumes purchased subsequent to his migration include books written by his former pastor, John Robinson, as well as classic works of the English reformed Protestant community, such as four devotional books by the popular religious author William Sibbes. Such books held obvious interest to both Brewster and Winslow, as well as to others in the young plantation.

The majority of Brewster's books consisted of religious works—doctrinal, practical, or scriptural exposition—but other sorts—historical, philosophical, and the like—were also enumerated. Many of them, like those by Robinson and Sibbes, were typical acquisitions for well-read English Protestants. His book ownership leaned sharply toward the Reformed faith, with books by John Calvin (who designed the government and church of Geneva), Theodore Beza (a French theologian and disciple of Calvin's), and other reformed theologians. Brewster also acquired numerous anti-Catholic works, including one identified as "a book of Pope Joan," which may have been Alexander Cooke's 1610 work attempting to prove that one pope in the distant past had in fact been a cross-dressing woman.[11] Although his Protestant books far outnumbered his anti-Catholic texts, Brewster did gather notable examples of the genre, including Thomas Beard's *Antichrist the Pope of Rome* (1625), which he acquired after migrating to New England. His copy of the *Swedish Intelligencer's* reporting on the exploits of the Protestant hero Gustavus Adolphus, reprinted in London, proved to be among those that his son Love (otherwise not especially interested in his father's literary pursuits) kept after his death. The elder Brewster acquired one of the works of Sir Walter Raleigh, his *The Prerogative of Parliaments* (Middleburgh, 1628). He got his hands on some books written by William Prynne, who had become a hero among the "hotter sort of protestants" in England after the court ordered his ears cut off for his printed libels against bishops. Like any well-educated English man of the seventeenth century, Brewster was also interested in ancient Roman authors, and therefore he owned works like Thomas Lodge's translation of Seneca, from which Bradford quoted. While Brewster's collecting held to the dominant theme of religious text, he also used his purchases to remain up to date on the varied concerns animating the English reading public.[12]

Brewster's engagement in books (and Reformed Protestantism) had led him to run a printing press in Leiden for a few of his years there. The press operated briefly, issuing sixteen or seventeen books, before the Dutch authorities shuttered it at the request of the English government. In that time, Brewster along with his partner, Thomas Brewer, and eventually their young assistant, Winslow, printed religious books in English that could not be produced in England. Some made their way clandestinely to England, including one text that was critical of the king. Alerted, the English authorities demanded that the government in Holland close the press. These three men never used their skills in Plymouth to resume the production of books, and indeed Plymouth would not have a press until the late eighteenth century.

Forgoing the local creation of books—which was more than the small settlement had the time or the resources to manage—Plymouth men instead sent writings to be published in England. Their efforts tell us much of what we know about early Plymouth, as a number of these publications recounted events in the infant plantation. In the first years, various manuscripts penned by residents made the transatlantic crossing to be printed on London presses. These missives

THE WORKES both Morrall and Naturall of LVCIVS ANNÆVS SENECA Translated by T: Lodge D: of Phis:

London Printed by William Stansby

William Brewster owned the collected works of Roman philosopher Seneca the Younger. Well-educated Europeans during this era read ancient Roman authors, which explained the volume's presence in Brewster's collection. William Bradford and possibly others borrowed Brewster's Seneca volume during his lifetime, yet his heirs did not care to own it and instead sold it after their father's death. Thomas Lodge's translation of Seneca was one of many books circulating in Plymouth.

traveled with their authors, as was the case when Winslow returned to England with the manuscript of his 1624 publication, *Good Newes from New England: Or A True Relation of Things very remarkable at the Plantation of Plimoth in New-England*, or when Robert Cushman carried his 1622 sermon.[13] Other book manuscripts made the crossing in the hands of a friend. Cushman, for instance, carried, along with his own sermon's text, the multiauthored *A Relation or Journall of the Beginning and Proceedings of the English Plantation setled at Plimoth in New England* (1622). These accounts launched the New England practice of contributing to transatlantic conversations through the circulation of words. While Cambridge and later Boston hosted presses, most of the print materials penned by New England authors throughout the first century traveled, as did Plymouth's writings, in manuscript, to a London printer.

It took more than a decade and a half, but Plymouth eventually found itself under attack in print in England. Plymouth leaders and eventually those in Massachusetts, too, made an enemy of Thomas Morton, who set up a temporary trading outpost near Plymouth. Local authorities twice removed him from the region, once in 1627 (at the hands of Plymouth but with the backing of the region's few other English residents) and again in 1630 (through the efforts of the Massachusetts Bay government). Morton took his revenge in the 1637 "scurrilous" book *New English Canaan*.[14] Divided unequally into three parts, the book described the area, the lives of the Native inhabitants, and Morton's contentions with his neighbors. Written in a flippant tone, *New English Canaan* bestowed mocking names on various people. For instance, the short-of-stature Miles Standish was "Captain Shrimp."

Tucked into his satirical account were various assertions intended to tarnish the reputations of New England leaders. For instance, Morton depicted himself as a godly man, leading worship in his home for his family and servants according to the Book of Common Prayer.

Morton emphasized his supposed devotion to the Church of England in order to claim (erroneously) that his piety explained the feelings of annoyance that he prompted. While Morton did many other things—like welcome servants who had run from their masters and sell guns to Indians—to elicit opposition, he correctly asserted that the Book of Common Prayer—which conveyed the liturgy of the Church of England—did not circulate in New England in the 1630s.[15] No contemporary evidence survived to document Morton's use of it in his family worship, nor does evidence exist that either colony had any inkling that he promoted its use. When Bradford characterized Morton's effort as "an infamous and scurrilous book against many godly and chief men of the country, full of lies and slanders and fraught with profane calumnies against their names and persons and the ways of God," he acknowledged with his last point—his reference to "the ways of God"—that Morton attacked Plymouth's version of Protestant practice. Still it was only one (relatively minor) point of contention, although Morton emphasized it to galvanize Archbishop Laud, who opposed the church order emerging there.

Books were one of many things that circulated through the early seventeenth-century Atlantic. The people who came to Plymouth brought numerous books. Some of these had been produced on the Leiden English-language printing press that Brewster and others founded, but most issued from London presses that produced books suitable to Anglo-Protestant reading tastes. Many households held only one or two books—invariably including a Bible—while a number of church members amassed larger collections. When they packed to go to America, they brought books. Brewster at least worked to keep up his collecting practices by acquiring books from both England and Holland during the twenty-four years he resided in Plymouth. Books mattered in this small outpost because they connected the residents to the larger conversations and changes involving English people in Europe. Although Plymouth went many years without a minister to care for its church—because no man with adequate educational attainments came to the area where he could receive an invitation to preach from the church—it always had books that linked it to intellectual currents, spiritual edification, and events elsewhere.

Books mattered in Plymouth. Most fundamentally, a book carried the word of God, which was the reason the Bible was the most commonly owned work. Books also educated and edified. They gave readers a chance to participate in a broad community, one mostly, but not exclusively, English and reformed Protestant. Books matter to us as well: it is through Plymouth people's writings—especially their books—that we have come to understand Plymouth Plantation and its relationship to its larger world.

CONCLUSION

Plymouth's World

WILLIAM BRADFORD, who did more than any single author to shape the modern understanding of Plymouth Plantation, knew full well how thoroughly embedded that plantation was in the wider Atlantic world. While the first part of his great work "Of Plimoth Plantation" recounted the history of the settlers who came from Leiden (in a narrative that reached all the way back to the Protestant Reformation of the previous century to give their story context), the longer second part of his tale offered year-by-year accounts of key events in Plymouth through 1646. That narrative addressed a whole range of matters from Native diplomacy to church affairs, with attention to debt, commodities, migration, rumors, crimes, and every other matter that might capture the attention of a seventeenth-century colonial governor. No single source gives a greater sense of Plymouth's level of involvement with the world beyond Cape Cod Bay than this handwritten account.

A simple editorial decision in the preparation of the most readily available modern edition of his work makes it hard to see the extent to which Bradford engaged the wider world. The editor, Samuel Eliot Morison, altered Bradford's organization, removed most of the letters that he had inserted into the flow of the narrative, and moved them to an appendix at the back of the published volume. As Bradford composed it, "Of Plimoth Plantation" frequently interrupted its story to insert letters from various locations and authors, letters that demonstrated the connectedness of Plymouth and the importance of its interactions with those beyond its borders. Bradford relays the intrusion of various other English traders into the vicinity, the arrival of the privateering squadron sailing up from the West Indies, and the struggles to find an economic strategy for paying off the ballooning debt. His Plymouth Plantation rested firmly on the edge of the Atlantic, entangled in matters of trade, investment, religious reform, labor needs, rumors, and political infighting.

Approaching Plymouth from this broader perspective, in other words, recovers that sense of connection that Bradford himself felt. With Plymouth firmly in its place, we can better understand how a small settlement ended up in southern New England in 1620, why it developed as it did, and how it contributed to larger trends then emerging in the English Atlantic. A myriad of factors shaped Plymouth, not just the religious experiences of some of the first migrants, as showcased by Bradford in his first section. Certain features of New England—with its colder climate, its modest agricultural potential, its dense forests, its proximity to fishing grounds and the river systems in which the residents hunted for beaver and otter, its distance from the sites of Spanish colonization and the conflicts that prompted—profoundly affected Plymouth.

The plantation became what it did not only because of the Protestant Reformation in England and the desire of some English people resident in Leiden to leave Europe, but also because of its participation in many other contemporary trends. One of these changes was rising migration out of England into locations on the western shores of the Atlantic. When Plymouth was founded, it became England's third Atlantic settlement (after Virginia and Bermuda), but by the end of just one decade, it was one among many. Other outposts by 1630 included Providence Island, St. Christopher, and Nevis in the Caribbean, and Massachusetts Bay Colony as well as New Scotland (Nova Scotia) in the north. Plymouth hosted many visitors not only because the presence of the first English residents made it a known destination but also because of this broader uptick in the circulation of peoples. After Plymouth was planted, many more English people frequented southern New England.

Returning to the famous scenes that make up our national memory of Plymouth, these mythic images all included a component of Atlantic engagement. The Mayflower Compact—treated by later writers as the birth of American democracy—had parallels elsewhere. In every English colony, residents worked out local governance and argued over questions of political legitimacy. Plymouth viewed its "civil combination" at the time as a temporary measure that would allow self-governance until the plantation could secure its status as a bona fide colony with a royal charter. Having landed north of Virginia (which stretched as far north as the Delaware River but not all the way to New England), the *Mayflower* passengers were not included under the Virginia charter, as they had planned. They knew that by settling at Plymouth (which was necessitated by the lateness of the season as well as the difficulties of navigating around Cape Cod), they were putting their enterprise at risk. If they stayed there, their leaders were aware that they would need to sort out their status in England. Very quickly they moved to do so, gaining a patent from the newly established Council for New England that allowed them to settle under its jurisdiction. They failed utterly—despite repeated attempts—to gain a charter. That they desperately wanted one linked them outward from southern New England into a transatlantic context of legal documents and government authority far more than it linked them forward to a time when their democratic stopgap measure would be elevated to a founding moment.

Given that the migrants failed to gain a royal charter, the agreement signed on the *Mayflower* took on greater significance. When Bradford wrote the first part of his history, he skipped over the signing as inconsequential. By the time he returned to his account more than a decade later, the significance of the civil combination had grown. In order to explain the event, which had become (in the absence of anything better) one piece of the basis for the settlement, he backed up in his story—writing, "I shall a little return back, and begin with a combination made by them before they came ashore; being the first foundation of their government in this place"—in order to recount the agreement. It had not rated a mention in his first section, but by the time he penned the second book, it assuredly did.

Not only Bradford but other early Plymouth leaders had by that time come to appreciate the importance of the combination. The man who kept the Plymouth record book eventually recounted its signing, but only in 1636, when it had been identified as fundamental to the legitimacy of the government. Plymouth used the combination, along with the patent that granted limited land rights but no rights of governance, to fend off others who had moved into the region with far better political authorization. Bradford and others were acutely aware that more powerful and populous colonies pressed around them. Far from being a triumphal moment, the signing garnered attention in the somewhat desperate scramble to bolster Plymouth's claims. Places like Rhode Island and Connecticut were able to gain royal charters eventually. Others, like New Haven, never did and subsequently disappeared. Plymouth would last longer than New Haven, persisting as a separate although charterless plantation until the 1680s. In the end, it was, as its early leaders feared it might be, absorbed into Massachusetts. It remains a county in that state to the present day.

The purported landing on Plymouth Rock also supported wider themes in Atlantic history. Those who designated a rock as the landing site in the 1740s conveyed an astonishing ignorance about sailing (which was somewhat surprising since it continued as the main mode of seaborne travel). They also apparently failed to read the surviving sources, which recorded complaints of the health dangers of wading through the surf fully clothed. The women with wet skirts and the men with sodden breeches had not stepped out of a boat onto a rock but had struggled through water to the shore. The imagined landing—regardless of how ludicrously it has been portrayed—linked Plymouth to the ocean crossing and the maritime connections that made the English settlement of southern New England possible.

The prominence given to the ship itself similarly highlights these maritime connections. The new arrivals were tied to other places by the sea. Boats and men to sail or row them were essential for local transportation along the coast and in the streams and rivers since overland transportation was slow and cumbersome. Ships visiting the settlement kept residents supplied with various items, informed them of events elsewhere, brought passengers to join or visit the plantation, and allowed the indebted residents to load fish, timber, and furs that went toward paying their debts. Long before privateers arrived via the West Indies with money to spend, Plymouth was firmly linked to maritime networks. Ships came to Plymouth from England, the fisheries to the north, the Dutch colony to the west, and Virginia to the south. All of necessity came by sea, connecting Plymouth to distant places.

The meeting with Squanto (or Tisquantum) also offered insight into Atlantic trends. As a kidnapped captive, he joined other indigenous people who had been transported to Europe, a practice that began with the first voyage of Columbus. Native people were transported to prove the existence of indigenous Americans; they were often paraded about or made to pose for viewers so that interested parties could catch a glimpse. The kidnapper, Thomas Hunt—judged at Plymouth to be a man who "cares not what mischief he doth for his profit"[1]—carried off Tisquantum and his companions in order to sell them. Among those captured were three brothers; Plymouth men described a heart-wrenching meeting with their bereft mother. Hunt carried his captives to Spain, which had a market for slaves, and he tried to sell his victims there. When the local religious authorities realized that the captives were Natives of the Americas, they challenged the sale. With indigenous Americans legally acknowledged by Spain's king as his vassals, they could not be held as slaves unless they declined the king's care. Tisquantum and at least some of the others were freed as a result. Getting hauled into a distant labor market but also coming under a particular legal regime first threatened Tisquantum with slavery and then led to his unexpected release. Both slave markets and laws entangled this Patuxet man in Atlantic trends. That he eventually made it all the way home was a tribute to his own ingenuity but also evidence of the increasing traffic in ships coming to New England.

Tisquantum's role as an interpreter between the Plymouth planters and the local peoples was also reprised elsewhere. Certain key players throughout the history of European-American encounters served as go-betweens. The meeting with Squanto, retold endlessly, connected the Plymouth experience to all the other places up and down the coast of both American continents where Native inhabitants encountered newcomers.

Finally, the image of the first Thanksgiving connected Plymouth to the wider Atlantic. Described as a multiday harvest festival that gave an opportunity for the English to host their new allies and to take a much-needed break from their grueling labor, the gathering invoked the seasonal festivals of English rural culture that granted laborers a holiday. Popular representations of it—in nineteenth-century paintings, for instance—add religious overtones, with an emphasis on giving thanks to God. The name bestowed on the event in the nineteenth century, the "First Thanksgiving," reflected that understanding. Plymouth residents and other seventeenth-century

This imaginative recreation of "the first Thanksgiving" by Jennie Brownscombe contains some obviously inaccurate elements, most glaringly structures and Native attire from other places and periods. The 1875 painting emphasizes some standard representations of Plymouth: the devout nature of its society and the significance of its family bonds, not to mention the harmonious relations between English newcomers and Native residents. Little that matches the original written sources can be found in this depiction.

Christians did stage days of thanksgiving consisting of worship services in order to thank God for good occurrences, among them a successful harvest. Although this was not the type of event Winslow described, which was clearly a simple harvest celebration, both understandings of the gathering relate to larger themes. The harvest celebration reminds us of the settlers' efforts to import their own cultural practices. Marking a successful harvest helped to honor their new home as a "new England." The second idea—a day set aside for prayer and reflection—relied on the importation of European religious practices. Travelers always carried their religious beliefs and practices. Despite variations across the English Atlantic—the biggest division being between those who tried to recreate the Church of England in America and those who did not look to the Book of

Common Prayer as the pattern for their church services—every settlement tried to transplant English religion. Settlers could not prevent themselves from bringing with them their understanding of how the world worked. Every time a planter had a theological conversation with a Native person, European Christianity and Native belief met.

The subtext for both Plymouth Rock and the Thanksgiving story—as developed by later authors—is of course the twin (if somewhat contradictory) ideas of religious purity and religious freedom. These issues too played out throughout the Americas. Despite Bradford's record, which tells the story as one of English separatism, European exile, and American conclusion, Plymouth was like every English colony in that it played host to people with a range of religious views and varying levels of commitment. Working out how to live together and deciding where to draw the lines of inclusion and exclusion was part of the Plymouth project. Some people were not welcomed. That was certainly true of Sir Christopher Gardiner, who tried to hide his Roman Catholic faith. Despite its reputation as strictly separatist, the Plymouth church did welcome a variety of Reformed Protestant viewpoints. Following the advice of the Leiden minister John Robinson, it willingly held communion with those in the Church of England and did not require any prospective minister to renounce a previous ordination in that church. It did not, however, use the Book of Common Prayer. Plymouth's archnemesis Thomas Morton probably made more of that issue when trying to rouse Archbishop William Laud than was ever the case in New England itself. Morton did have a point, however: the prayer book was one easily transported aspect of English religiosity, so it was significant that the Plymouth people did not introduce it. Its absence would have placed Plymouth on the side of those reformers who would settle other parts of New England later, as well as many inhabitants in every other English colony—rather than on the side of those trying to recreate the national church.

Plymouth's toleration had its limits. The colony excluded those it saw as troublemakers. The church regretfully let Roger Williams go because his preaching, although inspiring, became too radical. More obscure people were made to feel unwelcome too. Such was the case with "one Manton": the men of Yarmouth church asked Edward Winslow's help in removing Manton after they decided he was "a discontented man" who was "unsettled and opposing God's people."[2] It is not clear how Winslow responded to their plea, but their letter documented that the tolerance of Plymouth's people had limits.

On every point, Plymouth's history can be woven back into a wider story. These connections provide a framework for understanding labor systems (like slavery and servitude), Native relations, religious practices and policies, and every other aspect of Plymouth life. In Plymouth Plantation, as elsewhere, existence was shaped by why people came, what they hoped to build, what features shaped the place where they settled, and how they thought of and treated those they encountered. These questions animated all the history of the Americas at least from the moment Columbus arrived in the Bahamas in 1492.

Some advocates of Plymouth Plantation might say that presenting that settlement as participating in larger events and trends minimizes its significance. Rather, I would suggest that Plymouth remains important, but not for what it contributed to the United States. An Atlantic perspective does challenge the narrative of American exceptionalism, but it also elevates small and marginal places to new importance by showing that they took part in the movements and events of their own day. Unlike those who debunk the myths associated with the plantation (and, as Francis Stoddard's complaints show, have done so for at least seventy years), my intention is not to prove wrong those famous tableaux—signing an agreement, stepping onto a rock, meeting a Native man, or celebrating a meal. Instead I would like to suggest that an emphasis on firstness and uniqueness needlessly limits our understanding of the experience of these early settlers. Plymouth, neither first nor unique, participated in a growing network of people, ideas, and things that slowly pulled southern New England and many other places into a newly connected world.

ABBREVIATIONS

NOTES

ACKNOWLEDGMENTS

ILLUSTRATION CREDITS

INDEX

ABBREVIATIONS

Alexander, *Encouragement*	Sir William Alexander. *An Encouragement to Colonies.* London, 1624.
"A Descriptive and Historical Account"	"A Descriptive and Historical Account of New England in Verse: from a MS of William Bradford, Governour of Plymouth Colony." *Collections of the MHS, for the Year 1794.* Vol. 3 (Boston, 1810): 77–84.
Dialogue	William Bradford. *A dialogue or third conference between some young men . . . and some ancient Men . . .* Edited by Charles Deane. Boston: John Wilson, 1870.
Good Newes	E[dward] W[inslow]. *Good Newes from New England: Or A True Relation of Things very remarkable at the Plantation of Plimoth in New-England.* London, 1624.
JWJ	*The Journal of John Winthrop, 1630–1649.* Edited by Richard S. Dunn, James Savage, and Laetitia Yeandle. Cambridge, MA: Belknap Press of Harvard University Press, 1996.
James, *Three Visitors*	Sydney V. James Jr., ed. *Three Visitors to Early Plymouth: Letters about the Pilgrim Settlement in New England during its first seven years, by John Pory, Emmanuel Altham, and Isaack de Rasieres.* [n.p.]: Plimoth Plantation, 1963.
Josselyn, *Account*	John Josselyn. *An Account of Two Voyages to New-England.* London, 1674.

Letter Book   *Governor Bradford's Letter Book*. In *Collections of the Massachu-setts Historical Society*, 1st ser., vol. 3 (1794); reprinted Boston, 1810. Reprinted as *Governor William Bradford's letter book*. Boston: Massachusetts Society of Mayflower Descendants, 1906.

Levett, *A Voyage*   Christopher Levett. *A Voyage into New England Begun in 1623. and ended in 1624. Performed by Christopher Levett, his Majesties Woodward of Somerset-shire, and one of the Councell of New England.* London, 1624.

McIntyre, *Debts*   Ruth A. McIntyre. *Debts Hopeful and Desperate: Financing the Plymouth Colony.* [Plymouth, MA]: Plimoth Plantation, 1963.

Morrell,   [Morrell, William.] *New-England, or a Briefe Enarration of the*
New-England   *Ayre.* London, 1625.

Morton,   Nathaniel Morton. *New-Englands Memoriall: Or, A brief*
New-Englands   *Relation of the most Memorable and Remarkable Passages of the*
Memoriall   *Province of God, manifested to the Planters of New-England in America; with special Reference to the first colony thereof, Called New-Plimouth.* Cambridge, Massachusetts, 1669.

Morton, *New*   Thomas Morton. *The New English Canaan or New Canaan.*
English Canaan   Amsterdam, 1637. Reprinted as *New English Canaan of Thomas Morton, with Introductory Matter and Notes.* Edited by Charles Francis Adams, Jr. Publications of the Prince Society, 14. Boston, 1883. Reissued in the Research and Source Work Series, 131; American Classics in History and Social Science, 2. New York: Burt Franklin, 1967.

New-Englands   [Francis Higginson]. *New-Englands Plantation. or, A Short and*
Plantation   *True Description of the Commodities and Discommodities of that Countrey.* London, 1630.

OPP   William Bradford. *Of Plymouth Plantation, 1620–1647.* Edited by Samuel Eliot Morison. New York: Alfred A. Knopf, 1952.

Pratt

Phineas Pratt. "A Declaration of the Affairs of the English People that first Inhabited New England" [1662]. Published as *A Declaration of the Affairs of the English People that first Inhabited New England*. Massachusetts Historical Society, *Collections*, 4th ser., vol. 4 (1858): 474–87; available online at https://pilgrimhall.org/pdf/Phineas_Pratt_Narrative.pdf.

RCNP

Records of the Colony of New Plymouth. Edited by Nathaniel B. Shurtleff. 12 vols. Boston: Commonwealth of Massachusetts, 1855–1861.

A Relation or
Journall

A Relation or Journall of the Beginning and Proceedings of the English Plantation setled at Plimoth in New England. London, 1622.

Smith,
Advertisements

John Smith. *Advertisements for the Unexperienced Planters of New England, or Any Where*. London, 1631; reprinted in *The Complete Works of Captain John Smith (1580–1631)*, 3 vols., edited by Philip L. Barbour. Chapel Hill: UNC / Institute of Early American History and Culture, 1986, 3: 253–307.

Smith, A
Description

John Smith. *A Description of New England*. London, 1616; reprinted in *The Complete Works of Captain John Smith (1580–1631)*, 3 vols., edited by Philip L. Barbour. Chapel Hill: UNC / Institute of Early American History and Culture, 1986, vol. 1: 291–370.

Smith, New
Englands Trials
(1622)

John Smith. *New Englands Trials*. London, 1622, reprinted in *The Complete Works of Captain John Smith (1580–1631)*, 3 vols., edited by Philip L. Barbour. Chapel Hill: UNC / Institute of Early American History and Culture, 1986, vol. 1: 413–48.

Wood, New
Englands
Prospect

William Wood. *New Englands Prospect. A true, lively, and experimentall description of that part of America, commonly called New England*. London, 1634.

WP

Winthrop Papers, vol. 3: 1631–1637. Edited by Allyn Bailey Forbes. Boston: Massachusetts Historical Society, 1943.

NOTES

Introduction

1. Samuel Sewall, *Phaenomena quaedam Apocalyptica* (Boston, 1697), 33; Jedidiah Morse, *The American Universal Geography*, part I (Boston, 1802), 316.

2. George Bancroft, *The History of the United States*, 15th edition (Boston, 1855), I:309–10.

3. Francis R. Stoddard, *The Truth about the Pilgrims* (New York: Society of Mayflower Descendants in the State of New York, 1952; Baltimore, MD: Clearfield, 1995), x. His biography appears in a family history he authored, *The Stoddard Family* (New York: The Trow Press, 1912), 112–13.

Wives

1. The name "Massasoit" is a title of respect, for a political leader. Although we don't know for certain what his personal name was at the time he first met the Plymouth settlers, as Native names often changed over a lifetime, we do know that later in life he was called Ousameyuin, which is rendered in the Wopanâak language as 8sâmeeqan. The English sources typically refer to the leader as "Massasoit," and that practice has been followed here.

2. *A Relation or Journall*, 38.

3. Ibid., 4.

4. Smith, *New Englands Trials* (1622), 431.

5. Robinson to church, 30 June 1621, Leiden, *Letter Book*, 45.

6. *A Relation or Journall*, 64.

7. *OPP*, 444.

8. The phrase, originally a comment about proper comportment for early New England women in a scholarly article, went on to have its own cultural life,

prompting Laurel Thatcher Ulrich to write about its strange history; see *Well-Behaved Women Seldom Make History* (New York: Knopf, 2007).

9. Morton, *New-Englands Memoriall*, 108.

10. *OPP*, 167.

11. Morton, *New-Englands Memoriall*, 58.

12. *OPP*, 222.

13. Morton, *New-Englands Memoriall*, 81.

14. Charles Francis Adams, Jr., in his introduction to Morton's volume, reviews these histories; Morton, *New English Canaan*, 24.

15. Letters dated 19 and 20 December 1623, *OPP*, 375, 376.

16. Edward Winslow to John Winthrop, 17 April 1637, *WP*, 391–93.

17. 1639, *RCNP*, 1:128–29.

18. Governor and Assistants of Plymouth to Governor and Assistants of Massachusetts Bay Colony, 6 February 1631[/32], *WP*, 64.

19. *Good Newes*, 56–57.

20. Morrell, *New-England*, 19–20.

21. Levett, *A Voyage*, 16.

22. *A Relation or Journall*, 45.

23. [] to the Council for New England, 9 June 1628, *Letter Book*, 62.

PLANTATION

1. *A Relation or Journall*, 43.

2. Ibid., 62.

3. *Good Newes*.

4. Smith, *Advertisements*, 253, 283; Morton, "Dedicatory epistle to Plymouth governor Thomas Prince," in *New-Englands Memoriall*, n.p.

5. *Good Newes*, A3.

6. Josselyn, *Account*, 152.

7. [John] Higginson, *New-Englands Plantation* (London, 1630).

8. Altham to his brother, Sir Edward Altham, dated September 1623, James, *Three Visitors*, 29.

9. Smith, *New Englands Trials* (1622), 428.

10. Morton, *New-Englands Memoriall*, 28.

11. Wood, *New England Prospect*, 94.

12. *Good Newes*, 59.

13. *A Relation or Journall*, 25.

14. *OPP*, 121.

Guns

1. *A Relation or Journall*, 15. The author erred in naming the culprit the son of Francis Billington; his father was in fact John, and the boy (probably age fourteen) was named Francis.

2. Ibid., 29.

3. *OPP*, 234; *JWJ*, 40, n.50.

4. Letter signed E. W., 11 December 1621, *A Relation or Journall*, 64.

5. *A Relation or Journall*, 13–14.

6. Ibid., 31.

7. See ibid., 26.

8. Ibid., 36–37.

9. *Good Newes*, 33.

10. James, *Three Visitors*, 77.

11. *OPP*, 165. Thomas Morton also described it in *New English Canaan*, 264.

12. *Good Newes*, 3.

13. *A Relation or Journall*, 19.

14. Ibid., 38.

15. Ibid., 44.

16. James I & IV, *A Proclamation prohibiting Interloping and Disorderly Trading in New England in America*, dated 6 November 1622, in *British Royal Proclamations Relating to America, 1603–1783*, ed. Clarence S. Brigham, Burt Franklin: Bibliography and Reference Series #56 (New York: Burt Franklin, 1911), 33–35.

17. Pratt.

18. *OPP*, 204.

19. Ibid., 206–7. For some of his attacks, see Bradford to Sir Ferdinando Gorges, 15 June 1627; and [ ] to the Council for New England, 9 June 1628, *Letter Book*, 57, 62. Morton also recapitulates some of his main points in *New Englands Memoriall* 76–71

20. *A Relation or Journall*, 37.

21. *JWJ*, 395.

Transients

1. For percentages, see Susan Hardman Moore, *Pilgrims: New World Settlers and the Call of Home* (New Haven: Yale University Press, 2007), 55. Moore calculates between 9 and 15 percent returned but may underestimate the astounding birth rate.

2. *OPP*, 441–48.

3. Josselyn, *Account*, 259.

4. *OPP*, 101–2.

5. *Good Newes*, 26; Pratt.

6. On de Rasieres, see James, *Three Visitors*, 63–80.

7. *OPP*, 443.

8. C. G. Pestana, "Peirce, William (1590?–June or July 1641)," *American National Biography* (New York: Oxford University Press, 1999).

REFUGE

1. *A Relation or Journall*, 66.

2. John Bunyan, *The Pilgrim's Progress* (London, 1678).

3. His first compilation, *Purchas his Pilgrimage or Relations of the World and Religions observed in all ages* (London, 1613), makes this point in his "epistlie dedicatory," 2v.

4. *OPP*, 47.

5. *Dialogue*, 55–56.

6. Quotations in this narrative taken from *OPP*, 11–14.

7. Ibid., 47.

8. Ibid., 442; *A Relation or Journall*, 16.

ANIMALS

1. *Good Newes*, 25–31.

2. *A Relation or Journall*, 29, mentions a little spaniel in 1621. Dogs are described in Pratt (in both Native and English communities). Morrell, *New-England*, n.p., recommended bringing mastiffs to hunt "light-footed Natives."

3. Smith, *A Description*, 334.

4. *A Relation or Journall*, 52.

5. *New-Englands Plantation*, C3v.

6. Morton, *New-Englands Memoriall*, 49.

7. Sherley et al. to Bradford et al., 18 December 1624, *Letter Book*, 33.

8. Morton, *New-Englands Memoriall*, 53; Josselyn, *Account*, 250.

9. Smith, *Advertisements*, 283.

10. "A Descriptive and Historical Account," 78.

11. Morrell, *New-England*, n.p.

12. *JWJ*, 40–41.

13. Higginson, in his catalog of what to bring, *New-Englands Plantation*, n.p.

14. 2 January 1633 / 4, *RCNP*, 1:23.

15. Pratt.

16. 1 July 1633, *RCNP*, 1:13.

17. *OPP*, 310, 311, 314–15.

TRADERS

1. Morton, *New-Englands Memoriall*, 36; Morton also summarizes the history of that endeavor generally, 40–41. Bradford discusses both Weston and his venture; see *OPP*, 37–40, 56, 119–20, 109–10, 113–19.

2. For Robinson's letter against Standish's actions, see ibid., 374–75.

3. "Of Plimoth Plantation" does not use the term "lazy," but Bradford describes them wasting what they had and doing little for themselves; see 114–17. Thomas Morton dubbed "many of them lazy persons"; Morton, *New English Canaan*, 249.

4. Phineas Pratt married Mary Priest, daughter of Degory Priest (who arrived in 1620 but died shortly thereafter) and of Sarah (who came later with her daughters and her new husband).

5. Morton, *New-Englands Memoriall*, 43.

6. The idea was initially broached in James Sherley to William Bradford, 17 November 1628, *Letter Book*, 58–59; and the Articles of Agreement between the people of Plymouth and Bradford, Standish, Allerton, and others who would join in the terms with the new partners, n.d., 60–61.

7. Charles M. Andrews, *The Colonial Period of American History*, vol. 1: *The Settlements* (New Haven: Yale University Press, 1926), 288.

8. *OPP*, 245, 246, 289.

9. Morton, *Dobie*, 50 50 1.108 1460 1 702 708–908 807–805.

GOD

1. *Good Newes*, 52–56.

2. Smith, *New Englands Trials* (1622), 428.

3. *A Relation or Journall*, A3, 10, 14, 15, 19–20, 29.

4. *Good Newes*, A2v.

5. *Letter Book*, 48.

6. *JWJ*, 395.

7. *Good Newes*, 6.

8. Samuel Fuller and Edward Winslow to Bradford, Ralph Smith, and William Brewster, 26 July 1630, Salem, *Letter Book*, 75.

9. *A Relation or Journall*, 48.

10. Hilton letter, in Smith, *New Englands Trials* (1622), 431.

11. 1624, *Letter Book*, 28.

12. Samuel Fuller to William Bradford, 2 August 1630, Charlestown, ibid., 76.

13. *Good Newes*, A2.

14. Mr. Sherley, dated 25 January 1623 / 4, *OPP*, 372.

15. Thomas Harriot, *A Briefe and True Report of the New Found Land of Virginia* (London, 1588).

16. *OPP*, 114.

17. *A Relation or Journall*, 48.

18. *Good Newes*, 55.

19. Morton, *New English Canaan*, 141, 150–51, 167; *A Relation or Journall*, 61.

20. Morrell, *New-England*, 23; Levett, *A Voyage*, 18–19; *New-Englands Plantation*, n.p.

TOBACCO

1. *A Relation or Journall*, 38.

2. Ibid., 34, 38.

3. Ibid., 34.

4. Ibid., 37.

5. Ibid., 48.

6. Ibid., 54–55.

7. Ibid., 45.

8. Ibid., 46.

9. James I, *A Counterblaste to Tobacco* (London, 1604); Levett, *A Voyage*, 28—rather than women, he in fact said "whores."

10. Benjamin B. Roberts, *Sex, Drugs and Rock'n'Roll in the Dutch Golden Age* (Amsterdam: Amsterdam University Press, 2017), 127–29, 134–35, 136–37. My thanks to Melissa Morris for bringing this reference to my attention.

11. *Good Newes*, 61–63.

12. 4 September 1638, *RCNP*, II:27–28.

13. Dated 5 March 1638 / 9, ibid., I:118.

14. 1 September 1640, ibid., II:36.

15. Altham to Altham, 1625, James, *Three Visitors*, 58–59. Two years before he mentioned the gift of a pipe to the same brother (35), presumably a different one.

ESCAPEES

1. *OPP*, 167.
2. Ibid., 119–20.
3. Ibid., 322.
4. *OPP*, 247. *JWJ*, 51, n.4; *OPP*, 248–49, and see *American National Biography*: Philip Ranlet, Gardiner, Sir Christopher (1596–February 1662). Gardiner was also the subject of a Longfellow poem: "The Landlord's Tale: The Rhyme of Sir Christopher."
5. On Fells, "packed him away," see *OPP*, 192.
6. 7 August 1638, *RCNP*, 1:93.
7. 2 November 1640, ibid., 1:164.
8. 7 August 1638, ibid., 1:93, 94.
9. 3 September 1639, ibid., 1:132.
10. Smith, *A Description*, 348.

A NEW ENGLAND

1. *OPP*, 301 (second murder); more generally, 299–301. And see *RCNP*, I: 96–97.
2. Isaack de Rasieres to Samuel Blommaert, 1628 or 1629, James, *Three Visitors*, 77; Morton, *New-Englands Memoriall*, 111.
3. *OPP*, 301n.1.
4. Anon., *A briefe Relation of the Discovery and Plantation of New England* (London, 1622); Alexander, *Encouragement*.
5. Morton, *New-Englands Memoriall*, 25.
6. [Robert Cushman], *A Sermon Preached at Plimmoth in New-England December 9. 1621* (London, 1622), A2.
7. Morton, *New English Canaan*.
8. *A Relation or Journall*, 35.
9. Morrell, *New-England*, 24.
10. Roger Williams to Governor John Winthrop, 26 October 1637, *The Correspondence of Roger Williams*, ed. Glenn W. LaFantasie, 2 vols. (Hanover and London: Brown University Press / University Press of New England, for The Rhode Island Historical Society, 1988), 126.
11. Levett, *A Voyage*, 22.
12. *Good Newes*, A2.
13. Anon., *A briefe Relation*, B3; *A Relation or Journall*, 50.

14. Bradford to the Council of [for] New England, 15 June 1627, *Letter Book*, 56.

15. Sherley to Bradford, 24 June 1633, *OPP,* 392.

16. Morton, *New-Englands Memoriall,* 14.

STOCKINGS

1. August 1638, *RCNP,* 1:93.

2. James Sherley, William Collier, Thomas Fletcher, and Robert Holland to Bradford, Allerton, Brewster, and "the rest of the general society of Plymouth in New England," 18 December 1624, *Letter Book*, 33.

3. *OPP,* 182.

4. Isaack de Rasieres to "Monsieur Monseignieur, William Bradford, Governeur in Nieu-Plemeüen" 4 October 1627, James, *Three Visitors,* 53.

5. *A Relation or Journall,* 63.

6. *OPP,* 66n.

7. James Sherley to William Bradford, 8 March 1629, *Letter Book*, 68–69.

8. 24 November 1633, *RCNP,* 1:20; 2 September 1634, *RCNP,* 1:31.

9. 5 June 1638, ibid., 1:87, 91.

10. *A Relation or Journall,* 11.

11. Ibid., 34.

12. Ibid.

13. *OPP,* 219.

14. *A Relation or Journall,* 45.

15. Ibid., 32.

16. Francis Kirby to John Winthrop, Jr., 22 June 1632, London, *WP,* 82.

17. "A Descriptive and Historical Account," 78.

SERVANTS

1. Leviticus says simply "And if a man lie with a beast, he shall surely be put to death: and yᵉ shall slay the beast." Leviticus 20:15, from the King James Version of the Bible. English laws on this, beginning with the first civil enactment under Henry VIII in 1533, do not appear to be the source of the punishment. The ritual execution of the animals along with the perpetrator occurred on the European continent as early as the fifteenth century, according to E. P. Evans, *The Criminal Prosecution and Capital Punishment of Animals* (New York, 1906), 147–8, 151. Cotton Mather, in his *Magnalia Christi Americana,* describes a scene quite similar to the

one in Plymouth, with the perpetrator made to watch the animals die, in New Haven in 1662. (London, 1702), Book VI: 38–39.

2. *OPP,* 320–21 (dated 1642).

3. February 1632 / 3, *RCNP,* 1:8.

4. *Good Newes,* 65.

5. *RCNP,* 1:16.

6. 24 December 1636, ibid., 1:46–47.

7. August 1638, ibid., 1:94.

8. 2 September 1634, ibid., 1:31.

9. 24 June 1639, ibid., 1:128–29.

10. See Governor and Assistants of Plymouth to the same of MBC, 6 February 1631[/32], *WP,* 64–65.

11. 7 November 1636, *RCNP,* 1:46.

12. 2 October 1637, ibid., 1:68.

13. *OPP,* 62, 204–10, 216.

14. 1633, *RCNP,* 1:23; 1636, 44; 11:18 [1639?].

15. 10 January 1632 / 3, ibid., 1:7.

16. Incidents in this paragraph are all in ibid., vol.1, dated 23 July 1633 (15), 11 June 1639 (128), 3 March 1639 / 40 (143), and July 1635 (35).

17. August 1637, ibid., 1:64; for the serving woman, see 65.

18. 8 February 1638, ibid., 1:113.

19. Alexander, *Encouragement,* 37.

20. *RCNP,* 6:153. The date was 5 May 1685, and within a few years Plymouth would cease to be a separate colony.

APPARAISM

1. Sherley et al. to Bradford et al., 18 December 1624, *Letter Book,* 29–30.

2. *OPP,* 171.

3. Smith, *Advertisements,* 270, 297.

4. Morton, *New English Canaan.*

5. *OPP,* 273–74, 422–23. Also see *JWJ,* 159, n.63.

6. Morton, *New English Canaan,* 262–63.

7. *OPP,* 171–72.

8. *Dialogue,* 22.

9. Morton, *New-Englands Memoriall,* 79.

10. Sherley to Bradford, 18 May 1641, *OPP,* 399.

Furs

1. *JWJ*, 131.
2. *OPP*, 262–68.
3. Ibid., 263.
4. Smith, *A Description*, 323; also see Anon., *A Briefe Relation of the Discovery* (London, 1622), C2. Winslow discussed them in his natural history chapter (8) in *Good Newes*.
5. Smith, *A Description*, 324, 336.
6. *A Relation or Journall*, 33, 37–38.
7. Ibid., 50.
8. Ibid., 46.
9. Ibid., 35, 41.
10. 7 March 1636 / 7, *RCNP*: 1, 54.
11. *OPP*, 254–55, 176. Morton, *New-Englands Memoriall*, 62.
12. *OPP*, 286–87.
13. Bradford to Sir Ferdinando Gorges, 15 June 1627, *Letter Book*, 57.
14. *Good Newes*, 18.
15. *OPP*, 206–7.
16. Ibid., 319, n.4.
17. William Cronon, *Changes in the Land: Indians, Colonists and the Ecology of New England* (New York: Hill and Wang, 1983).

Privateers

1. *OPP*, 345–46. *JWJ*, 626–27.
2. James, *Three Visitors*, 42. William Bradford, Governor, and Isaac Allerton, Assistant [to James Sherley], 8 September 1623, ed. R. G. Marsden, *AHR*, 8:2 (1903): 296, for wages and "taker."
3. *Letter Book*, 53.
4. Wood, *New Englands Prospect*, 54.
5. John G. Reid, *Acadia, Maine, and New Scotland: Marginal Colonies in the Seventeenth Century* (Toronto: University of Toronto Press, 1981), 84–87, 94.
6. "Complaint of Certain Adventurers and Inhabitants of the Plantation in New England," printed in Edward Arber, *The Story of the Pilgrim Fathers, 1603–1623 A.D.* (London: Ward and Downey, 1897), 506–8.
7. *OPP*, 175–76.
8. Sherley to Bradford, 6 December 1632, ibid., 251.

Kingship

1. *A Relation or Journall*, 36–37.

2. Ibid., 58, 69.

3. Ibid., 61.

4. *RCNP*, 11:20.

5. *Good Newes*, A2.

6. Pratt.

7. *Good Newes*, 26; Morton, *New-Englands Memoriall*, dedicatory epistle, n.p.

8. *A Relation or Journall*, 3.

9. *Good Newes*, 36.

10. *OPP*, 62.

11. Governor and Council to Director and Council of New Netherland, 19 March 1627, *Letter Book*, 51–52.

12. *RCNP*, 11:20.

13. *A Relation or Journall*, 36, 40, 45, 49, 53; the queen, 57.

14. Levett, *A Voyage*, 21.

Books

1. *OPP*, 248; Morton, *New-Englands Memoriall*, 86 87; also see *JWJ*, 51, 51n.4.

2. [Henry Martyn] Dexter, "Elder Brewster's Library," *Proceedings of the Massachusetts Historical Society* 5 (1899–1900): 82.

3. *New-Englands Plantation*, D3.

4. Thomas Goodard Wright, *Literary Culture in Early New England, 1620–1730* (New Haven, 1920), 26–29.

5. James Deetz and Patricia E. S. Deetz, *The Times of Their Lives: Life, Love, and Death in Plymouth Colony* (New York: W. H. Freeman, 2000), 195.

6. Smith, *Advertisements*, 285–86.

7. David A. Lupher, *Greeks, Romans, and Pilgrims: Classical Receptions in Early New England* (Leiden: Brill, 2017), 185.

8. *OPP*, 113.

9. H. Kirk-Smith, *William Brewster: 'The Father of New England': His Life and Times, 1567–1644* (Boston: Richard Kay, 1992), 248, 275.

10. The discussion that follows is based on Dexter, "Elder Brewster's Library," 37–85, and Jeremy Dupertius Bangs's effort to check and update Dexter, in *Plymouth Colony's Private Libraries: As Recorded in Wills and Inventories, 1633–1692*, transcribed and edited by Bangs (Leiden: American Leiden Pilgrim Museum,

2016; revised edition, 2018), 38–178. Bangs also surveyed other book lists for Plymouth.

11. Alexander Cooke, *Pope Joane: A Dialogue between a Protestant and a Papist* (London, 1610).

12. For specific works mentioned, see Dexter, "Elder Brewster's Library": Robinson (48, 49–50), Sibbes (51, 75, 78), Beard (49), *Swedish Intelligencer* (58), ballads (60, 68), Raleigh (69), Prynne (56, 68).

13. [Robert Cushman], *A Sermon Preached at Plimmoth in New-England December 9. 1621* (London, 1622).

14. Morton, *New English Canaan*, published in London in 1637; Nathaniel Morton called it scurrilous: *New-Englands Memoriall*, 72.

15. Morton, *New English Canaan*, 283, 332, 260, 259–60n.1.

CONCLUSION

1. *A Relation or Journall*, 33.

2. Yarmouth church to Edward Winslow, 12 April 1639, printed in Jeremy Dupertius Bangs, *Pilgrim Edward Winslow: New England's First International Diplomat, A Documentary History* (Boston: New England Historic Genealogical Society, 2004), 186–88.

ACKNOWLEDGMENTS

The idea for this book arose after Richard Pickering at Plimoth Plantation invited me to participate in a reassessment of the museum's programming funded by the National Endowment for the Humanities. My few days there prompted my thinking about the way we isolate Plymouth when we consider its history. The book benefited from readings by Emily Cahill and Don Pestana. They provided the perspective of the nonacademics, whom I hope this book will reach. As always, both Sharon Salinger and Michael Meranze read much of the book in draft form and discussed my goals and concerns. Nicole Gilhuis helped catch errors and infelicities. Eric Hinderaker and an anonymous reader for Harvard University Press gave me helpful ideas for how to improve it. The talented Isabelle Lewis made the maps. Individuals at various institutions aided my search for images or sources, including the staffs at the Congregational Library and Archives; the Huntington Library; the John Carter Brown Library; the National Museum of American History (Smithsonian Institution); the Pilgrim Hall Museum; Plimoth Plantation; and the State Library of Massachusetts.

Like most people educated in U.S. public schools, I first encountered Plymouth in grade school, particularly around the holiday of Thanksgiving. It therefore seems fitting to dedicate this book to my many excellent history teachers, from grade school through graduate school.

ILLUSTRATION CREDITS

7   "Pilgrim Brand Oranges," Jay T. Last Collection, ephJLC_CIT_000538, The
      Huntington Library, San Marino, California.
10   Plymouth Rock fragment with painted inscription, 1830, Virginia L. W. Fox,
      National Museum of American History, Smithsonian Institution.
20   William Bradford, "Of Plimoth Plantation." Courtesy of the State Library of
      Massachusetts.
32   "Map of New England," in John Smith, A Description of New England,
      London, 1616. RB3409, The Huntington Library, San Marino, California.
42   Engraving, "The March of Miles Standish," Harry T. Peters "America on
      Stone" Lithography Collection, National Museum of American History,
      Smithsonian Institution.
49   Artist unknown, Edward Winslow, 1651. Courtesy of Pilgrim Hall Museum,
      Plymouth, Massachusetts.
70   Good Newes from New England, London, 1624. RB17923, The Huntington
      Library, San Marino, California.
84   William Bradford, "Of Plimoth Plantation." Courtesy of the State Library of
      Massachusetts.
91   The Booke of Common Prayer, with the psalter or Psalmes of David,
      London, 1619. RB17023, The Huntington Library, San Marino, California.
98   "The Landing of the Fathers at Plymouth, Dec. 22: 1620," Harry T. Peters,
      "America on Stone" Lithography Collection, National Museum of American
      History, Smithsonian Institution.
116   John Smith, A Description of New England, London, 1616. RB3409, The
      Huntington Library, San Marino, California.
126   Courtesy of Plimoth Plantation.
140   Thomas Morton, New English Canaan, Amsterdam, 1637. RB3389, The
      Huntington Library, San Marino, California.

155   Edgar Parker, based on Robert Weir, *Embarkation of the Pilgrims*, 1875. Courtesy of Pilgrim Hall Museum, Plymouth, Massachusetts.

169   "The South part of New-England," in William Wood, *New Englands Prospect*, London, 1634. RB17980, The Huntington Library, San Marino, California.

177   *Hollandiae chorographia*, Amsterdam, 1611. Courtesy of the John Carter Brown Library.

189   Thomas Lodge, *The workes of Lucius Annaeus Seneca*, London, 1614. RB69402, The Huntington Library, San Marino, California.

199   Jennie A. Brownscombe, *The First Thanksgiving at Plymouth*, 1875. Courtesy of Pilgrim Hall Museum, Plymouth, Massachusetts.

INDEX

Adey, Web, 127

Adolphus, Gustavus, 187–188

adultery, 111–112

adventurers, 81, 87, 130; support from, 55, 71, 125, 139, 170; history of, 77, 89–90, 141–142, 147–148; debt owed to, 82, 145, 164, 173; Lyford and, 105–106. See also Altham, Emmanuel; Weston, Thomas

Advertisements for the Unexperienced Planters, 29

Ainsworthy, Henry, 185

Aldrich (widow), 21

Alexander, John, 144

Alexander, Sir William, 117, 145

Allerton, Isaac, 51, 80–81, 83, 85, 187, 171; trader, 55, 80, 81, 82, 85

Allerton, Mary Norris, 18–19

Almanac (Peirce), 186

Altham, Emmanuel, 55, 101, 170

Andrews, Charles McLean, 81

animals, 33, 68–74, 119, 135, 143. See also beaver; otter

Anne (ship), 17, 23

Anne of Denmark, 25

Annotation on the Fourth Book of Moses (Ainsworthy), 185

Antichrist the Pope of Rome (Beard), 187

Ashley, Edward, 129

Bahamas, 52–53, 201

Baker, William, 26, 120, 136–137

Bancroft, George, 6, 123

Beard, Thomas, 187

beaver, 82, 130, 158–164, 172, 192

Bermuda, 50, 51, 194

Beza, Theodore, 187

bigamy, 107, 108–109, 113

Billington, Francis, 37–38, 44

Billington, John, 38

Bishop, James, 143

Boardman, Luce, 109, 110, 113

Boardman, Thomas, 109, 110, 111, 113

Book of Common Prayer, 91, 111, 153, 191, 200; Thomas Morton and, 149, 190–191

Boston, England, 63

Boston, Massachusetts, 22, 85, 124, 190

Bourne, Plymouth Plantation, 83

Bradford, Alice Southworth, 23, 126

Bradford, Dorothy, 23

Bradford, William, 5, 23, 81, 89, 129; writing "Of Plimoth Plantation," 3,

Bradford, William (*continued*)
29, 60, 196; on Mayflower Compact,
5–6, 196; on women, 16, 21, 34–35,
63; on deaths, 18, 52, 56; on births,
19, 20, 26; his correspondence, 22,
147, 154–155, 193–194; on guns, 38, 42;
on Wessagussett, 54, 122; on trade,
55, 83, 84, 162, 163, 194; narrative arc,
60–62, 150, 153, 194, 200; on religion,
61, 87, 88, 89, 90; using term "pilgrim,"
61, 65, 66; on departure, 62–65; on
Thomas Morton, 79, 122, 139, 144,
149, 180, 191; on bad influences,
107, 122, 135–136; on Christopher
Gardiner, 108–109, 183–184; on
murder, 114, 121, 157; rivalry with
Massachusetts, 115, 196; on sin, 135,
143, 170; on servants, 135–136, 139;
on privateers, 167, 170–171, 174, 194;
and books, 184, 185, 189
Brewer, Thomas, 188
Brewster, Fear, 80
Brewster, Jonathan, 185–186
Brewster, Love, 185–186, 187
Brewster, William, 22, 40, 147, 153, 185;
printer, 176, 184, 188, 189; library of,
184, 185–189
Brian, Thomas, 142
Brooke, 2nd Baron, Robert Greville, 157
Browne, Robert, 147, 148, 150
Bunyan, John, 60

Calvin, John, 187
Cambridge, Massachusetts, 186, 190
Cape Ann, 53, 83, 117, 162, 170
Cape Cod, 23, 37, 83, 117, 127, 195; Bay, 15,
47, 48, 108, 118, 193

Caribbean, 56, 73, 74, 96, 99; trade with,
73, 74; privateers in, 173, 194, 197
Carver, John, 17, 19, 52
Charles I, 115, 149, 180; as Prince
Charles, 115–116, 118
Charles River, 117
Chrysostom, 186
church, 89, 105, 121, 182, 191; Scrooby, 8,
62, 150; Leiden, 17, 51, 54, 59, 80, 150,
153; of England, 91, 147–149, 155,
176, 191, 199; Plymouth, 105–106,
148, 150–155, 200, 201; commu-
nion with the Church of England,
150–151, 153–154, 200; Huguenot,
151; Salem, 152; Catholic, 183;
Geneva, 187
Church, Richard, 143
Clarke, Thomas, 127, 138
cloth, 114, 125–126, 128, 130–131
clothing, 34, 72, 82, 124–131
Conbatant, 39–40
Connecticut, 4, 53, 141, 162, 196
Connecticut River, 53, 83, 130, 161, 163
Cooke, Alexander, 187
Cooke, Francis, 138
Cooke, Hester, 19
Cooper, Humility, 17, 52
corn, 5, 87, 137, 138, 143; traded, 42, 161,
163; Native use of, 24, 71, 99, 119
Council for New England, 107, 117, 122,
161, 168–169, 184, 195
Counterblaste to Tobacco, A (James I &
VI), 89
Cronon, William, 164
Crosse, Daniel, 114
Cushman, Robert, 54, 118, 176, 178, 190;
on "Pilgrims," 59–60, 61, 65, 67

debt, 73, 82, 194; undertaken, 81, 83, 141, 142; questioned, 83, 84, 164; covered by trade, 83, 85, 160–162, 178, 197; Weston's, 107, 113; servants', 137, 139, 144
Delft Haven, Netherlands, 61–62
Derby, Richard, 138
Description of New England, A, 115–116
Dialogue or third conference, A, 89
Dotey, Edward, 138
Droitwich, England, 143
Dunford, John, 53–54
Dutch West India Company, 55, 171
Duxbury, Plymouth Plantation, 108, 110, 135, 142

Eaton, Francis, 18
Eaton, Samuel, 18
Eaton, Sarah, 18
Eedy, Samuel, 142
Ely, 56
Emerson, Edward, 143
Encouragement to Colonies, An, 145
English civil wars, 5, 55, 168, 170
Englishness, 27, 35–36, 114–123
epidemics, 28, 30–31, 48, 50, 87, 88

Farrell, Thomas, 143
Fells, (Mr.), 109
"First Comers," 4, 6, 9, 16
Ford, John, 18
Ford, Martha, 18
Forefathers' Day, 3, 6, 7, 27
Fortune (ship), 18, 172
Fuller, Edward, 21
Fuller, Samuel, 17, 89, 184

furs, 80, 85, 130, 157–164; competition for, 42, 122, 163; shipped, 56, 173, 197; hopes for, 99, 128, 173

Gardiner, Sir Christopher, 107–109, 113, 183–184, 200
Gardner, Richard, 56
gender, 23, 32, 34–35; male, 16, 28, 111, 141; female, 35
God, 86–94, 143, 178–180; Word of, 152, 191, 192. See also Providence, divine
Good Newes from New England (Winslow), 2–3, 5, 29, 70, 190; assesses Plymouth, 89, 99, 137
Gorges, Sir Fernando, 107–108, 149, 183–184
Gorton, Samuel, 21, 53
Granger, Thomas, 143
Graves, (Master), 71
Grinder, Alice, 127
gun control, 38, 41
guns, 37–44, 56, 63, 69, 82; and Natives, 77, 79, 122, 160, 191

Hallowell, Thomas, 124–125, 131
Hampden, John, 54–55
Handmaid (ship), 72
Harmon, Edmund, 138
Harmon, John, 138
"Harmony of Confessions," 151
Harriot, Thomas, 90, 120
Hawthorne, Nathaniel, 112
Higginson, John, 33, 71, 92, 93, 184
Hilton, William, 17
Hingham, Massachusetts, 21
Hocking, John, 157–158, 161, 162

Holland, 155, 185, 191; journey to, 8, 49, 61, 64–65, 152; living in, 17, 119, 120, 153; press in, 176, 188
Hooke, John, 17
Hopkins, Damaris, 18
Hopkins, Elizabeth, 18, 65
Hopkins, Oceanus, 56, 65
Hopkins, Stephen, 18, 39, 51–52, 65, 111, 139
household, 139, 141–143; ideal, 23, 34–35, 143–144; female-headed, 22; patriarchal, 34, 106, 111
Howland, Elizabeth Tillie, 19
Howland, John, 17, 19, 157, 162
Hudson River, 55, 99, 160
Hunt, Thomas, 48, 121, 158, 197–198

Indian Ocean, 79
Ireland, 62, 105

Jackson, Thomas, 115
James I and VI, 97, 116, 175–176, 177, 181
Josselyn, John, 53, 71

Kennebec, Maine, 43, 83, 157–158, 161–163
King Philip's War, 141, 145
Kingship, 171, 175–182, 188; Natives and, 15, 95, 101, 129–130

language, 57, 86, 179; adepts, 47, 57, 120–121; learning, 62, 129
Latham, William, 52
Laud, William, Archbishop, 149, 151, 154, 191, 200
Leiden, 17, 61, 62, 120, 177, 184; time in, 48, 65, 80, 96, 154, 194; location of church, 59–60, 150, 165; tobacco in, 96, 98, 100; migrants from, 119, 126, 153, 179, 184, 193; site of press, 184, 186, 187, 188, 191. See also church; Leiden
Levett, Christopher, 25, 88, 92, 93, 97, 121, 181
Lincoln, Abraham, 4–5
Little James (ship), 55, 170–171, 172, 173
London, 8, 49, 97, 100, 106, 163; presses in, 2, 59, 62, 184–191; living in, 52, 54, 65, 110–111, 137; investors in, 77, 81, 84, 87, 89, 126
Lupher, David A., 185
Lyford, John, 21, 53, 56, 105–107, 148, 151; rapist, 88, 105–106, 113
Lyford, Sarah, 21, 106

Maine, 43, 48, 109, 121
Manomet, 142
map, 32, 117–118, 169, 184–185
marriage, 11, 18, 23, 106, 111, 143; subsequent, 17, 21, 23; children outside of, 23, 113; native practices characterized, 24, 25; sex outside of, 26, 109, 110, 143
Marshfield, Plymouth Plantation, 65
Martin, Mary, 17
Massachusetts (people), 108
Massachusetts (state), 8, 196
Massachusetts Bay Colony, 30, 31, 53, 56, 85, 195; government, 4, 24; founding of, 22, 73, 88, 108, 139, 162; Wars of, 53, 141; religion in, 66, 148–149, 152, 153, 154; foe of Morton, 109, 149, 190; contention with, 115, 142; working with, 135, 139, 157–158, 183–184
Massasoit, 95–96, 97, 129–130; as leader, 15, 50, 209; his people, 15, 51, 68; on wives, 16, 25, 97; meeting with, 39, 54–55, 68, 71, 95; treaty with, 43, 82,

95, 160, 175; as king or emperor, 175, 176, 181

Mayflower (ship), 7, 18, 38, 44, 56

Mayflower Compact, 2, 5, 8, 179; democratic nature, 1, 3–4, 6, 182, 195

Mayflower descendent, 1, 6, 9, 52

Mayflower passengers, 6, 37, 51, 56, 58, 65, 156

Mendame, Mary, 112

Mendame, Robert, 112

Mendloue, William, 142–143

Minter, Desire, 17, 52

Moorecock, Mary, 23, 138

Moral Epistles (Seneca), 185, 188, 189

Morison, Samuel Eliot, 193

Morocco, 172

Morrell, William, 24, 25, 33, 72, 93, 119

Morse, Jedidiah, 5

Morton, Nathaniel, 29, 77–78, 88, 118–119, 152; using "Of Plimoth Plantation," 3, 6, 8; on conditions, 31, 71, 122, 123

Morton, Thomas, 79, 81, 118–119; allegations against, 25–26, 42, 122, 139, 144, 180; on religion, 92–93, 149–151, 190–191, 200; as foe, 109, 149, 150, 151, 163, 180, 190; author of New English Canaan, 140, 190–191

Mount Wollaston, 42, 79, 108, 162

Nantasket, Massachusetts, 21

Narragansett Bay, 160

Narragansetts, 41, 108, 115

Nevis, 195

Newcomen, John, 38

New-England Memorial (N. Morton), 3

New English Canaan (T. Morton), 118, 140, 190

Newfoundland, 48

New Haven Colony, 81, 196

New Netherland, 55, 80, 125, 162, 171, 180

Nova Scotia, 171, 195

"Of Plimoth Plantation," 6, 20, 29, 88, 150; writing, 3, 52, 60–61, 185, 193, 194

Oldham, John, 21, 40, 53; wife of, 21

otter, 130, 159, 164, 194

Palmer, William, 138

Peach, Arthur, 111, 114

Peirce, William, 56, 186

Penowanyanquis, 115

Penwatechet, 142–143

Pequot, 53

Pequot War, 141, 145

Pickworth, John, 24

Pierce, John, 88

Pilgrim, 1, 4, 7, 61, 66; concept, 59–61, 65, 66–67

Pilgrim's Progress, 60

plantation, 28–36, 79, 83, 184

Plimoth Plantation (museum), 1–2, 66, 126

Plymouth, England, 117, 172

Plymouth Rock, 3, 8, 200, 202; tourists and, 1, 8, 67; improbable, 4, 9–10, 196–197

Pocahontas, 1, 4

Pory, John, 54, 185

Pratt, Phineas, 42, 55, 78, 179

Prence, Thomas, 114, 186

Prerogative of Parliaments (Raleigh), 188

Priest, Digory, 17

privateers, 167–174, 182, 194, 197

Privy Council, 63

Providence, divine, 5, 87–89, 174; as
punishment, 21, 31, 88, 92, 93, 106;
as mercy, 37–38, 39, 78, 198–199
Providence Island, 195
Prower, Solomon, 17
Prynne, William, 188
Purchas, Samuel, 60

Quaddequina, 41
Quincy, Massachusetts, 79

Raleigh, Sir Walter, 90, 97, 188
Rasieres, Isaac de, 55
"Reasons and Considerations," 59
refuge, 59–67, 113, 118–119, 153
Relation or Journall, A (anon.), 2, 29, 33,
54, 87, 92–93, 97, 190
Rhode Island and Providence Planta-
tions, 22, 29, 30, 85, 114, 196
Roanoke, 1, 38, 90, 120
Roberts, Thomas, 144
Robinson, Bridget, 65
Robinson, John, 17, 22, 65, 77, 187;
theology, 150–151, 153–154, 200
Rogers, Thomas, 17
Rolfe, John, 26
Roman Catholicism, 48, 67, 86, 183, 200;
anti-Catholicism, 67, 187
Runaways, 24, 109, 113, 122, 139,
144–145, 191

Saint Christopher, 195
Samoset, 15, 50, 120–121, 128
Satan, 86–87, 93
Saye and Sele, 1st Viscount, (William
Fiennes), 157
Scarlett Letter, The, 112

Scituate, Plymouth Plantation, 108, 142
Seekonk, MA, 115
Seneca, 185, 188, 189
separatism, 147–156, 200
Sermon Preached at Plimmoth, A, 54,
178
servants, 17, 19, 26, 52, 79, 135–146; in
household, 22, 23, 34, 35, 53, 105, 190;
runaway, 24, 113, 145, 191; time as, 26,
52, 78, 79; and sex, 109, 143–144;
care of, 126–127
Sewall, Samuel, 5
sex, 53, 143–144, 145; abusive, 26, 79,
88, 106; premarital, 109, 110–111, 143;
adulterous, 111–112, 143; with native
women, 120, 144; with animals, 135,
143
sexual assault, 26, 79, 88, 105–106, 113
Sherley, James, 122, 126, 147–148, 154
Shetle, William, 127, 138
Sibbes, William, 187
slaves, 30, 33, 35–36, 123, 145–146,
201; Native, 5, 48, 141, 146, 198;
African, 29–30, 80, 141, 145;
English, 30, 172
Smith, John, 1, 4; writing on New
England, 29, 31, 69–71, 71–72,
84–85, 123, 1158; map, 32, 115–116,
169; naming, 32, 115–118, 119; on
New Englanders, 112–113, 119–120,
148, 149
Smith, Ralph, 29
Snow, William, 138
South America, 96
Spain, 48, 98–99, 198
Sparrow, Pandora, 23, 138
Sparrow, Richard, 23, 138

Squanto. *See* Tisquantum

Standish, Alexander, 185, 186

Standish, Miles, 39, 42, 51, 77, 95, 190

Stinnings, Richard, 115

Stoddard, Francis Russell, 9, 201

Tempest, The, 51

Temple, Dorothy, 111, 144

Thanksgiving, 1, 3, 4–5, 7, 69, 198–200,
221

Thompson, David, 22

Thorpe, John, 138

Till, James, 143

Tillie, John, 19

Tinsin, 112, 113

Tisquantum, 41, 47, 48, 120; meeting
with, 3, 48, 57; interpreter, 15, 40,
50–51, 90, 120–121, 198; kidnapped,
30, 48, 57, 158, 197–198

tobacco, 80, 82, 92, 95–101, 159

traders, 50, 77–85, 97–98, 125, 159–160;
in Plymouth, 26, 55, 56, 128–129, 162;
rivals, 42, 108, 158, 161, 194

trading outpost, 28, 79–80, 81, 161;
Morton's, 25–26, 42, 79–80, 92,
139–140, 180, 190; Plymouth's, 43,
82–83, 157–159, 161, 164; Weston's,
54–55, 77–78, 107

Trevore, William, 56

Ulrich, Laurel Thatcher, 19

undertakers, 81, 141, 142, 145, 164; and
debt, 83, 162

vassals, 48, 198

Virginia, 25, 50, 52–54, 194, 197; contrast
with Plymouth, 4, 26, 66, 80, 81; and

John Smith, 29, 115, 116, 148; leaving
Plymouth for, 52, 53, 79, 107; compared to Plymouth, 77, 78; tobacco
and, 82, 97, 99, 159; intended destination, 179, 195

Virginia Company, 117, 118, 179

visitors, 30, 47–48, 160, 195; assessments
of, 31, 40, 73, 114, 181

Wampanoag, 25, 96; treaty, 15–16, 39, 95,
175; village site, 31, 108; leader,
68–69, 95

Wappatucke, Thomas, 146

Warren, (widow), 143

Weeks, John (and wife), 21

Wessagussett, 77–79, 108, 122, 162;
failure at, 42, 77, 107, 180

West, Francis, 110

West, Marjory, 110

West Indies. *See* Caribbean

Weston, Thomas, 17, 78, 107, 113; established post, 54–55, 77, 78, 81, 163,
179

Weymouth, Massachusetts, 77

White, Peregrine, 22–23, 58

White, Resolved, 22–23

White, Susanna, 18, 23, 65

White, William, 65

White Angel (ship), 172, 173

Williams, Mary, 22

Williams, Roger, 22, 53, 114, 120, 150,
152

Williams, Thomas, 143

Williamson, 39

Winslow, Edward, 23, 43, 47, 57, 87,
150; author of *Good Newes,* 2, 5,
29, 70, 190; negotiator, 15, 43, 80;

Winslow, Edward (*continued*)
on Natives, 24–25, 33, 86, 92, 93;
emissary to Europe, 43, 56, 101, 150;
mobility of, 47, 48, 49–50, 51, 57, 154;
journey to Massasoit, 54–55, 68, 71;
on Thanksgiving, 69, 199; in Leiden,
176, 184, 188
Winslow, Elizabeth, 23
Winslow, Gilbert, 5
Winslow, Josiah, 81
Winthrop, John, 22, 43, 87, 108, 183

Winthrop, John Jr., 130
wives, 15–27, 34–35, 113; beating of, 25,
88, 92
women, 7, 15–27, 78, 131, 177, 179; Native,
31–32, 33, 121, 141, 144; and work,
31–36; abused, 63–64, 79, 106.
See also wives
Wood, William, 33, 169, 171
Wright, William, 184

Yarmouth, Plymouth Plantation, 108